THE JEW
AS
OUTSIDER

Historical and
Contemporary Perspectives.

Jack Nusan Porter

UNIVERSITY
PRESS OF
AMERICA

Dedicated to creative, responsible rebels everywhere!

Several of these essays have appeared elsewhere, and I thank the editors and publishers for permission to reprint them: <u>The Jewish Spectator</u>, <u>Jewish Currents</u>, <u>Midstream</u>, and <u>American Jewish History</u>.

Permission from the Macmillan Publishing Company to reprint an excerpt from <u>Why They Give</u> by Milton Goldin, Copyright © 1976 by Milton Goldin.

Jny PORTER
12/05

TABLE OF CONTENTS

Prologue:
Insiders and Outsiders

The concept of marginality has had a long, distinguished, and controversial history within the social sciences. In essence, this book attempts to dust off the issue of the marginal man (and woman) and to breathe new life into it. In the past, Robert Park, W.I. Thomas, Florian Znaniecki, Georg Simmel, and Everett Stonequist concentrated on cultural marginality and the phenomenon of cultural and racial hybrids, that is, individuals who are biologically marginal, or of mixed racial stock, and those who are marginal due to their social or economic level of existence. (See Roucek, 1964.)

The aim of these essays is to expand this familiar concept of marginality by concentrating on a people that has been called the "classic minority group in history"--the Jews. Jews are an ideal type to study because they are marginal on so many levels, and they include perhaps more variety of marginality and more aggravated cases of marginality than many other groups in society. Furthermore, their marginality becomes more complex and sophisticated as they assimilate into modern cultures.

Strictly speaking, marginality among Jews is a fairly recent phenomenon, beginning with their emancipation from the ghettos of Western Europe in the 18th century and from those of Eastern Europe in the 19th century. (See Koenig, 1962 and Roucek, 1964.) With emancipation, they were confronted with the problem of accommodating to two cultures--the Jewish culture and the host culture. It may be true that emanicipation was a mixed blessing for the Jews--allowing them to enter and contribute to the host society but also making them vulnerable to its enticements and freedoms.

Recent writings have contributed sophisticated analyses of such marginality among emanicipated Jews. For example, Mintz (1972) has observed that the Jewish response to freedom was varied--some chose complete assimilation (that is, through conversion and inter-marriage); some chose co-incidence of Judaism with the great movements of the times--liberalism, socialism, and humanism; still others chose isolation and avoidance by returning to the ghetto and becoming ever more separated from the "outside" host society; and finally, some sought the hard path of integration, that is, combining the best elements of traditional religious culture with those of modern secular thought. Mintz goes on to present as an example of integration the case of Mordechai Kaplan, a Jewish philosopher and religious leader, who would be quite at home with modern sociologists.

Kaplan described the synthesis and integration of the minority group into the host culture through what can be called reverse assimilation--that is, like a permeable membrane, the Jewish community would absorb what was wholesome for its survival and reject any injurious aspects of the host culture. Mintz ends his essay by asking: Should a group assimilate completely? Is the group's collective will supple enough to resist assimilation? Has it retained sufficient elasticity to engage in this cultural exchange? Is it too late for some groups? Or has the group and its collective will atrophied because it has never been stretched far enough, that is, has never attempted such cultural exchange? (Mintz, 1972:62)

The essays in this book will show that the collective and individual will of Jews has not atrophied. There are numerous examples in the Jewish community, as well as in other minority groups (blacks, women, Indians, etc.), of individuals struggling with their marginality. Far from being outworn, marginality, as these essays prove, is still a creative and seren-dipitous concept, one that is useful when studying a wide array of groups, not only Jews.

These essays have been influenced by Robert Merton's article (Merton, 1972) "Insiders and Outsiders." Merton, taking a sociology of knowledge perspective, concentrates on the insider-outsider tension as it relates to American blacks, but his concepts are applicable to Jews as well. The following theoretical assumptions, influenced by Merton, underlie these essays.

First, marginality affects not only biological and social class, but intellectual, artistic, life-cycle, and political positions as well. The essay on the upper class and my other work on middleman-traders show aspects of marginality within the class structure. The essays on the Jewish homosexual and Jewish women highlight marginality as it functions sexually. Other essays show the effect of marginality on life-cycle developments (Jewish young adults); artistic concerns (the Jewish comic); political movements (Jewish radicals and radical Jews); and intellectual/academic areas (the Jewish intellectual and Jewish sociologist).

Second, marginality need not be lamented, ridiculed, or despised. Marginality can be viewed positively as a source of creative tension. The marginal person may be creative either because he or she is not fully integrated into either host or minority culture and, therefore, can view both with cynical and objective vision; or the tension of being doubly or even triply alienated leads to a kind of dissonance that can be relieved through radically innovative means. In essence, as Freud pointed out, the Jew, being an outsider and a newcomer to "insiders" (established ideas), need not support the status quo. He or she may in fact do just the opposite--present new ways of looking at old problems. Furthermore, as in the case of the comic, poet, or writer, the anguish of outsider status can be excellent grist for one's artistic mill.

Third, the nuances of marginality should be seen as process, not static event. They change over time, depending on such variables as class structure, societal freedom and openness, and historical-political setting. Thus, marginality, far from being a stagnant condition, is an ever changing, ever new device for understanding society. How a society treats its deviants, its marginals, its middlemen, and its "outsiders" tells us a great deal about that society.

If one utilized a theological perspective, one might call the Jews "eternal outsiders," a people whose mission in life is to stand back from society and not simply observe and record it (the "sociologist as Jew") but to build a new world (the "revolutionary as Jew") or turn away from such a world and build an internal spiritual abode (the "mystic as Jew").

This book is not simply a collection of research essays; it is also an intellectual autobiography. Most

writing reflects in one way or another the life of an
individual, and these essays reflect my life as
student, radical, intellectual, and Jew. Writing is
also a form of self-analysis and self-discovery.
Writing about marginality helps illuminate the problems
facing me in all my many roles: teacher, citizen,
American, Jew, insider/ outsider.

These essays represent an entire opus. There is a
leit-motif that runs through them--the study of marginality and identity from a critical, conflict-oriented
perspective. They are the thoughts of an "outsider"
sociologist looking at both a people and at individuals
who are also outsiders. While written at different
times and for separate occasions, these essays should
in fact be seen as a whole, both intellectually and
personally.

References

Koenig, Samuel, "Living on the Edge of Two Cultural Worlds," Indian Journal of Social Research, vol. 3, January, 1962, pp. 88-92.

Merton, Robert K., "Insiders and Outsiders: A Chapter in the Sociology of Knowledge," American Journal of Sociology, vol. 78, no. 1, July, 1972, pp. 9-47.

Mintz, Alan, "Is Our Schizophrenia Historically Important?" Response: A Contemporary Jewish Review, no. 15, Fall, 1972, pp. 54-62.

Roucek, Joseph S., "The Marginal Man as a Sociological Phenomenon," Indian Sociological Bulletin, vol. 1, no. 2, January, 1964, pp. 39-46.

Part I
Political and Intellectual Rebels

Chapter 1

The Jewish Rebel

The following essay, the first, sets the stage for the others. It is a refinement of my thinking on the subject of Jewish rebels that began with my research on Jewish student activism in 1969-1970 and continued with my book on Jewish radicalism, with Peter Dreier, in 1973. It has evolved out of both political and intellectual soul-searching while attempting to understand the interface between universalism and particularism. Of all forms of religious marginality, the political radical is the most explosive example of such tension, from Karl Marx until today. This essay grew out of a search for meaning after the student protest movements of the 1960s had spent themselves in the 1970s and while a newly emerging Jewish counterculture was reaching maturity. Most of this essay is entirely new, but it draws upon ideas that first appeared in my article "The Jewish Rebel," The Jewish Spectator, vol. 38, no. 6, June 1973, pp. 15-17, portions of which are reprinted by permission of the editor, Trude Weiss-Romarin.

* * * * *

How does one bridge the gap between universalism and Judaism? The answer burns in my mind...and may never be resolved. The struggle between universalism and particularism is not a new one. Though the roots of Jewish radical universalism go back to the prophetic vision of the Bible and Talmud, the real dialogue began in the modern era, with the 19th century Haskalah--the Enlightenment--when European Jews left the ghetto and entered the non-Jewish world. The struggle between allegiance to one's people and community and to outside cosmopolitan ideals and ideology comes into play only when there are options. The response to these options set the stage for the confrontation between Judaism and secularism.

Other questions trouble me: who or what is a rebel? Why are the Jew and the rebel often seen as one and the same? How does one become a rebel? Why are Jews predisposed to becoming rebels? In short, why are there so many Jewish rebels--political, cultural, artistic, and intellectual?

The obvious answer is: marginality. One could see the Jews as "eternal outsiders" who, because of anti-Semitism, are "strangers" (Georg Simmel's term) or "pariah people" (Max Weber's term) even if they try to assimilate into the host society. Then, as Thorstein Veblen observed, they may be cut off, first from their own people, their own traditions, and their own community, and, then, from the rest of society. Thus, they are doubly alienated.

If one were a strict Freudian (another alienated Jew turned rebel), one might say that the Jews' creative tension is due to powerful sublimation of the libido and Oedipus drive channeled into areas such as art, science, politics, or literature. For example, the Jew, unlike the Christian, yet similar to the Buddhist, learns his or her social and moral responsibilities not because of fear of sin, but because of fear of what his or her family might think. Take the example of crime. Jews and Japanese have very low crime rates. Their low crime rate is not due to theological reasons (the "sin syndrome") but because of the dishonor it may bring to the family's name and to the community's prestige (the "guilt" syndrome). Crime is dishonorable--it causes a "black eye" to be cast upon the family, and such social control is a powerful deterrent. It works. Conversely, honor is bestowed upon the family if a child does well in life, learns well, does well in business, gains wealth, prestige, and status. Jews call such honor _nachas_, an untranslatable word that means joy, respect, and admiration--as in the phrase: "my son or daughter brings us _nachas_."

Nachas also implies obedience, obedience to family, synagogue, rabbi, and community, to bourgeois goals and ideals, to the status quo. For if the child obeys his or her parents' desire to bring honor to his or her family, he or she thereby honors himself. The power of the Jewish family, especially the mother, is

-4-

incalculable in motivating the Jewish child to succeed. Consider for a moment the impact of the mothers of Moses, Jesus, Marx, Trotsky, Freud, and Einstein on each of these great men.

Two forces are major motivators in Jewish life: respect for one's parents ("Honor thy father and thy mother") and respect for the Jewish community ("Do not cut thyself off from thy people"). How often have Jewish parents admonished their children: "Don't do that! What will the goyim (non-Jews) think? Don't dishonor our name!" Sin was never mentioned; God was rarely mentioned. To honor one's parents was to honor God.

Along with the family and the community came the concept of "chosenness." The Bible uses the term Am Segula, a nation like no other nation. This concept has historically aroused controversy. Why were the Jews chosen? For what purpose? What does "chosen" mean? How did this concept influence the self-image of the Jew and the collective image of the Jewish people? Is this a clue to the Jews' creative tension?

I believe it is. The covenant between God and "His" people is a contract binding both parties. God will care for and protect the Jewish people, and in return Jews must be a holy people, by carrying out God's wishes, upholding His moral code, and carrying His message to the world. For the Jewish rebel, this moral code in a religious sense becomes too constrict-ive, yet the moral force behind it remains, such that Jewish rebels may reject the "narrowness" of the covenant with God, yet find a way out of the ensuing guilt and dissonance by finding secular substitutes for the religious calling (radical politics, avant garde cultural and artistic modes, intellectual/academic pursuits). These rebels go beyond Judaism in their search for a more humane and just world after rejecting their "ghetto mentality," yet the origins are still Jewish--the prophetic vision of an ideal world.

These are broad statements, attempting to cover the lives of many kinds of rebels and many kinds of rebellions. I would like to analyze these theories of Jewish radicalism--the psychoanalytic and the theological-substitute by examining three different approaches to the subject: the first by an Irish-American sociologist, John Murray Cuddihy, in his book The Ordeal of Civility: Freud, Marx, Levi-Strauss, and

the Jewish Struggle with Modernity (1974); the second
by a Jewish writer, the late Maurice Hindus, in an
article written fifty years ago entitled "The Jew as a
Radical" (1927); and the third by a young, gifted
Jewish historian from England, Robert Wistrich, in his
book Revolutionary Jews From Marx to Trotsky (1976).
Each of these men grapples with the question of Jewish
rebellion and creativity from a different perspective.
Later, the theories of Isaac Deutscher and American
sociologists will also be analyzed and compared.

     Cuddihy's book is an excellent example of a
brilliant idea gone haywire. It also shows how one
can, in attempting to understand the Jewish component
in radicalism or academia, go off onto a tangent that
is not only wrong but immoral. Yet, Cuddihy's book
should be read by scholars and students, because it,
nevertheless, raises important issues that should be
pursued. More on this later, but first a short overview of his theoretical position. (For a good, critical review of the book, see Kitch and Mayer, 1976.)

     Cuddihy's controversial thesis is that Jews as
revolutionaries (political, cultural, and intellectual)
can best be understood by viewing their lives as a
confrontation between the "uncivil, pre-modern, and
vulgar", shtetl Jew with the civil, modern, refined
Christian society. (See Kitch and Mayer, 1976:23.) In
Cuddihy's often fascinating, but ultimately tedious,
terminology, it is a clash between the "Yid" and the
"Id." Now to take a Freudian approach to this question
can be useful. I have done so at the beginning of this
essay. Nevertheless, Cuddihy shows how outlandish one
can become by reducing complex social-political variables to psychological reductionism. My thesis--that
Jewish creativity may be due to a powerful sublimation
of the libido and repressed Oedipus drive into other
areas such as art, science, and politics--is intriguing
but almost impossible to prove. Until the day comes
when one can test such hypotheses, it might be better
to leave them aside and concentrate on social-
psycholgical constants such as self-hatred (also a difficult concept) and on sociological concepts such as
assimilation. Furthermore, one must understand the
context of the Jewish rebel's thought. Marx had a
well-defined ideology that precluded a positive
approach to Judaism. Freud too was little concerned
with Judaism in his work, yet he had great respect for
Zionism and for Zionists such as Herzl. He belonged to
the B'nai Brith. He had many Jewish friends. He loved

Jewish humor. He was, however, an assimilationist and he transcended Judaism for more "universal" concerns.

Cuddihy, by analyzing only some elements in the lives of three "representative" Jewish rebels (Marx, Freud, and Levi-Strauss), will have us believe that the clash between vulgarity and refinement is the best solution to the question of why Jews rebel. It is not. The major problem with Cuddihy's thesis is that (a) it ignores many other factors; (b) it attempts to generalize to all rebels; and (c) it ignores many other kinds of Jewish rebels.

Cuddihy is to be congratulated for placing the problem in the context of modernity, but his analysis is entirely off-base and even smacks of anti-Jewish sentiment. The Jew, according to him, resisted the modernization process. As Kitch and Mayer note (1976: 23), as a "premodern ethnic he is unsuited for civil society....(and) no amount of education, active repression, or, indeed, assimilation will 'convert' the Jew into a polite, 'nice' citizen of the modern world. The shtetl mentality--the Yid, in Cuddihy's expression --cannot be suppressed under the veneer of the parvenu. It is the need to come to terms with their Yiddishkeit that informs the work of Freud, Marx and Levi-Strauss."

Delving into the Jewish confrontation with modernity is important, but Cuddihy shows a woeful lack of knowledge of the Jewish experience and those of his "vulgar" rebels. For example, Marx was not a "premodern ethnic" but a doubly, even triply, alienated and assimilated Jew. Marx rejected both Judaism, the faith of his grandfathers, and Christianity, the faith of his parents. He was, like Cuddihy, woefully ignorant of Jewish history and tradition and bitterly hateful of Jews and Judaism, despite the fact that he clothed such hate in a general disgust for the entire bourgeoisie. (See Wistrich, for example, 1976:27-45.) In fact, Marx is the example par excellence of the self-hating Jew. He was not indifferent, but spiteful of Jews and Judaism. His anti-Jewishness is still reflected one hundred years later in some Jewish radicals today.

As Marx emphasized: "In the last analysis, the emancipation of the Jews is the emancipation of mankind from Judaism." (Marx-Engels Werke, vol I, East Berlin, 1964, p. 377)

To Cuddihy, Marx is the vulgar Jew. To Marx, it is the "haggling, egotistical" Jew who is the truly vulgar one. It is the materialistic Jew who was the object of so much disgust on the part of Karl Marx, the descendant of refined Jewish rabbis. Marx rejected not only "vulgar shtetl Judaism" but "capitalist, money-hungry haggling Jews," as well as Christians who also fit his description. Furthermore, Cuddihy reveals his ignorance about shtetl life. Despite the grinding poverty, there was great dignity among the Jews and not only among the rabbis. All Jews strived to be edel (refined), not prost (vulgar). To be prost was to be considered a goy. To act like a goy (a non-Jew) was to be prost. There were prosteh Jews, yet prosteh Jews were not held in high esteem (and one could suppose that to many Jews, Marx was also prost--but then again Marx had converted and had become a goy--so his prost-ness was inevitable in his assimilation). There may be some value in Cuddihy's thesis that to be a good Jewish rebel one had to rebel against much of Judaism and Jewishness, and one at times had to act like a prosteh goy in order to do so. I also agree with Cuddihy that many Jewish rebels rebelled against the structure of orthodoxy in the shtetl and against the clannish Jewish community. They had to break away in order to ultima-tely transcend Judaism. Jewish rebels clashed against their fate as Jews and against their Jewishness, as much as they clashed against the Protestant "esthetic" and the Protestant "etiquette," to use Cuddihy's terms.

Furthermore, Cuddihy must certainly understand that there are many kinds of Jewish rebels; one kind is the rebel from within the Jewish ranks (Baal Shem Tov, Theodore Herzl, Franz Rosenzweig, Martin Buber). What variables will explain these kinds of Jewish rebels? Cuddihy's theories will not.

Cuddihy's approach is a valiant try but also a good example of a non-Jew attempting to understand Jews and failing miserably. (Luckily, there are many examples of non-Jews who do understand the Jewish "psyche"). He is also a good example of a sociologist who attempts to explain a very complex issue in an overly simplified, rigid, and ultimately ludicrous theoretical manner. What follows are much better and more useful sociohistorical analyses of the question: why are Jews drawn to revolutionary and radical ideas? And what are the circumstances under which they are?

Maurice G. Hindus, a Jewish writer and novelist, wrote a sensitive and beautifully written answer to these questions fifty years ago, called "The Jew as a

Radical." Hindus, who lived in both the USSR and the United States, was quite aware of the nuances of being a Jewish radical. He outlines several distinct, yet overlapping, reasons.

First, he emphasizes that such radicalism, while nurtured by certain prophetic and humanitarian beliefs within Judaism, actually came from outside it. It was not the cheder (classroom), the shul (synagogue), or the rebbe (rabbi) that influenced young Jews to become radicals--it was non-Jewish intellectual sources outside the confines of the ghetto. In fact, orthodox Judaism frowned upon (and feared) modern intellectual thought from literature to politics. In short, according to Hindus, radicalism was not only tref (impure, nonkosher), it was also a form of assimilation. In that sense, both the left and the right wanted to "do away" with the Jews--the fascist right through extermination and exile, the Marxist left through disappearance as a distinct people, through assimilation, and through social dissolution. As Wistrich (1976:8) notes:

> The tragic irony....was that both the Jewish revolutionary and the pathological anti-Semite who feared and hated him, starting from wholly different general premises, desired the ultimate disappearance of the Jew.

Second, the ancient Hebraic prophetic influence fit perfectly into the new radical clothing either consciously or unconsciously. The Jewish prophet had much in common with modern radicalism:

> Both scorn the wrongdoer. Both would show no mercy to the unrepentant foe....The prophets continually hurl threats and curses on the despoilers of the widow and the orphan, the exploiter of the poor and the weak, as does the modern radical, though in terms of his own, coarser, more vitriolic than those of his ancient forebearers, also less awesome and less majestic.
> (Hindus, 1927:372)

Third, there is the intellectual tradition of the Jews. That too was a radicalizing force according to Hindus. The Jews have always been the Am Hasefer, the people of the book. They have combined a love of learning with a love of intellectual debate and speculation. The radical ponders and tests just as the learned Jew does. One could extend this thesis to say that the works of Marx and Freud are "Talmudic" in their endless maze of inquiry. Marxists and Freudians, like Hassidim, continually analyze the works of their "secular rebbes", Marx and Freud, attempting to find intricate answers to their questions. Furthermore, the followers of such Jewish rebels as Marx and Freud defend their "rabbis" with as much vehemence as Hassidim did when attacked by Mitnagdim or when per-secuted by non-Jewish anti-Semites. Hindus also makes an interesting analogy of radicalism to sports, echoing Irving Howe (1976) some fifty years later. To the Jews, radical politics was a sort of substitute for sport. It was, as he puts it, its "intellectual equivalent":

> Watch the crowds of garment workers during the lunch period as they parade in groups up and down Fifth Avenue and the surrounding side streets. The vehement controversy in which they are invariably engaged rages not over the prospects of Babe Ruth beating his home run record, or of Dempsey snatching the heavyweight championship from Gene Tunney, but over the fight between the Forwarts and the Freiheit (two New York Yiddish news-papers--JNP), the Mensheviks and the Bolshe-viks in their unions, or over the merits of some new social idea or theory.
> (Hindus, 1927:375)

For Jews, long locked out of the private hunting clubs, dueling societies, and private athletic associa-ciations of Europe, their need for "combat" turned from the physical to the mental, and radical politics was an excellent showcase for displaying such prowess.

A fourth factor in the Jewish heritage that made them susceptible to the call of radical causes was their burden of personal and group suffering. Jews were sensitive to the plight of the exploited, the oppressed, and the unliberated because of their own history of oppression. Moreover, radicalism promised the Jew more than deliverance from physical tribula-tion--it offered him a world where all discrimination and inequity would disappear forever. Radicalism was appealing because it was intellectual; it was redemp-tive; it was combative; and it was humanitarian. Yet, Hindus also alludes to an issue that weaves in and out

-10-

of this essay--the question of self-hatred.   The
embrace of radicalism implies the negation of Judaism,
but modern Jewish history is also replete with examples
of Jews who could not totally reject their heritage and
had to find a way out of their dissonance. Out of this
struggle came such movements as the Jewish Bund,
socialist Zionism, and the so-called radical Jew (as
opposed to the Jewish radical).   I will return to the
concept of self-hatred, but here is what Hindus says
about the phenomenon:

> Inordinately   sensitive,   the   Jew   in   this
> country often finds his Jewishness such a
> source of torment that he would fain flee
> from it.   He would root out of himself that
> something   which   the   late   Shalom   Aleichem
> called dos pintele yid, that innate inesca-
> pable all-pervading self-consciousness that
> constantly tugs at his heart-strings.   He
> would deny or disguise his Jewishness, join a
> Christian church, move to a non-Jewish neigh-
> borhood and in other ways seek to shuffle off
> his racial identity, all because of the dis-
> favor that the word Jew courts.   Unless he
> can sublimate his Jewishness into an ideal, a
> vision, or a cause, the modern Jew must be
> prepared to bear it as a cross that often
> lacerates the soul even while it leaves the
> body unharmed.   But radicalism promises to
> relieve him of this cross.   It promises to
> root out the cause and source of racial ill-
> feeling and thus lift the burden of disgrace
> that still attaches to the racial identity of
> the Jew.   Is this promise merely a bombastic
> bid for support?   Even so it holds forth a
> reward which intrigues the imagination of the
> Jew.   It soothes his ego.   It flatters his
> self-respect.   In fact, there is no other
> movement in existence, not even religion,
> which so audaciously attacks racial ill-
> feeling as does modern radicalism.
>   (Hindus, 1927:376-377)

Hindus goes on to state that the assimilationist
tendency of radicalism makes the radical Jew "at home"
in the company of his associates. He compares him to
the ghetto Jew in Poland and Soviet Russia, who is
forever an "outsider, an intruder...a thorn in the
flesh of the outside world and to himself."   Here
Hindus is treading on fragile ground, getting carried

-11-

away with his prose. Yet he makes an interesting point: namely that the Jewish rebel will stay and fight as, let us say a Russian, for the Russian people despite the dangers and the abuse, while the poor shtetl Jew, the eternal outsider, will forever have to wander in exile or be condemned to his oppressed position. Hindus, however, forgets that there were other movements (Zionism, Jewish socialism, etc.) that attempted to give Jews both pride and tradition. Such movements succeeded in breaking away from the "outsider" stigma while maintaining historical memory, religious integrity, and cultural creativity.

Hindus ends his essay echoing the thoughts of sociologist Nathan Glazer writing four decades later. Glazer (1969:112-113 et seq) felt that Jewish radicals, because they were more intellectual-minded than their non-Jewish compatriots, would shrink away from their movements if and when these movements turned violent. (He was partially correct--some Jews did, some didn't.) Hindus feels for similar reasons (which he adduces to the Jews' "love of life") that Jewish radicals will also compromise their ideals. He was prophetic--one of the first observers to notice the effect of social mobility into the middle class on one's radicalism. As he puts it: "Given favorable conditions of life he (the Jewish radical) often loses his interest in revolutionary movements." (1927:379) Such loss of interest is because Jews are pragmatic compromisers. American democracy would eventually inculcate a new set of loyalties which would come into conflict with radical propensities. Even anti-Semitism will not slow this inexorable movement away from radicalism. In fact, it will hasten it. Yet, radicalism will continue in truncated forms--the ex-radical may continue to read radical journals and papers; he may transform his radicalism into liberalism, intellectualism, or academism. "Basking in affluence," Hindus continues, "(the Jewish radical) may find radicalism--or its milder brother, liberalism--intriguing, but usually as a diversion, as a means of intellectual escape, rather than a method of social change or a code of social behavior." (1927:379) In short, it is the material conditions of life that will propel the Jew into radicalism, and when such conditions improve, the Jew will tend to leave radical movements except for certain vestigial aspects.

Robert Wistrich, a young pro-Zionist British scholar, picks up several of the themes that Hindus had

discussed and amplifies them. To Wistrich, revolutionary Jews were the heirs of the dream of assimilation
first proclaimed by the French revolution in 1789.
Socialism became their substitute for Jewish identity.
However, the logic of Marxism led the Jews into a
cul-de-sac. In the USSR, the "promised land" turned
out to be a 20th century Egypt. Communism led them
back into bondage, not to freedom.

Wistrich greatly enlarges our understanding of
European intellectual history by examining ten
outstanding revolutionaries or radicals of Jewish
origin--from Germany (Marx, Lassale, Eduard Bernstein,
and Rosa Luxemburg); from Austria-Hungary (Victor
Adler, Otto Bauer); from France (Bernard Lazare, Leon
Blum); and from Russia (Julius Martov and Leon
Trotsky). Accented by a short but enticing introduction, "The Jews and Socialism," his book is a
refreshing alternative to Cuddihy's The Ordeal of
Civility.

Wistrich is skeptical about the parallel between
Jewish and socialist messianism as it is customarily
formulated. (1976:3-6) He feels that, however interesting this "theological position" may be, it ultimately
distorts the general attitude of Marxism to religion,
as well as the true nature of Jewish messianism. He
writes:

> Marxism transformed the critique of religion
> into a political issue, making it a reflex of
> the secular contradictions in civil society.
> By politicizing religion and deifying human
> consciousness, by reducing spiritual phenome-
> non to a function of impersonal economic
> laws, Marxism broke completely with the
> Judeo-Christian tradition and the teachings
> of the Hebrew prophets. Nor should the
> universality of Marxist and traditional
> messianism be regarded as comparable. The
> universalistic thrust of prophetic Judaism
> always co-existed in a polarized tension with
> belief in the chosen-ness of Israel, its par-
> ticular mission among the nations. Socialist
> assimilationism, on the other hand, expressly
> derided this Jewish messianism, which it
> regarded as a reactionary movement to pre-
> serve the independent existence of a 'chimer-
> ic' nationality. Jewish nationalism and
> Zionism as secular forms of this traditional

messianism (although they should also be viewed as a revolt against the quietism of orthodox belief) were treated with disdain and contempt by many Marxists....The crucial point, then, is not that there are no affinities between Judaism and socialism, but that within the framework of Marxist theory there could be no scope for such rapprochement.
(Wistrich, 1976:4-5)

He then goes on to emphasize that certain individuals who did in fact make an attempt to synthesize socialism and Judaism (Moses Hess, Bernard Lazare, Chaim Zhitlovsky, Aron Liebermann) eventually were led not into the forefront of Marxism but to the emergence of socialist Zionism or Jewish socialism. In the case of Chaim Zhitlovsky and Aron Liebermann, it led to Jewish socialism and Bundism. And these four men had little influence on the development of international socialism. On the other hand, "non-Jewish Jews" (Marx, Trotsky, Lasalle, and Rosa Luxemburg), Marxist Jews who were intensely antagonistic to the Jewish tradition including its messianic impulse, turned out to be a powerful force in modern history and international socialism. Yet from the standpoint of Jewish life, they were a tragic aberration and an embarrassment. (See Wistrich, 1976:5-6 and Wistrich, 1977:13.)

In a critique of his book, Hyman Maccoby (1977:14) takes issue with Wistrich. Maccoby feels that Wistrich ignores the "myriad subtle ways in which cultural attitudes are handed on, even unintentionally." It is these subtle influences of Judaism on Jewish radicals that led them to transcend Judaism and Jewish values for substitute movements, movements that would provide "the intellectual orientation and stimulation, and the universalist idealism, previously provided by Judaism." Maccoby asserts that such Jewish radicals had the knowledge and love of Judaism in the first place, then became disillusioned and sought out secular substitutes. Maccoby is correct if he refers to Leon Trotsky or Isaac Deutscher. They both had Jewish educations which they later rejected, but what of Karl Marx? He had no Jewish education even to reject and find a substitute for. He was converted to Lutheranism at the age of six. No, in this case, it is Wistrich who is correct when he says: "My position is that one cannot transcend something which one does not know. It is this ignorance of the Jewish tradition, so evident in the careers of the great Jewish revolutionaries, that

-14-

makes me skeptical of attempts to see in them a positive modern manifestation of 'Judaism'." (Wistrich,
1977:14)

Next, Wistrich raises the problem of self-hatred
among Jewish radicals, namely the role it played in
activating latent prejudices in the socialist movement:
"Self-hatred can take many forms, and is often
difficult to detect, let alone diagnose. Frequently it
is hidden from the self-hater himself, and not visible
to his closest colleagues." (Wistrich, 1976:6)

He goes on to note that "gifted individuals from a
minority," such as Jewish rebels, are often exposed to
self-hatred because their abilities, while giving them
greater possibilities of recognition and success, also
expose them to rejection and hostility. Wistrich then
notes that such self-hatred is often translated into a
form of an "ethnic death wish" within Marxist theory.
This issue was inseparably joined with the question
(Das Judenfrage) of nationality, or in modern terminology, the question of ethnicity versus class consciousness. (See Schappes, 1970; Novick, 1977; and Wistrich,
1976:8-22 and 26-45.) This is a complex question that
can only be briefly raised here. It deserves and has
gotten much greater coverage.

The standard Marxist analysis of the Jewish
"question" is as follows: Jews were seen as a parasi-
tic class (Marx), a caste (Kautsky-Lenin), a historical
fossil (Stalin, Toynbee), or a nation in the process of
irreversible dissolution (Otto Bauer). The Jews were
therefore denied the right to preserve and recreate
their national identity. The best solution for them
would be to leave behind their ghetto "mentality,"
their undesirable "Jewish" characteristics, and their
"reactionary" religion (all of which provoked anti-
Semitism anyway) and become internationalists.

Furthermore, with regard to anti-Semitism, or
Judeophobia as it has been called, this would disappear
in a classless society, since it was a specific product
of capitalist society and furthermore was a diversion
from the class struggle itself. (It was known as the
"socialism of fools.") Anti-Semitism could only exist
in a class-divided society, and it served primarily to
create dissension within the working class. Thus, the
general struggle against capitalism would eventually
eliminate anti-Semitism.

-15-

But anti-Semitism did not magically disappear even in socialist societies, and the Jews did not miraculously lose their distinctiveness. In fact, during Lenin's time and after, the problems that Jewish nationality posed for Marxists were immense. At first Lenin was completely against the idea, as he explained in 1903:

> The idea of a Jewish 'nationality' is definitely reactionary, not only when expounded by its consistent advocates (the Zionists) but likewise on the lips of those who try to combine it with the ideas of Social Democracy (the Bundists). The idea of a Jewish nationality runs counter to the interests of the Jewish proletariat, for it fosters among them, directly or indirectly, a spirit hostile to assimilation, the spirit of the 'ghetto'. (Originally appeared in V.I. Lenin, "The Position of the Bund in the Party," in Collected Works, Moscow/London, 1961, vol. 7, p. 100 ff., and quoted in Wistrich, 1976:11).

But Wistrich fails to note that Lenin, while strongly critical of the Bund (a powerful, secular, anti-Zionist socialist movement of the Jewish working class before 1939), also expected national differences to exist for a long time, even after world socialism had been achieved. (See Schappes, 1970:3-4.) Lenin tried, unsuccessfully, to cope with national realities in light of the Marxian vision of the future. As he wrote in 1920:

> ....as long as national and state differences exist among peoples and countries--and these differences will continue to exist for a very long time, even after the dictatorship of the proletariat has been established on a world scale--the unity of international tactics of the Communist working class movement of all countries demands, not the elimination of variety, not the abolition of national differences (this is a foolish dream at the present moment), but such an application of the fundamental principles of Communism....as will correctly modify these principles in certain particulars, and will properly apply them to the national and national-state differences....(From V.I. Lenin, "Left-Wing"

Communism: An Infantile Disorder; New York: International Publishers, 1934, pp. 71-72 as quoted in Schappes, 1970:4)

Manifestations of Jewish nationalism, whether the Diaspora nationalism of the Bund or the Israel-centered nationalism of the Zionists, were eventually vilified and persecuted in the Soviet Union and later exterminated by Nazi Germany. The question of Jewish nationality especially now that there exists a national state of Israel, will, as I will discuss soon, still continue to be a controversial and unsettling issue.

To recapitulate this long section, Wistrich is aware that there are many types of Jewish rebels of various shades--revolutionaries and anarchists such as Moses Hess and Bernard Lazare who became Zionists; assimilated bourgeois Jews like Herzl who became Zionists; socialists and humanists who were Jewishly committed such as Leon Blum, Abraham Cahan, and many others; and even Marxists who seemed to be friendly to Jewish rights--Engels, for example.

Wistrich has shown the diversity of Jewish revolutionaries as well as the complex web of factors leading to such radicalism. Cuddihy, however, is bent on emphasizing only the Jewish struggle with civility. His discussion of the confrontation with modernity, is a more fruitful approach. Nevertheless, if there was guilt and the "guilt of shame" among Jewish radicals for abandoning their ancient heritage, it was not because Jews were guilty over the "vulgarity" of shtetl Yiddishkeit, but over rejecting the strict moral code of the ghetto; of rejecting and abandoning the chosenness and the fate of the Jewish people; by being perceived by fellow Jews as traitors and turncoats; and by rejecting the ideals of one's mother and father. But all this presupposes that they knew enough to reject; many Jewish revolutionaries did not. They rejected an infantile concept of what Judaism was all about because they themselves had stopped their Jewish education at an "infantile stage," if they had any to begin with.

Furthermore, I question whether Judaism is as "narrow" as Cuddihy perceives it. I do not believe that it is. I question whether even shtetl Yiddishkeit was as "vulgar" as he believed it to be. The shtetl life contained many examples of dignity and refinement. Too often, the Jewish rebel threw out the "baby along with the bath water." They too often rejected too

-17-

much--the good along with the bad in Jewish life,
ignoring the humanitarian and universal aspects of
Judaism. Cuddihy nevertheless brings up an important
issue (namely the struggle with modernity) but botches
it in a plethora of psychoanalytical and sociological
jargon--his own made-up jargon, much of it confusing
and unnecessary. Furthermore, he stretches the evi-
dence for his assertions almost to the breaking point.
(See Rothman and Horowitz, 1976:109-115.)

Generally, I am uncomfortable with psychohistori-
cal, psychoanalytical, and theological interpretations
of Jewish radicals. There may be some truth in them
and they are titillating to debate, but they are almost
impossible to prove. How does one, for example,
measure "guilt," "ghetto mentality," "chosen-ness," or
"the Protestant aesthetic?" They may eventually become
useful, but I do not see it now, especially as Cuddihy
has described these concepts. Far sounder and more
robust are the interpretations and good sense found in
the works of Hindus and Wistrich.

Two Types of Jewish Rebels:
Insiders and Outsiders

The very definition of the term galut, diaspora,
implies that the Jew lives in two cultures, and this
"cultural schizophrenia," marginality, alienation, and
possible self-hatred or self-denial has existed since
the times Jews were emancipated from their ghettos some
200 years ago. For many Jews, this marginality has led
to creativity as well as to anxiety. To be marginal,
is of course, not always healthy. It can lead to a
neurotic division of the soul and mind. Yet out of
this neurosis can emerge a richly creative contribution
to society.

As was shown earlier, Wistrich disagrees with
Isaac Deutscher regarding socialism as a secular
messianism, but for some radicals, while they came to
revolutionary politics and to socialism from different
paths without respect for the prophetic tradition
(Marx, for example), still, they transformed their
alienation from Judaism and Christianity into an asset
by transcending both and thereby contributing vastly to
Western thought. The essence of this process is dis-
tilled in a Talmudic story told surprisingly by the
Marxist (Trotskyite) scholar Isaac Deutscher in his
book The Non-Jewish Jew (1968):

I remember that when as a child I read the
Midrash (the Biblical commentary), I came
across a story and a description of a scene
which gripped my imagination. It was the
story of Rabbi Meir, the great saint and
sage, the pillar of Mosaic orthodoxy, and co-
author of the Mishnah (codified Jewish law),
who took lessons from a heretic, Elisha ben
Abuyah, called Akher (The Stranger). Once on
a Sabbath, Rabbi Meir was with his teacher,
and as usual they became engaged in a deep
argument.

The heretic was riding a donkey, and Rabbi
Meir, as he could not ride on a Sabbath,
walked by his side and listened so intently
to the words of wisdom falling from the here-
tical lips that he failed to notice that he
and his teacher had reached the ritual boundary which Jews were not allowed to cross on
a Sabbath.

The great heretic turned to his orthodox
pupil and said: "Look, we have reached the
boundary--we must part now; you must not
accompany me any further--go back!" Rabbi
Meir went back to the Jewish community, while
the heretic rode on--beyond the boundaries of
Jewry.

The Jewish heretic who transcends Jewry
belongs to a Jewish tradition. You may, if
you like, see Akher as a prototype of those
great revolutionaries of modern thought:
Spinoza, Heine, Marx, Rosa Luxemburg,
Trotsky, and Freud....They all found Jewry
too narrow, too archaic....They all looked
for ideals and fulfillment beyond it.

This is an unusual passage for a Marxist--finding
a Jewish causation for one's radicalism. Many Marxists
(Rosa Luxemburg, Trotsky, for example, and the New
Leftists of the 1960s) rarely were so involved with
such religious selfexamination. They most likely would
have agreed with it, nevertheless, even though it would
have struck them as unnecessarily sentimental.

However, Deutscher points a way to the understanding that there is not one, but two basic types of
Jewish rebels (with several subtypes in each major

category). The first form is the insider rebel, that is, the radical from within the Jewish community. This can either be a person who initiates radical innovations from within the tradition (such as Baal Shem Tov, the founder of Hassidism) or who "returns" to the fold after a period alienated from the Jewish community (such as Theodore Herzl, founder of political Zionism). Other major figures who might fit this description are Moses, Shabbetai Tzvi, Jacob Frank, Franz Rosenzweig, Martin Buber, David Ben-Gurion, Zev Jabotinsky, Meir Kahane, Arthur Waskow, and the Jewish activists, poets, "mystics," and radicals of the Jewish countercultural movements of the past ten years. (See Porter and Dreier, 1973; Sleeper and Mintz, 1971; and Siegel, Strassfeld, and Strassfeld, 1973.)

They are the innovators from within who engage in a process of reverse assimilation whereby the host culture is encountered, Judaized, and employed for further elaboration and enrichment of Jewish expression. The Jewish rebel from within is an essential part of Jewish life. He or she makes it possible for Judaism and Jewishness to revitalize itself, adapt itself, and survive--by riding the "surfboard of history." While often attacked by fellow Jews, the Jewish rebel from within is eventually accepted and his or her contribution is then incorporated into the corpus of Jewish historical memory.

On the other hand, there is the outsider rebel, the rebel most often discussed when one speaks of "Jewish rebels." Here, one finds Jews who, though coming from Jewish parents or grandparents, have found Judaism too confining, narrow, parochial, and exasperating and have embarked on a search for new paths outside the confines of traditional Jewish life. Some have drifted far afield. Some have been consumed with great self-hatred and self-denial. Like blacks, they have attempted to "pass," though the attempt has rarely been successful--they are still labeled as Jews despite their efforts. Their lives are filled with secular and non-Jewish substitutes for the faith they have found too restrictive, yet that same faith had the ingenious ability to create heretics in the first place.

There are so many Jewish rebels it would take an encyclopedia to list and describe all of them. Some drifted away; some stayed close to home. But like children leaving home, they knew they would have to "break away" if they were to "make it" in the host

culture. What theory can possibly embrace all these
rebels? This essay has essentially concentrated on
political radicals; some theories may hold true for
other kinds of Jewish rebels--religious, artistic,
literary, poetic, and scientific. Furthermore, some
outsider Jewish rebels made their mark in the outside
non-Jewish world yet were loved and accepted by the
inside Jewish community and even saw themselves as part
of that community. (Albert Einstein and Franz Kafka
are good examples.)

The outside rebel probably started with Jesus and
continued with Spinoza, Karl Marx, Freud, Trotsky,
Heine, Rosa Luxemburg, Emma Goldman, Daniel de Leon,
Wilhelm Reich, Herbert Marcuse, and Gertrude Stein.
Among contemporary artists and rebels one could
add--Abbie Hoffman, Jerry Rubin, Bob Dylan, Lenny
Bruce, the Babba Ram Dass (Richard Alpert), Fritz
Perls, Anais Nin, Paul Goodman, Saul Alinsky, and
Abraham Maslow; plus Bernadine Dohrn, Mark Rudd, and
several other well-known SDS revolutionaries; and one
could end this incomplete list with such names as
Norman Mailer, Robin Morgan, Alan Ginsburg, Gloria
Steinem, and Shulamith Firestone.

It is quite easy to overgeneralize about all
Jewish rebels, as Cuddihy does. For example, there are
cases of intense self-denial among some--Marx being the
best example. Trotsky too (see Carmichael, 1973:43-45)
went so far as to deny or to gloss over in his own
biography that he was even bar-mitzvahed, which he
probably was. This denial carried over when he was a
young man of twenty-five and was asked whether he was a
Russian: "No!", "A Jew?"--"No!", "Then what?", and came
the proud retort--"A Social Democrat!" And later when
he came to power and was approached by a Jewish delega-
tion, he said similarly that he was not a Jew but an
internationalist! Such a blatant example of denial led
Carmichael (1973:44-45) to say:

A more Jewish response can hardly be imag-
ined. Other internationalists can be German,
French, Russian, etc., and will say so; only
Jews are just plain internationalists!
(Original emphasis).

As opposed to Trotsky, on the continuum of Jewish
identity might be the case of Sigmund Freud. Though he
later assimilated and his children intermarried, Freud
did in fact have a Jewish education; he was bar-

mitzvahed; he was sympathetic to Zionism even to the point of considering and rejecting the position of president of the Hebrew University in Jerusalem in 1925; Freud was acquainted with and deeply respected the work and vision of Theodore Herzl. He once sent Herzl a copy of one of his works with a dedication. Freud's son was a member of Kadimah, a Zionist youth group, and Freud himself was an honorary member of the B'nai Brith lodge in Vienna and occasionally gave lectures to its members. Yet despite these close ties, his own work rarely dealt with Jewish issues. He had successfully transcended Judaism.

The same could be said about several of the Jewish rebels of the 1960s American counterculture. For example, Jerry Rubin, the political leader, and Bob Dylan, the folk singer, have both had alienating experiences with Judaism and Jewish life, but they may be turning back to it quietly. Both had a Jewish education and were bar-mitzvahed. Both have been to Israel, Dylan reportedly several times. Dylan has been studying with a Hasidic rabbi and he has quietly supported Rabbi Meir Kahane and the Jewish Defense League with some financial support. All these events are kept in the background and rarely interfere with the public image of these two young Jewish men. Their Jewishness is really inconsequential to their acceptance, yet, I believe, it is crucial to understanding their ultimate creative alienation. (Dylan, however, has recently converted to a "born-again" Christianity. How complex these Jewish rebels are.)

In short, one can be a Jewish outsider-rebel and still maintain some interest and involvement in Jewish affairs. The essential point I am making is that we are discussing a highly complex and varied group of individuals, and there is, at times, a great deal of overlap in the interface between Judaism and radicalism.

In discussing the rebel from within versus the rebel from outside, I do not mean to imply that there is a strict separation of the two. It is probably better to see them as a continuum--from completely assimilated to completely involved with Jewish life. Neither extreme is easily maintained, so there is room in the center of the continuum and on each side of the center.

Deutscher's earlier Talmudic tale of the apikoros Akher, the intellectual atheist, stresses that Judaism has both compassion and pity for the rebel. A kind of ambivalence emerges, a form of ambivalence that appears in many Jews, the tightrope between one's own people and traditions and the universalistic impulses that abound in society. These are tempting impulses. The core of the dilemma can be found in the famous saying by Rabbi Hillel:

If I am not for myself, who am I?
But if I am only for myself, what am I?
And if not now, then when?

The answer is not an easy one and Judaism recognized that many centuries ago. Thus, it had compassion for the rebel, especially if he or she made an attempt to return to the fold. There is, however, a golden midpoint and a way out of the dilemma. As the Jewish novelist Elie Weisel observes: the deepest and richest teachings within the Jewish tradition are also its most universalistic. For those rebels, writers, and intellectuals who tap into that source and present the world with Judaism's deepest teachings, the world in turn will accept and respect those lessons as universal ones.

The Jewish Rebel Today

Suffice it to say, the ambivalence and tensions of one hundred years ago still exist in the present. Yet, two modern events have had a cataclysmic impact on Jewish life: the European Holocaust and the establishment of the state of Israel. Two other factors that also seem salient are the emergence of developing nations in Asia, Africa, and the Middle East and the rise of black and Third World liberation movements both in the United States and around the world. These factors, culminating in student protest and countercultural eruptions, led to what later would be referred to as the Jewish liberation movement. (See Porter, 1970 and Porter and Dreier, 1973.)

In the introduction to their anthology, Jewish Radicalism, Porter and Dreier (1973:xx-xxvii) attempt to answer the question: why were so many young Jews attracted to the New Left? One approach, the so-called "continuity theory" proposed by such social scientists as Kenneth Keniston and Richard Flacks, suggests that radicals share, rather than repudiate, the basic value commitments of their left-liberal parents by receiving both covert and overt support from their parents. Many Jewish parents are highly educated, urbanized, and cosmopolitan professionals, service workers (teachers and social workers), and intellectuals. In rearing their children they stressed sensitivity to injustice and discrimination, and distrust of irrational and bureaucratic authority and urged their offspring to question and challenge the status-quo.

The concept of self-hatred, however, was challenged by Porter and Dreier (1973:xxii-xxiii). They felt that the label of "self-hating" Jew, which they defined as a conscious attempt to escape one's Jewishness, to change one's name, or to pass as a non-Jew, was inappropriate, misleading, and much more a characteristic of second-generation American Jews than of third- or fourth-generation Jewish radicals. A better explanation, they felt, was Isaac Deutscher's "non-Jewish Jew" concept, radicals who were singularly unselfconscious about their Jewishness and even ignorant of the radical tradition of the prophets, of the Maccabees, and of the Jewish component of the "Old Left" in Europe. To use Leonard Fein's phrase, they were "religious and cultural amnesiacs": they were ahistorical. (This was true for many Jewish radicals but not all of them, it must be added.)

Porter and Dreier also clarify the premise that it was universalism which caused these Jewish rebels to turn away from Jewish concerns. The answer, according to them, was far more subtle, because it does not explain New Left support for national and racial liberation. In that sense, the New Left was a major break from the Old Left in that it unabashedly recognized national and ethnic differences and even glorified them. The New Left thus supported Third World movements which were attempting to overcome years of colonialism and imperialism, including the negative stereotypes imposed on them by the colonialists. Cultural and national groups, whether they were Vietnamese, blacks, Canadian Quebecois, Chicanos, American Indians, or others--showed that one could be proud of one's group identity despite years of oppression. On the other hand, American Jews were passively and quietly watching their culture drift away with only a trace of outrage or anguish. At the same time, Jews were increasingly being seen as a visible enemy and barrier to freedom. Jewish concentration in middle-men occupations, especially in the black and Puerto Rican ghettos, was singled out as an example of Jewish "colonialism." Porter and Dreier go on to quote New Left leader Jerry Rubin:

> I personally feel very torn about being Jewish. I know it made me feel like a minority or outsider in Amerika (sic) from my birth and helped me become a revolutionary. I am shocked at Julius Hoffman and Richard Schultz (Chicago 7 prosecutor) 'cause they try to be so Amerikan. Don't they know they're still Jewish no matter how much power or security in Amerika they have?....
>
> But despite this....Judaism no longer means much to us because the Judeo-Christian tradition has died of hypocrisy; Jews have become landlords, businessmen and prosecutors in Amerika.
>
> (Rubin, 1971:74-76)

Compare this to the self-denial of the 19th century Jewish revolutionary Ferdinand Lassale: "There are two classes of men I cannot bear: journalists and Jews--and unfortunately I belong to both." (Quoted in Wistrich, 1976:46) Rubin is almost sad that Jews are assimilating into an "Amerika" that will never accept them as Jews. Jews have become like everyone else rather than joining the vanguard that will fight such conformity and oppression. Rubin is sympathetic to Judaism and to Jewishness only if it will throw off its "hypocrisy" and "join the revolution." While Rubin was and is sympathetic to many aspects of Judaism, quite a few New Leftists were indifferent, even callous, to the sensitivities of Jews. There existed self-hatred, to be sure, but the modal quality of today's Jewish rebel is indifference to Judaism.

The issue of self-hatred or indifference to Jewish identity on the part of Jewish New Leftists in the 1960s and 1970s became increasingly intertwined with the "nationality question": the issue of Israel--its right to exist, its alleged colonialism, its alleged persecution of Arab citizens, and its alleged discrimination of Sephardic Jews. Jewish New Leftists willingly supported the liberation movements of Palestinians, Africans, and other Third World revolutionaries at the expense of Israel and Israeli interests. As I.L. Horowitz so pungently put it, just as the Jew had been the classic pariah throughout history, so now Israel had become the classic "pariah state" among the nations

of the world.   Thus, New Left anti-Semitism took on a
new form: anti-Zionist and anti-Israel.

The heroes of the New Left--Che Guevara, Franz
Fanon, Mao Tse-Tung, Fidel Castro, and Yasser Arafat--
were all identified with anticolonial liberation
movements in countries that are still relatively
nonindustrial. Such movements were characterized by an
anti-white orientation, yet some of their most fervent
supporters were Westernized and white members of the
New Left, and a solid proportion of the leadership of
the New Left was Jewish. Such "outsider" Jewish rebels
still retained their millenial vision of the new world:
a world free of prejudice and hatred; a world free from
colonialism and imperialism; and a world organized by
workers who will be able to control their own lives.
The increasingly anti-Zionist position of many New
Leftists, especially of Jewish radicals, brought forth
diverse reactions from sectors of the Jewish community.
The established Jewish leadership both feared and was
embarrassed by such rebels. Right-wing Jews established the Jewish Defense League in order to defend
Jewish rights in America as well as in the Soviet Union
and in Israel; and the liberal and left-liberal student
and young adult Jewish population, while sympathetic to
the left over Vietnam and black civil rights, became
alarmed over the anti-Zionist thrust of the New Left
and began to organize movements midway between the
Jewish establishment and the anti-establishment left.
These movements had several names: radical Jews, the
Jewish counterculture, the Jewish student movement,
radical Zionists, and the Jewish left.

Since the 1967 Six-Day War and the New Left anti-
Israel reaction to that war, a new but tiny movement of
militant and activist Jews arose. In essence, what
distinguished these activities was a proud regard for
Judaism and Jewish history and a critical stance toward
Jewish and Israeli leadership. The Jewish community
now had two kinds of rebels to contend with--rebels
from outside (Jewish New Leftists) and rebels from
inside (radical Jews and radical Zionists). The former
were condemned and isolated; the latter were condemned
and coopted.   (See Porter, 1970; Porter and Dreier,
1973; and Gershman, 1970, 1973.)

Lipset (1974), some time after the New Left had
gone into eclipse, wrote the following sophisticated
analysis of the situation:

The linkage of the Jewish community historically with the left stemmed from a historical
linkage of European conservatism allied with
anti-Semitism, exclusion of Jews from citizenship rights, while the left from the
French revolution on, through the Revolution
of 1848, the rise of socialism movements, the
Russian revolution, all supported social,
political and economic equality for the Jews.
This anti-left conservative tie reached its
zenith of anti-Semitism during the Nazi
regime, where the most vital anti-Nazi forces
were predominantly on the left. And conversely, the historical experience of being
an oppressed minority led many Jews to identify with the egalitarian ideologies and universalistic principles upheld by the left.

Although conflicts between the policies of
leftist groups and Jewish interests occurred
at various times, i.e. the Hitler-Stalin Pact
and the emergence of overt anti-Semitism in
the Soviet Union and Czechoslovakia in 1948,
and continuing until this day, these events
had little bearing on U.S. conditions.

The situation however in the U.S. began to
change in the 1960s, initially with respect
to Black-Jewish relations, and subsequently
with regards to Israel. Although Jews had
formed the principal source of white financial and activist support for civil-rights
and integrationist movements, a variety of
circumstances flowing in part from the fact
blacks had moved into previously Jewish urban
areas and began with increased racial
consciousness to seek to take over local
institutions still manned by Jews, and to
some degree because blacks sought to force
whites out of "their" organizations and
causes, Jewish and black interests began to
diverge and conflict. This became apparent
in the New York City Teachers' strike, the
Forest Hills housing controversy, and most
important and durable of issues, in the
sharply conflicting position of the two
groups with respect to the issue of quotas
for minority groups versus the historic
Jewish and liberal emphasis on meritocracy,
on judging individuals by personal standards
rather than group membership.....

-27-

Israel was to present an even greater dilemma for leftist Jews. Increasingly in the 1960s, particularly after the Six Day War, a new image was created, an image of a powerful wealthy Jewish state exploiting its own Arab minority in conflict with a mass of weak impoverished Arabs, part of the anti-imperialist Third World. Perhaps even more important in alienating Israel from its leftist supporters was the divergent political roles of the allies of the two parties in the Middle East conflict. Israel was to suffer greatly from the fact that its principal foreign supporter, the United States, achieved the status of the great international reactionary villain as a result of the Vietnam War. Conversely the Arab cause was taken up by almost every Communist nation and faction, not only the Soviet ones, but China, Korea, North Vietnam and Yugoslavia and the various Maoist and Trotskyite parties as well. Hence, with the exception of some older Social Democratic leaders and groups, almost all of the left outside the United States became strongly pro-Arab. This was particularly true of the New Left....

The Yom Kippur War clearly created a drastically different environment. Israel was once again clearly the weaker party. The Israelis reproduced the historic Jewish predicament of a small weak community surrounded by a powerful world of enemies, with few friends among the Gentiles willing to aid them. And their only real support comes from other Jewish communities, today, mainly the American.

How is this situation affecting opinion in this country? First and foremost, the Jewish community, particularly its older and more well-to-do members, have responded with an outpouring of funds and willingness to try to exercise political pressure on Israel's behalf. These efforts have clearly played a role in holding politicians who may have waivered in line. On the other hand, most of the organized left, including a number of veterans of the antiwar movement among the Christian clergy, such as the Berrigan brothers, have taken overt pro-Arab positions, or have adopted a nominally "evenhanded" stance, which calls on Israel to give up much or little, with no security assurances. Fortunately for Israel, however, the dramatic decline of the "movement" in the dramatic "street action" sense, in the past three years, has considerably lessened their ability to affect the body politic. But given the disproportionate strength of ideological liberal and left forces on the leading campuses of North America, with their heavily Jewish faculty and student concentrations, there does exist some cross-pressures, to some degree, between their Third World orientations and their Jewishness. As in previous crises, a threat to Jewish survival has revived Jewish identification, but others retain their universalistic orientations to the point of being pro-Arab.

Others, however, those that Lipset calls "Jewish radicals", strongly Jewish yet still radical, were forced to find some compromise to the Mid Eastern problem yet with a socialist or socialist-Zionist perspective. Out of this dissonance emerged such groups as the Radical Zionist Alliance, Breira, and Israeli groups such as Matzpen and Moked. One of the most well known of the "Jewish radicals" who attempted to forge a third force between socialism and Judaism was Arthur Waskow, a New Leftist of the 1960s who became an insider Jewish rebel after 1967. Waskow's views are best represented in an article he called "Judaism and Revolution Today":

> The Question that we must answer at this moment of crisis in our history is, indeed... Does the Jewish tradition impel us to believe that at this moment we must become committed as Jews to the radical transformation of America and the world? And, closely connected with that question, a second one of overwhelming import: Does the Jewish people stand utterly alone--or are there other peoples who share our needs, face much the same disasters as do we, and might, in concert with us, act to transform the world so that we and they are freed? (Original emphasis).

(1973:11-28)

Thus, in one stroke, Waskow combined the particularistic and the universalistic. Not only were Jews asked to transform radically the world out of their own tradition but they were to do so in concert with the needs and aspirations of others. For Waskow, the source for such transformation was to be the halachah, the codified Jewish law, but in his case, a new halachah would have to be developed and new-halachic communities would have to be built on the basis of democratic socialism.

The key symbol for Waskow of this blending of the universal and the particular is the Holocaust, the utter destruction of the world. This is the reason that one must increase one's efforts to radically transform the world:

> But to some Jews the twin message got lost. Some focused on Auschwitz as if no other people were in danger, while others focused on Hiroshima as though all the differences between people had been annihilated in that blinding flash. The truth is that both Auschwitz and Hiroshima threatened the Jewish people and that both threatened all the peoples of the Earth. Auschwitz threatened all of us in our differences, Hiroshima threatened all of us in our sameness."
> (Waskow, 1973:17)

Out of this awareness could emerge a revolutionary alliance of Jews and non-Jews that can one day bring about what Waskow calls the "Age of Shabbat;" what religious people have called the paradise of life after death, and what Marxists have called the final stage of Communism. In any case, it is a vision of a world free from destruction, poverty, and prejudice. This has been the essential historical goal of all rebels, Jewish or otherwise. Some of these lofty visions have become distorted, bringing misery and fear in their wake. That Jewish rebels, with all their good intentions, have at times been party to such misery is also true. Jewish law respects messianic visions, but it also curses those who bring a Messiah too soon. The Jewish rebel is thus both an approbation and a curse; in his or her hands lies the power to do both good or evil and, sometimes, a little of both.

References

Carmichael, Joel, "Trotsky: The Alienated Jew," Encounter, May, 1972, reprinted in Jewish Digest, January, 1973, pp. 43-45.

Cuddihy, John Murray, The Ordeal of Civility (New York: Basic Books, 1974).

Deutscher, Isaac, The Non-Jewish Jew and Other Essays (New York: Oxford University Press, 1968).

Gershman, Carl, "Countering Anti-Israel Propaganda on the Campus," January 31, 1970; Privately Printed.

_____, "Neither Jewish Radicals Nor Radical Jews," ADL Bulletin, May, 1972; reprinted in Jewish Digest, January, 1973, pp. 46-48.

Glazer, Nathan, "The Jewish Role in Student Activism," Fortune Magazine 79, January, 1969; pp. 112-113 et seq.

Hindus, Maurice G., "The Jew as a Radical," The Menorah Journal, vol. 13, no. 4, August, 1927, pp. 367-379.

Kitch, Laura and Mayer, Egon, book review of The Ordeal of Civility by J.M. Cuddihy in Jewish Sociology and Social Research, vol. 2, no. 2, Spring-Summer, 1976, pp. 23-25.

Lipset, S.M., personal memo to author January 28, 1974.

_____, "The Left, the Jews, and Israel" in his Revolution and Counter-Revolution: and Persistence in Social Structures, Rev. ed. (New York: Anchor-Doubleday Books, 1970) pp. 375-400. Originally appeared in Encounter 33, December, 1969; pp. 24-35 under the title of "The Socialism of Fools: The Left, the Jews, and Israel."

Maccoby, Hyam, Letters to the Editor section, "Jews and Revolution, Commentary, vol. 64, no. 1, July, 1977, pp. 13-14.

Novick, Paul, "Lumer vs. Lenin on the Jewish Question," Jewish Currents, vol. 31, no. 7 (343), JulyAugust, 1977, pp. 22-28.

Porter, Jack Nusan, "Jewish Student Activism," <u>Jewish Currents</u>, vol. 24, no. 5 (264), May, 1970, pp. 28-34. Also appeared as a booklet.

Porter, Jack Nusan and Dreier, Peter, <u>Jewish Radicalism</u> (New York: Grove Press, 1973).

Rothman, Stanley and Horowitz, I.L., Review Symposium on J.M. Cuddihy's book <u>The Ordeal of Civility</u>, in <u>Contemporary Sociology: A Journal of Reviews</u>, vol. 5, no. 2, March, 1976, pp. 109-115.

Rubin, Jerry, <u>We are Everywhere</u>, (New York: Harper and Row, 1971).

Ruchames, Louis, "Jewish Radicalism in the United States," in Peter I. Rose, (ed.) <u>The Ghetto and Beyond</u> (New York: Random House, 1969).

Schappes, Morris U., "The Jewish Question and the Left-Old and New", <u>Jewish Currents</u> 24, June, 1970, pp. 4-13, 29-37.

Siegel, Richard, Strassfeld, Michael and Strassfeld, Susan, <u>The Jewish Catalog</u> (Philadelphia: Jewish Publication Society, 1973). Another <u>Catalog</u>, Part II, came out in 1976, and a third volume appeared in 1980.

Sleeper, James A. and Mintz, Alan L., (eds.), <u>The New Jews</u> (New York: Random House-Vintage Books, 1971).

Waskow, Arthur, "Judaism and Revolution Today" in J. N. Porter and P. Dreier (eds.), <u>Jewish Radicalism: A Selected Anthology</u> (New York: Grove Press-Random House, 1973) pp. 11-28.

Wistrich, Robert, <u>Revolutionary Jews from Marx to Trotsky</u>, (New York and London: Barnes and Noble, Harper and Row, 1976).

_____, Letters to the Editor section, "Jews and Revolution," in <u>Commentary</u>, vol. 64, no. 1, July, 1977, pp. 13-14.

Chapter 2

The Jewish Intellectual

The Jewish intellectual and, more particularly, the Jewish academic, like the poet and radical, exhibit a unique sort of marginality from the Jewish community. For a very long time, Jewish academics were not very much involved with the Jewish community. Like Jewish intellectuals generally, academics tended to be less observant than their fellow Jews outside of academia, and they also tended to be more liberal, more opinionated, and more tolerant politically. The intellectual and academic subculture stresses its own values, and these often are at odds with Jewish values. Over time, Jewish intellectuals become less observant, more liberal, and more isolated the longer they stay within such subcultural environments, until they discover that they have emerged outside the mainstream of Jewish life. However, after the 1967 Israeli-Arab War, important changes took place among academics and intellectuals: they became more Jewishly-concerned--but still able to provoke controversy because of their provocative criticism of Israel and the Jewish community. Their critical impulse could not be squelched entirely even after their subsequent involvement in Jewish and Israeli affairs. This article is a revised version of a paper read at Brandeis University for the Bicentennial Lecture Series, sponsored by the American Jewish Historical Society. It was, solicited by the late Louis Ruchames and presented January 8, 1976. Another version was published in Midstream, January, 1979, pp. 18-25 and is reprinted by permission of the editor.

* * * * *

This analysis will concentrate on who the major Jewish intellectuals are, the divisions and conflicts among them, and, most crucially--the new and powerful role Jewish intellectuals play in modern society. They have become an important reservoir of power as well as a potent source of change. The pen is more powerful than the sword, at least in the long run, and who knows that better than the people of the book themselves?

What is an intellectual? To profess being an intellectual is to undertake a sacred task. It is the intellectual who speaks, or attempts to speak, for the people he or she "represents" and for the "truth" as he or she sees it. In the process one makes oneself vulnerable. To be an intellectual, then, is to be someone who loves ideas, who peddles ideas, who helps put ideas into power, who sacrifices for ideas.

Sociologists might define intellectuals as members of a society who are devoted to the development of original ideas and are engaged in creative pursuits. Such intellectuals (writers, editors, professors, publishers, some journalists) constitute a small creative segment of the intelligentsia, and they provide the intellectual leadership for the remainder of the intelligentsia as well as being advisers to the power elite.[1]

Since World War II the role of the intellectual has grown. Since Roosevelt's time, especially, the intellectual, and the academic in particular, has entered into the decision-making that goes on at the highest levels of government. It could not be otherwise: since World War II modern societies have grown very complex. Highly educated specialists have become necessary in various areas of government: military experts, foreign policy advisers, economic and social problem specialists, lawyers, agronomists, and others. Paralleling the rise of these new roles educated "information class" and the phenomenal growth of higher education.

More and more often, governments have to go to the "experts" in academia in order to find their advisers, and they have usually gone to the most prestigious universities in the land in order to do so: Harvard, Yale, Columbia, Chicago, Michigan, Princeton, and Berkeley. And it is at these universities where one finds Jewish professors and researchers in greatly disproportionate numbers.

Recent studies by S.M. Lipset and E.C. Ladd have shown that Jews are heavily represented on the facul-

-34-

ties of Ivy League schools, other elite private colleges, the "Big Ten" universities, and the various campuses of the University of California and are considerably underrepresented at other, less prestigious, state and private schools. Furthermore, they discovered that 32 percent of the Jewish professors are at schools which are in the highest quality category, in contrast to 9 percent of the Christian professors; conversely, over 40 percent of the Christians are in the lowest quality schools, as compared to only 13.5 percent of the Jews.[2]

Intellectuals, far from being the "effete and ineffectual snobs" that ex-Vice President Spiro Agnew called them, are far from ineffectual, although they may be snobs. On the contrary, they exert enormous power, more power than any of the 17th century Hof-Juden ever dreamed of.

At the same time, in the aftermath of the Holocaust and the establishment of a Jewish state--there has been a definite shift in their allegiance to Jewish causes. I have the impression--no doubt it should be backed up by research--that the "runaway" Jewish intellectual (despite a high intermarriage rate and low level of religious observance) is returning to the fold. There are several reasons for this return, which in sheer numbers is unique in modern Jewish history: the state of Israel and issues that revolve around it, especially New Left, black Left, and Third World anti-Zionism and, at times, anti-Semitism. These issues and events confused and disillusioned many Jewish intellectuals and opened up an opportunity for involvement within the Jewish community. The rise of the Jewish student and countercultural movement acted as a bridge and helped these intellectuals and their students to become a "Third Force" between Jewish apologists and conservatives on the one hand and radical New Leftists who happened to be Jewish on the other. There were other factors as well: the rise of Jewish pride, the growth of Jewish studies, memories of the Holocaust as reflected in the turmoil in Vietnam, and a new sensitivity to religious expression. Whatever the reasons, one sees more and more Jewish intellectuals involved in Jewish affairs.[3]

Historically, Jewish intellectuals have acted as a two-edged sword, critical of both the general society and the Jewish one. Jewish intellectuals have also acted as a positive force for Jews (Zionism, Reformism,

-35-

Haskalah) as well as a negative one (Communism, Enlightenment assimilationism, and even antiSemitism.[4]

Just as the Jewish intellectual will warily watch the Jewish community, so too will the Jewish community watch the intellectual. But historians will have to note that in America in the 1970s, Jewish intellectuals, while critical gadflys, have been reintegrated with the Jewish community. The overwhelming bulk of Jewish intellectuals are now within the fold.

But can these intellectuals be analyzed? They are members of the educated stratum of society, generally in professional and managerial occupations. The ambivalent role played by the Jewish intellectual is based on his or her precarious position of being both part of the Jewish intelligentsia and the non-Jewish one. Often, these dichotomous elements are in conflict.

According to Edward Shils there are four major and, at times, overlapping traditions that intellectuals are inspired by:[5]

(a) **Scientism**: This tradition insists on testing the validity of everything and rejecting it if it does not correspond to the "facts of experience." This tradition is critical of the arbitrary and the irrational. It is best exemplified by the academic scholar today.

(b) **The Romantic Tradition**: At first this seems to be the antithesis of scientism. At certain points-- for example, the value of impulse and passion--there are real and unbridgeable antagonisms, but in many important aspects there is a sharing of fundamental features. Both traditions value the originality of an idea, one that is produced by "genius," one that is "novel," in contrast to that which is stereotyped or mundane. This tradition is best exemplified by the artist or writer today.

(c) **The Apocalyptic Tradition**: This is the belief that the world is so corrupt that it will collapse and fall one day in the future, only to be replaced by one purer and better. This is the prophetic tradition; it is best exemplified by the political revolutionary and the religious mystic. It has fascinated many intellectuals and draws much from the romantic tradition.

(d) **Populism**: Again, akin to the revolutionary tradition, this too has attracted many intellectuals during the past 150 years. It rests on the assumption that there is an innate creativity and, moreover, a superior moral worth in ordinary "oppressed" folk--the people, the uneducated, the nonintellectual, even the antiintellectual. In the simplicity of the folkways, such simple people are thought to hold values that are morally superior to those found in the educated and higher social classes.

Jews, including this author, find themselves heir to all four traditions. They find aspects of all four in their intellectual and political heritage. Jews, given their history, are often wary of the populist, frightened by the revolutionary, troubled by the apocalyptic, and frustrated by the scientistic. There is an old Yiddish saying: "Yidden must tansen oif a sach chasenes"--"Jews have to dance at many kinds of weddings."

The picture, plainly, is becoming complex; historic and sociological strands are becoming tangled. When one looks to the American scene, one must agree with Michael Novak that "to draw a map of intellectuals is to draw a map as primitive as a Viking's map of America."[6] Still, Novak attempts to distinguish the following "families," those who are the foremost creators as opposed to the distributors of intellectual culture in the United States. (Some have died since he complied this list.)

Ivy League pragmatists and humanists (Henry Steele Commager, Arthur Schlesinger, Jr.)

Literary Modernists (Lionel Trilling, Louis Kampf, Irving Howe, Leslie Fiedler)

Pluralists (Nathan Glazer, Daniel Moynihan, David Reisman, Talcott Parsons, Will Herberg)

New Radicals (Noam Chomsky, the New York Review of Books gang)

Conservative Liberals (Sidney Hook, Norman Podhoretz, Irving Kristol)

Europe-oriented Humanists (Hannah Arendt, Philip Rahv, George Lichtheim, Saul Bellow)

It is an interesting division but peculiar to Novak. Not surprisingly, Jews overwhelm the list just as they overwhelm intellectual life in America. ("Dominate" is too controversial a word to describe the power of Jewish intellectuals within intellectual circles. Their "domination" in other spheres of inluence--political, economic--is a more tangled issue.) Novak's "families" are shifting, changing, getting older. Furthermore, there is a natural over-lap: some of his intellectuals synthesize in themselves more than one viewpoint and all share some elements of every viewpoint. Before I present my list of Jewish intellectuals, I shall attempt to grapple with the impossible task of defining who, exactly, is a Jewish intellectual. It is a diverse and wondrous collection of individuals: I.F. Stone and Meir Kahane; the Rav Soloveitchik and the Lubavitcher Rebbe; Betty Friedan and Eugene Borowitz; Nat Hentoff and David Brudnoy; Norman Mailer and Herman Kahn; Elie Weisel and Arthur Waskow; Jerry Rubin and the Babba Ram Das (nee Richard Alpert).

What single typology could include all these varied individuals? What single definition of an intellectual could encompass all these people? I will define an intellectual as a man or woman whose occupation, career, or mission is to influence people in creative and original ways either politically, morally, psychologically, or sociologically. Jewish intellectuals, whether rabbis, writers, journalists, novelists, pamphleteers, or teachers, do this in two arenas, either influencing the general society or the Jewish/Israeli community in particular. Some attempt to influence both.

Secondly, one must also divide these Jewish intellectuals into two broad groups, the "insiders" and the "outsiders." The former is by far the larger of the two and consists of those who vigorously support the integrity and survival of the Jewish people and the state of Israel. The latter, a much smaller group yet at times quite influential, are those who neither support the continuity of the Jewish people nor the state of Israel, or who support one but not the other (for example, the American Council for Judaism supports Jewish survival in the Diaspora but not the state of Israel). Here then is my typology:

"Insiders"

Conservatives (David Brudnoy, Milton Friedman, Meir Kahane)

Liberal Conservatives (Norman Podhoretz, Irving Kristol, Milton Himmelfarb)

Liberals (Nathan Glazer, Leonard Fein)

Left-liberals (I.L. Horowitz, Irving Howe, the author)

Radicals, including New Left and Old Left members committed to Israel and Jewish survival (Arthur Waskow, Morris U. Schappes, Paul Jacobs)

"Outsiders"

Conservatives (the American Council for Judaism plus other anti-Zionists of a nonsocialist perspective)

Liberals (any assimilated and/or anti-Zionist liberal Jews)

Radicals (New Left and Old Left Jews who are anti-Zionist and anti-Jewish survival)

This is, admittedly, a provocative typology; some named may feel uneasy with their assigned labels. I ask the reader to pay close attention to small but crucial differences. The most important is that nearly all Jewish "insiders" despite their political differences agree on two essential points: the survival and integrity of the Jewish people and the survival and integrity of the state of Israel. If any intellectual opposes either one of these, he or she stands outside the Jewish people!

However, one can be a principled non-Zionist (though not anti-Zionist), that is, a Diasporist, and still be accorded a respected place in the Jewish community, since such Diasporists believe in a secular form of Judaism and in a sovereign Jewish state. They may _not_ believe that Israel is, or ought to be, the cultural and spiritual center of the Jewish people. They are the Bundists of the past and the neo-Bundists of the present. Most Bundists today support the integrity of the state of Israel, even though they are Diasporist in ideology.

I will not go into a discussion of the "outsider" camp, even though they may deserve discussion. More and more, such "outsiders" are recognizing the weakness

of their political position and are asking for a
passport back to the Jewish people. I have met such
intellectuals; I feel thay have an important contribution to make as Jews once they have been reinstated in
the community.

Now we come to the Jewish "insiders." Despite the
crucial similarities, one finds tension, though it has
somewhat diminished in the post-Vietnam, post-radical-
student period. But the conflicts are still there. No
doubt Murray Kempton is right when he writes: "... What
distresses me, underneath all this nastiness, is the
impression that you're in nothing but a personal
quarrel....They're continuously bleeding from scars
where no one ever touched them."[7]

The marathon mano a mano between the right and
left factions of New York intellectuals still rages.
(Some are no longer in New York, but in Boston,
Washington, and San Francisco). Suffice it to say, the
battle has been over Israel; here, the liberal and
left-liberal intellectuals are "winning" over the
conservatives and liberal conservatives. The con-
stellation of issues revolve around the question of
recognizing the Palestinians and the question of how
public criticism of Israel should become. One important reason for the debate is because the Diaspora has
"grown up"--there is a more mature relationship today
with Israel. In the past, it was literally "collect
the money and keep quiet." This attitude is changing
and there are growing pains in such a changing relationship. In any case, it is over Israel, or rather
which tactics and strategies Israel should use in
seeking peace, that is dividing American Jewish
intellectuals. (There are, of course, other issues,
such as democracy in Jewish decision-making, the role
of women in Jewish leadership and within religious
life, the Jewish family, intermarriage, Jewish education, etc., but interestingly, there seems to be more
unanimity among "insider" Jewish intellectuals on these
issues than most people realize.)

Recently, the clash over the Palestinian question
has exacerbated the differences among Jewish intellectuals. On one side, stands a group formed several
years ago by Jewish "leftists" and a number of Reform
and Conservative rabbis, including a large number of
Hillel directors, called Breira (Hebrew for "alternative"); and on the other side, opposing it, are many
establishment Jewish organizations, most vocally, the

-40-

Anti-Defamation League, the Zionist Organization of America, the Jewish Defense League, and a group of revisionist-Zionist, Likud-aligned, American intellectuals called Americans for a Safe Israel.[9]

This clash was probably inevitable and has been building up since the 1973 war, though it had its origins in the 1967 clash when a Jewish student/radical movement emerged. Breira was a direct descendant of Jewish radical and radical Jewish activists. Jewish radicals "returned" to Jewish concerns but came with their baggage of criticism in hand. Being relative newcomers to the Jewish scene, some of them were not often trusted by the Jewish masses or the Jewish establishment. They hadn't yet "proven themselves" as confirmed friends of Israel or of the Jewish people. Furthermore, their messianic fervor, their bold and innovative strategies, and, at times, their insensitivity to Jewish nuances made them both feared and praised. The best example of such a radical Jew is Arthur Waskow.[9]

It was Waskow who, like a lightning rod, charged the atmosphere in intellectual circles when in November, 1976 he, acting as an unofficial representative of Breira, along with several other Jews, met with Palestinian leaders secretly in Washington and New York.[10] This was viewed as an unheard of act, and when news of the meeting leaked to the press, Waskow himself went public in the New York Times.

Arthur Waskow, an "outsider" who became a radical "insider," is a much maligned man. He has been called an "evil son" as well as a "rabbi's rebbe." He is quite devout and not the "raving, self-hating leftist" that he is often pictured. He prays every day. He studies Talmud and Torah. He keeps the Sabbath. And he dynamically applies religious teachings to current political problems in a very innovative way. His enemies are both the Jewish establishment and the Jewish assimilationist.

While influential within Breira, he is not the dominating force. A brilliant organizer and writer, heavily influenced by Buber and Heschel as well as Mao Tse-Tung and Paul Goodman, he is often criticized even by his own sympathizers for "calling for the messiah too soon." He forces people to move beyond their narrow visions, and people feel he pushes too far and too fast. And they rebel against his vision which they often find too utopian to accept.

-41-

Even though most Breira members are not as radical
as Waskow, they are radical enough in proposing a
Palestinian state on the West Bank and in recognizing
the PLO as a legitimate voice for their people. The
attack against Breira has come from conservative and
liberal-conservative Jews and from what Irving Howe
calls "Jewish neo-Conservatism":

> We've seen the rise of a very sharp and clear
> articulation of what has been called Jewish
> neo-Conservatism, and this has been reflected
> most prominently in the pages of Commentary.
> I find this development distressing. I was a
> longtime contributor to Commentary and during
> the late '60s my personal and political rela-
> tions with its editor, Norman Podhoretz, were
> quite close. We shared an interest both from
> Jewish and general political premises in
> polemicizing against the New Left, or against
> its excesses. I wanted to attack the New
> Left from the perspective of democratic
> socialism and liberalism and it began to seem
> to me that under Norman's editorship...
> Commentary was moving increasingly toward a
> conservative position. In the name of
> attacking the New Left, it soon began to take
> all kinds of swipes against liberal
> views..[11]

Howe goes on to say that in the absence of significant opposition, the increasingly strident conservatism of Commentary came to be seen by influential
others as representative of the political and cultural
outlook of all American Jews. And that, to Howe,
seemed "highly unfortunate."

Yet, at the time of Howe's comments, Breira had
not yet come to prominence, and Howe had not yet come
to be one of its most influential and valuable supporters. Commentary attacked Breira in April, 1977 in an
article by Joseph Shattan, based heavily on an earlier
pamphlet written by a spokesperson for Americans for a
Safe Israel, Rael Isaac.[12] Jewish liberalism, best
personified by Moment magazine, founded by a Brandeis
University political scientist, Leonard Fein and edited
by the past editor of Response, William Novak, had not
found its true voice and had not yet made a deep enough
impact.

Breira and its newsletter, Interchange, edited by
Arthur Samuelson, had emerged, on the other hand, as

one of the most important journals of independent, critical and Jewish liberal-leftist thought in the country. (Interchange was to have a short lifespan, however, because of Breira's troubles nationally.)

The clash among these intellectuals implied an important, if not crucial, change in Israeli-American relations, namely that Jews outside of Israel would from now on clamor to be taken seriously and to be seen as equal partners. No longer could Israel dictate to world Jewry--"give us your philanthropy and shut up!" A more mature, more provocative, and therefore more difficult period lay ahead as Diaspora Jewish intellectuals confronted Israel with private and sometimes public criticism of both its foreign and domestic policies. As Irving Howe, one of the most prominent of American Jewish intellectuals, emphasized:

> ....whatever our views, we claim it as proven friends of Israel. And we ask that right in behalf of all opinions within the Jewish world that accept the necessity of Israeli survival--a right to be exercised without fear, without pressure, without retribution, without excommunication. In that respect, surely, we speak for what is best in the traditions of American Jewish life.[13]

Whether it be in the "best traditions" of Jewish life or not, such criticism of Israel did not sit well with many Jewish leaders and some Jewish intellectuals, especially those intellectuals who were ideologically supportive of the Jewish middle class. Breira came under severe attack and had to suspend operations nationally because of financial difficulties. It was ironic, however, that soon after Breira's demise nationally (local chapters still exist, one must emphasize) in April, 1978, a group of thirty seven prominent American artists, writers, rabbis, and Jewish professionals gave support to the dovish, grassroots "Peace Now" movement in Israel by placing ads in the New York Times and Boston Globe, calling upon Prime Minister Begin to be more flexible and to seek peace rather than a Greater Israel. These writers and intellectuals also came under fire from some Jewish quarters.

Why have such new "Breira's" arisen and why will they arise in the future? The answer is because the Jewish community is not monolithic. There are doves and hawks--there are Jews who support President Carter's "New Deal" in the Middle East and those who oppose his position. Intellectuals are also split, but the vast majority are on the liberal to left side of the spectrum and support the American president's new initiatives. Opposition to Begin's "hard line" is found both in America and in Israel, and Jewish intellectuals will continue to be in the forefront of such opposition.

And what of the future? How will Jewish intellectuals and the Jewish communities of the Diaspora and Israel confront each other? How will Jewish intellectuals themselves confront each other? Most surely, relations will continue as they have been traditionally --provocative, exasperating, and touchy. The split among Jewish intellectuals will also continue. Some Jewish intellectuals speak for the masses and wish to heighten their vision. They are usually leftists or left-liberal. Others speak to them in order to justify, clarify, or support their Jewish paranoia. They are usually conservatives, neo- or liberal-conservatives.

As Lenin emphasized long ago, the intelligenty of a society must be neither too far ahead of the people nor too far behind them. However, the role of the intellectual is essentially radical, while the role of the community is essentially conservative, that is, to restrain the utopian dreams and overzealous politics of the leftist intellectual and to conserve the tradition-al and the status quo.[14] While most Jewish intellectuals are consistently leftist or left-liberal, a conservative Jewish faction has arisen and says that it speaks for the people. The true role of the intellectual, however, is more prophetic, to give the people and their intellectual supporters a vision of the "promised land." The tension between the two will always exist and will always be necessary. In short, each needs the other.

Notes

1. George and Achilles Theodorson, _Modern Dictionary of Sociology_ (New York: Thomas Crowell, 1969), p. 210.

2. S.M. Lipset and Ladd, E.C., Jr., "Jewish Academics in the United States: Their Achievement, Culture, and Politics," in the _American Jewish Year Book_, vol. 72, 1971, pp. 89-128.

3. See for example, Jack Nusan Porter, "Jewish Student Activism," in _Jewish Currents_, vol. 24, no. 5, May, 1970, pp. 28-34; Jack Nusan Porter and Peter Dreier (eds.), _Jewish Radicalism_ (New York: Grove Press, 1973); and Peter Dreier and Jack Nusan Porter, "Jewish Radicalism in Transition," in _Society_, vol. 12, no. 2, January-February, 1975, pp. 34-43.

4. For an extension of this position, see Jacob Neusner, "The Absence of Jewish Private Lives," in _The Jewish Advocate_ (Boston), June 17, 1976, p. 3, section 2.

5. Edward Shils, "The Intellectuals and the Powers: Some Perspectives for Comparative Analysis," in Philip Rieff (ed.), _On Intellectuals_ (New York: Doubleday-Anchor Books, 1970), pp. 47-51. For further elaboration of these issues, see Aleksander Gella (ed.), _The Intelligentsia and the Intellectuals_ (London and Beverly Hills, California: Sage Publications, 1976).

6. Michael Novak, _The Rise of the Unmeltable Ethnics_ (New York: Macmillan, 1971), p. 160.

7. Philip Nobile, _Intellectual Skywriting: Literary Politics and The New York Review of Books_ (New York: Charterhouse, 1974), p. 134.

8. For a more wide-ranging analysis of this issue see Eugene B. Borowitz, "For Dissent on Israeli Policy--Part 1 and 2," _Sh'ma: A Journal of Jewish Responsibility_, 6/116 and 6/117, September 3 and 17, 1976.

9. The best of Waskow's ideology at his most radical
    stage, somewhat modified now, is The Bush is
    Burning: Radical Judaism Faces the Pharaohs
    of the Modern Superstate (New York: Macmillan,
    1971), and The Freedom Seder (New York: Holt,
    Rinehart, and Winston, 1970). He has toned down
    his excesses since that time.

10. For repercussions of this meeting see William
    Novak, "The Breira Story," Genesis 2, March-April,
    1977; Alexander Cockburn and James Ridgeway, "Jews
    Against Jews: An American Witch Hunt and Israel's
    Survival," Village Voice, vol. 22, no. 10, March
    7, 1977, pp. 26-29; and Rael Isaac, Breira:
    Counsel for Judaism (pamphlet) (New York:
    Americans for a Safe Israel, January, 1977); Alan
    Mintz, "The People's Choice?: A Demurral on
    Breira," Response, vol. 10, no. 4, (#32), Winter,
    1976-77, pp. 5-10; and Rael Jean and Erich Isaac,
    "The Rabbis of Breira," Midstream, vol. 23, no.
    4, April, 1977, pp. 3-17.

11. Quoted in an interview in Moment, vol. 1, no. 8,
    March, 1976, p. 27.

12. See Joseph Shattan, "Why Breira?" Commentary, vol.
    63, no. 4, April, 1977, pp. 60-66.

13. From Breira literature, Breira Inc., 200 Park Ave.
    New York, NY 10003. See Irving Howe, "For Free
    Discussion in the Jewish Community," Interchange,
    vol. 1, no. 10, June, 1976, pp. 1, 7-8.

14. For more on the complex and intricate role of the
    modern intellectual, see S.M. Lipset and R.
    Dobson, "The Intellectual as Critic and Rebel with
    Special Reference to the United States and the
    Soviet Union," Daedalus (101:3, 1972), pp.
    137-198; and Karl Mannheim, Ideology and Utopia,
    Louis Wirth and Edward Shils, trans. (New York:
    Harcourt, Brace and World, 1936 (1929)).

Chapter 3

The Jewishness of Karl Marx

This essay emerged out of my interest in the social-psychological concept of self-hatred, and I saw in Karl Marx a perfect example. When I have presented this paper at sociological conferences, many people have no problem in seeing how determined Marx was in erasing the Jewish features of his life. The only ones who respond with some anger are a few leftists in the audience who feel that by emphasizing the "psycho-history" of Marx, I am somehow missing the point, that what Marx felt in private about Jews or Judaism is tri-vial and should be forgotten or overlooked. But this is exactly what Soviet publishers have been doing for years, and, in a way, I feel that the terrible treat-ment of the Jews in Russia is and was exacerbated because they have attempted to camouflage Marx's Jewish ancestry. For how could Soviet officials harm Jews if Marx himself was a Jew? Then again, perhaps it would not have helped. Look at Jesus. In any case, the evi-dence mounts, as shown in a recent collection of Marx's letters edited by the renowned scholar Saul K. Padover. In these letters, Marx outdoes himself in his vitupera-tion of Jews and Jewish personalities. I have also discovered that no matter how much evidence one pre-sents, there are apologists out there, no matter how intelligent, who will never be convinced and will be totally blind to the facts. I pity them. This essay is original and has never been published before.

* * * * *

Introduction

Karl Marx was born in 1818 in the small, pre-dominantly Catholic city of Trier in the Rhineland,

Germany. His father, Heinrich (Hershel), was the son of Marx Levi (Mordechai ben Samuel Halevi) who was the rabbi of Trier. The name Marx itself derives from an abbreviated form of Mordechai, later changed to Markus. Marx's grandfather Mordechai was the descendant of a long line of rabbinical scholars, and his grandmother Eva Lwow had an equally illustrious ancestry. Thus, from both sides of his family tree, Marx had distinguished rabbis.

Marx's father, Heinrich, was a knowledgeable, industrious lawyer in the high court of Trier, but given the anti-Semitism of the times, he was forced to convert to Lutheranism (in 1817) in order to practice his legal profession. In 1824, when his children were of school age, Heinrich Marx had them all baptized into the Lutheran religion. (Wistrich, 1976:27-28)

Thus, at the age of six, Karl Marx became a Christian without having any say in the matter at all. His mother (nee Henrietta Pressburg) delayed her conversion until 1825 when her father, Isaac Pressburg, rabbi in Nujmegen, Holland, died. The reason for the delay was obvious: her parents were against such conversion. Perhaps, too, she had a greater love of her religion. Only with great reluctance did she finally convert.

Wistrich (1976:27) points out that though Marx completely rejected his background, it did not mean that it exercised no influence on his revolutionary career. As Wistrich says: "His intransigent hostility to Judaism should not blind one to the role which insecurity about his origins played in shaping the intellectual and moral character of his outlook.... Although Marx was to give his name to a secular, universalist ideology, as hostile to Christianity as it was to Judaism, he never freed himself from subjective prejudices which reflected the oldest anti-Semitic stereotypes of European Christian society." (1976:27) Wistrich feels that Marx came by his anti-Semitic feelings quite easily: he was raised as a Lutheran in Lutheran schools, and he could not avoid seeing Jews and the "Jewish problem" through the distorted lens of the Christian Judeophobia of his era. Often, as we will see, he continued to describe Jews and Judaism, not in a tolerant way, but in the emotional and often belligerent stereotypes of the day, that is, the Jew as international banker; the Jew as "money-grubber;" the Jew as "Capitalist;" all the while forgetting ignoring that most Jews in the world were poor, impoverished ghetto or <u>shtetl</u> dwellers.

Marxism and Judaism

By its very definition, orthodox Marxism is opposed to religion and nationality. Marxism is international, materialistic, and the very negation of religion. The optimism of Marxist theory is based on the idea that mankind can solve its problems without divine assistance because of man's essentially rational nature. Religion is seen by Marx as the "opium of the masses" because it drugs and clouds the vision of the masses with irraional, mystical thoughts, thus delaying the making of political revolution. Marx identified Jews and Judaism with capitalism, and Judaism he saw as antimaterialistic, chauvinistic, reactionary, and resigned to the scrapheap of history when the revolution of the proletariat was accomplished.

According to Marx, the elimination of capitalism will emancipate Jews along with the rest of the world that has been victimized by capitalism. The abolishment of both capitalism and, thereby, Judaism will therefore liberate the Jews from their religion. Under communism, the Jews will no longer have to live as Jews. Their real nature will be rejected, and Jews should actively facilitate this process by rejecting their Judaism and taking part in the rebellion against capitalism. Furthermore, Jewish nationalism (Zionism) is a bourgeois concept and diverts the attention of the Jewish workers away from revolutionary action. Later Marxists saw Zionism and its instrument, the state of Israel, as archaic vestiges of capitalism in the form of neocolonialism and imperialism. An important point to stress is that Marx's views of the Jews (and by extension as applied to Israel), written over one hundred years ago, have influenced the attitudes of many Marxists today. (See Lipset, 1969; Laqueur, 1971; Lichtheim, 1968; Bloom, 1942; and Gotlieb, 1978.)

Robert Wistrich (1976) in his <u>Revolutionary Jews from Marx to Trotsky</u> feels that the term self-hatred should be applied to Karl Marx and several other radical thinkers (i.e., Ferdinand Lasalle, Rosa Luxemburg, and Julius Martov). Wistrich emphasizes that Marx, the assimilated descendant of a distinguished line of rabbis, felt embarrassed and ambivalent about his Jewish "roots" and, furthermore, lashed out against Jews and Judaism in vulgar anti-Semitic stereotypes.

Being of Jewish parentage and never being allowed to forget that he was in fact a Jew, Marx turned upon not only the Christian society but against Jews themselves, attempting in the process to transcend both Christianity and Judaism with the ideology of revolutionary socialism. Since Marx was, according to Wistrich, an anti-Semitic Jew, he feels that the label of a self-hating Jew is applicable to Karl Marx.

Some writers (Friedland, 1978:1551-1552 and Deutscher, 1977:57-60) have disagreed with Wistrich. Friedland, for example, feels that Marx, Lasalle, Luxemburg, et al did not hate themselves. He will concede that many Jewish radicals had "reservations" about Jews and about their own Jewish antecedents, but he feels that the term "self-hatred" is essentially a psychological process, and Jews who assimilate or who are anti- or non-Zionist are not necessarily people who hate themselves. Friedland feels that the term self-hatred as applied to Marx is "incorrect;" an example of "name-calling;" and ultimately "inadequate and unsatisfactory." (1978:1552)

He maintains that Marx and other radicals of Jewish background rejected Judaism not out of self-hatred but because they felt that Judaism and Jewishness as a philosophy of life was too limiting a background. He sees assimilation as a rejection of the social group that one has come out of rather than as hatred of self. What Friedland may have overlooked is that it could be both reasons rather than either one. And does not rejection of one's group include disgust with the behavior of that group?

Deutscher (1977) takes exception with the self-hatred theory, because she feels that Marx was not concerned with the religion of the Jews but with the "exceptional" role that Jews played in feudal and early capitalist development where they represented the oncoming money economy in societies in transition from natural economy. Marx felt that Christian society had become "Judaized." According to Deutscher, he did not mean to apply anti-Semitic connotations to this fact, but only meant that money had become a world power, and as Christian society became more capitalist, it became more "Judaized." What both Marx and Deutscher forgot was that the bulk of the Jewish masses were not involved in banking or moneylending but were poor tradesmen. Because of the prominence of a few Jewish banking houses (most notably, the Rothschilds), Marx and other radicals accepted the prevailing anti-Semitic stereotype of the "money-hoarding Jew."

Despite the protestations of Friedland and Deutscher, there are other authorities who disagree with their formulations and do in fact feel that Marx's ideological system does contain some anti-Semitic elements:

From S.M. Lipset (1969:9):

Some socialists, including Marx himself, used the symbol of Jewish capitalism (of the Jews as merchants and "Shylocks") in their propaganda. Without going into the whole question of Marx's curious relationship with Judaism—it is certainly not a simple one—there can be little doubt Marx's belief system included some components which must be described as anti-Semitism.

From Walter Laqueur (1971:561):

Judaism for Marx was a totally negative phenomenon, something to be got rid of as quickly and as radically as possible. As far as he personally was concerned, his Jewish origin must have appeared an unfortunate accident of birth and a matter of considerable embarrassment. But this was by no means an original or specially "Marxist" attitude. Many of his antisocialist contemporaries reacted in exactly the same way. They were first and foremost citizens of the world and only secondarily German, Austrian, or Russian nationals.

However, Karl Marx often stepped beyond this thin line from internationalist sentiments to anti-Semitic statements, and it is here where I stress that self-hatred may not be too strong a term to describe aspects of Marx's personality. From Silberner (1949:43-45):

In his correspondence with Engels, Marx used a variety of expressions to designate Jews. In some instances, the proper names are preceded or followed by the word "Jew," "English Jew," "French Jew," etc. In other cases, "der Jud" (Yid), "der verfluchts Jude" (the damned Jew), or "Jud Suss" fulfill the same function....

A very rich vocabulary is displayed by Marx
in his comments on Ferdinand Lassalle....He
....designates Lassalle as "the Jewish
nigger," about whom he tells a very witty
story. Lassalle's head and hair, says Marx,
perfectly indicate that "he is descended from
the Negroes who joined Moses on the exodus
from Egypt" (unless his mother or grandmother
on the father's side were crossed with a
nigger). This union of Jew and German on a
Negro base must create a singular product.
The importunity of the fellow is also nigger-
like." (Though quoted in Silberner (1949),
the original quote is from Marx-Engels,
Gesamtausgabe, Dritte Abteilung. Der Briefwechsel zwischen Marx und Engels, Berlin,
1929-1931, III, pp. 82, 84 (July 30, 1862).

Marx makes his most concise statement on the Jews
in his 1843 essay "Zur Judenfrage" ("On the Jewish
Question") which is really a review of two articles by
the German philosopher Bruno Bauer, the leader of the
Young Hegelian movement. Marx's reply originally
appeared in the Deutsch-franzosische Jahrbucher in
Paris in 1844 when he was twenty-six years old. (The
entire essay has been reprinted many times in the
collected works of Marx and Engels and is quoted in
Padover, 1978:42-43; Bloom, 1942:7-8; and Silberner,
1949:24-25.) Marx dealt with the Jewish problem in
depth in only two writings--his 1848 essays mentioned
above and in an extension of those essays in his first
book with Engels, The Holy Family (1845). We will
quote only the most controversial section of "Zur
Judenfrage":

Let us consider the actual, secular Jew, not
the Sabbath Jew as does Bauer, but the every-
day Jew. Let us look for the secret of the
Jew not in his religion, but let us look for
the secret of religion in the actual Jew.

What is the secular basis of Judaism?
Practical need, self-interest.

What is the worldly cult of the Jew?
Huckstering (Schacher).

What is his worldly god? Money.

What actually was the foundation, in and of
itself, of the Jewish religion? Practical
need, egoism....

Money is the jealous god of Israel before
whom no other god may exist. Money degrades
all the gods of mankind--and converts them
into a commodity....

The god of the Jews has been secularized and
has become the god of the world. The bill of
exchange is the real god of the Jew. His god
is only an illusory bill of exchange....

What is contained abstractly in the Jewish
religion--contempt for theory, for art, for
history, for man as an end in himself--is the
actual conscious standpoint, the virtue of
the money-man....

The chimerical nationality of the Jew is the
nationality of the merchant...

And the last sentence of Zur Judenfrage reads:

The social emancipation of the Jew is the
emancipation of society from Judaism. (All
emphasized words are by Marx himself.)

It is this section from Marx's Der Judenfrage that
has been the cause of most of the controversy through
the years. Julius Carlebach (1978) has in fact written
a 466 page book with nearly ninety five pages of notes
and an annotated bibliography of ninety one books and
articles that deal with Marx's essays on, or associations with, Jews. These items are in six languages and
span viewpoints both for and against Marx. It is a
wonderment that Marx's short essays, which the great
scholar Isaiah Berlin (1963:99-100) called "dull and
shallow," could provoke such a number of responses. If
Marx were simply an anti-Semite like Hitler (see Runes:
1959), why all the debate? Why? Because Marx was not
a simple man. In his life, he showed signs that he was
also philo-Semitic. Furthermore, the many responses to
this essay have been colored by the writer's own personal ideology (whether for or against communism), his
desire to see or avoid seeing certain aspects of Marx's
life, or his own personal agenda (an "axe to grind").
Marx has this power to churn up intellectuals 150 years
later.

On the balance sheet, one should mention the apo-
logetical arguments in favor of Karl Marx. First, he
did speak out in favor of Jewish emancipation, and the

Rheinische Zeitung, a Cologne paper that Marx edited
from 1842 until its suppression in March, 1843, was one
of the strongest supporters of such emancipation as one
aspect of the struggle against the clerical monarchy.
It was because of the paper's strong support of Jewish
rights that the leading Jews of Cologne, early in 1843,
turned to Karl Marx to draw up a petition for Jewish
rights to be submitted to the government. Furthermore,
it should be noted that Marx wrote a moving passage
about the wretched condition of the Jews of Jerusalem
in the April 15, 1854 issue of the New York Tribune.
He also exchanged letters with the Jewish historian
Heinrich Graetz (1817-1891) and Graetz wrote back in
warm personal terms. Finally, Marx should be excused,
because he wrote those fateful essays at a young age
before his mature thinking had been published. He had
not yet developed his theory of the class struggle, and
his views of Jews were based entirely on a preoccupa-
tion with money and were influenced by the nonclass
perspective of Ludwig Feuerbach. He would shortly
discard such views. (See Harap, 1959:33-34.)

These are most of the arguments, but there are a
few others that should be mentioned. One has to do
with the translation or mistranslation of certain
phrases in Der Judenfrage. Marx meant that the "social
emancipation of the Jew (des Juden) is the emancipation
of society from Judaism (Judentum)." Some translators
(for example, Runes:1959) changed the wording of
"Judaism" and say "Jews" or "Jewry." This then would
make it sound genocidal, that is, "....the emancipation
of society from Jews." This would be false and misleading. Marx did not wish to rid the world of Jews
but the Jews of their Judaism. In essence, the
outcome, however, would be the same. By eliminating
Judaism, the cultural and religious sourceblood of the
Jews, one would assimilate Jews. If one destroys a
culture and a religion, one ultimately destroys a
nation. Still, we must be precise in what Marx wrote
and avoid mistranslations.

Furthermore, some apologists such as Ruchwarger
(1979) maintain that Marx's attitudes toward Jews were
no different from other liberals of his time, and that
his views should be placed in the context of Germany of
the 1840s, not America of the 1980s. Even those who
were in favor of Jewish emancipation for German Jews
held such anti-Semitic stereotypes. Ruchwarger even
goes so far as to say that many early Zionists held
similar positions, for example, Pinsker, Syrkin, Ber

Borochov, A.D. Gordon, and Hayim Greenberg. He quotes Draper (1977:602) that "to be a good Zionist one must first be somewhat of an anti-Semite," meaning that one must hate the "unclean" commerciality and speculation of Jewish businessmen and bankers in order to be a good socialist Zionist!

Yet, despite the many sophisticated and (almost) persuasive apologetics for Marx, I remain unconvinced. Marx was, in my estimation, an anti-Semite, and, despite his brilliance, he accepted the most vulgar stereotypes of his time. He did nothing to refute such views in his later, more mature works, and even Engels was embarrassed by Marx's anti-Semitic outbursts.

Was Marx blind to or ignorant of the Jewish situation? Was the Jewish question really insignificant within his overall philosophy? Was it disgust for his own identity as a Jew and with Jews in general? Was his "hysterical hatred of the Jews" based on a reaction to his mother (Feuer:1968)? Even when he favored Jewish emancipation, was he simply (and cynically) using Jews as part of his attack against the clerical monarchy and the bourgeoise? Or, should we not agree that the violently anti-Semitic tone of Marx's essays influenced untold generations of communists and, in Berlin's succinct phrase, became "one of the most neurotic and revolting aspects of his masterful but vulgar personality"? (See Berlin, 1959:17-18; Carlebach, 1978:439; and Berlin, 1963.)

Thus, aside from his personal anti-Semitic remarks regarding Lasalle and other Jews, we see that anti-Semitic stereotypes of a negative kind crept into Marx's philosophy-ideology as well. Padover (1978:43) notes the following: As a student of religion, Marx should have known that Jews did not worship Mammon but an all-pervasive deity, and that their rabbis were often profoundly mystical and otherworldly people with a dedication to saving souls rather than saving money. They worshipped a monotheistic God, not money. Furthermore, as a historian, Marx should have known that the founders and early practitioners of Judaism were not men obsessed with trade and money but with their deity. And that later, when Jews in Christian Europe were involved in money affairs, it was out of desperate necessity and not out of inner faith, because most other means of livelihood (farming, the military, etc.) were closed to them. Furthermore, Marx's concept of the "capitalist Jew" held true for some Jews in

Western Europe (Germany, France, England, and Holland) and not for the majority of world Jewry who lived in small towns or urban ghettos in Czarist Russia and in Poland.

If Marx and later Marxists would have been more aware of anti-Semitism and of the Jewish proletariat in Eastern Europe, they might have sympathized with their plight and written in a different manner about Jews and their economic situation. Edmund Silberner takes the view that Karl Marx was not only anti-Semitic, but that he was one of the major contributors to the antiSemitic "tradition" in modern socialism. He writes:

> Already half a century ago, Thomas G. Masaryk drew attention to what he plainly called "the anti-Semitism of Marx." More sympathetic commentators preferred not to use such a blunt term, and spoke of "an anti-Jewish prejudice" of the master. Still others, without adducing evidence, however, assert that "one cannot say that Marx was an anti-Semite," "that nothing is more erroneous" than to consider him as such, because he treated the Jewish problem "entirely without prejudice," and that after all he did not really have "such a bad opinion" of the Jews as his harsh attacks would suggest. Finally, there are those for whom the whole problem seemingly does not exist, and who pass over it in complete silence....It would obviously be futile to argue with those whose wishful thinking is stronger than verifiable facts. If the pronouncements of Marx are not chosen at random, but are examined as a whole...Marx not only can but **must** be regarded as an outspoken anti-Semite....(original emphasis)
>
> Basically the same contempt for the Jews, though couched in a different language, is to be found in the writings of Karl Kautsky, Victor Adler, Franz Mehring, Otto Bauer, and others. Their cumulative impact, added to that of the master, must have been a considerable one....Hundreds of thousands, if not millions, of his adepts read Zur Judenfrage with the same zeal and ardor as they read the Communist Manifesto. Those who accepted his views were much more numerous than those who ventured to formulate objections or qualifi-

cations. Thus, willingly or not, Karl Marx contributed powerfully to provoke or to strengthen anti-Jewish prejudice among his Christian followers, and to estrange from their own people a good number of his Jewish admirers. He thus unquestionably holds one of the key positions in what may, or rather must, be designated by a new but appropriate term as the <u>anti-Semitic tradition of modern Socialism</u>. (Original emphasis.)

(From Silberner, 1949:49-52)

Conclusions

While Karl Marx has had his apologists over the years, and while many have attempted to ignore, over-look, or whitewash his personal feelings, it can definitely be concluded that he did hold anti-Semitic attitudes. Some might say that one should not engage in "psychohistory," that is, one should ignore a man's personal life when one discusses his contribution to science, art, or politics, that it is at best interest-ing but irrelevant. Others might conclude that Marx's animosity toward individual Jews should not be confused with his attitudes toward Jews as a whole. Still others might say that one cannot become an "Anti-Defamation League of the past" and apply the same standards of today to Karl Marx's historical life and times.

While I will agree that Marx was a very complex man and that his attitude toward Jews and Judaism was likewise complex (see, for example, the works of Kurt Lewin, 1948, on the subject of Jewish self-hatred), I remain unconvinced. Through Marx's writings, his own words, and through the interpretations of important scholars in the field, I have attempted to show that a form of self-hatred toward his people and his Jewish identity did in fact occur. Contrary to Friedland (1978), Karl Marx went beyond simply having "reserva-tions" about Jews and his Jewish antecedents. He went beyond indifference and minor annoyance about his Jewish past. He had a real and palpable disgust for Jews!

Though he was born a Jew and came from a long line of rabbis, some of his writings show a deep embarrass-ment and antipathy toward that Jewish identity. Many respected authorities (Silberner, Padover, Lipset, Laqueur, Bloom) have all come to the same conclusion--

-57-

that Karl Marx's belief system had strong anti-Semitic components, and his view of the "Jew as Capitalist" has been echoing in anti-Semitic literature from both right-wing and left-wing anti-Semites. Such anti-Semitism, coming from a man like Karl Marx, can be considered a form of self-hatred regarding one's Jewish identity, an identity that Marx attempted to expunge during his entire life.

Marx's attitude toward the Jews was influenced by Bruno Bauer, but Marx went even further than Bauer by elaborating on Bauer's assertion that the Jews must overcome their religious parochialism (their Judaism) as a precondition for political and social emancipation. Marx went one step further and emphasized that the religious base of the Jews was essentially secular. To him, the natural role of Judentum, (a German word, difficult to translate, that means not only Judaism but also commerce, hucksterism, or mercantilism) was its secular "money-hustling." In order to be truly liberated, the Jews must give up their huckstering and their reliance upon the "Jewish god or money."

Interestingly, Marx wanted to liberate the Jews not simply from Judaism but from what he saw as a Judaized form of Christianity. He felt that Jews should return to a more primal form of Christianity, a Christianity of sharing, doing good, living for others --in short, a form of primitive communism. Then, in such an atmosphere of a "dissolved" communitarian Christianity and a disappearing Judaism could European Jews truly be emancipated. This is what he meant when he writes that the emancipation of the Jews is the emancipation of society from Judentum.

<u>Implications</u>

This essay has not been an exercise in "red-baiting" nor is it meant in any way to diminish Marx's enormous influence on Western civilization. I have simply attempted to point out a serious dilemma in Marxian philosophy regarding religion in general and Judaism in particular. While there have been numerous attempts, both within the Jewish world (Labor Zionism, Bundism, the Jewish student movement of the 1960s) and within the non-Jewish (the Catholic left, the New Left), to modify orthodox Marxism on the question of religion and Judaism/Zionism and to find some middle road or compromise, the dilemma continues to exist. The situation of the Jews in the Soviet Union and in

Israel and the leftist and Third World position on Zionism bears witness to Marx's legacy. The issue has not been resolved. (See Porter and Dreier, 1973; Dreier and Porter, 1975; Liebman, 1979; Porter, 1978: 25-34, 189-209, and Schappes, 1970.)

A Note on Sources

A comprehensive analysis of all of Karl Marx's references to Jews and Judaism would take five to ten times the number of pages allotted here. Readers should examine the secondary sources listed above and the primary sources listed below. A further problem is that most of Marx's manuscripts and correspondence were and still are in the possession of political parties, and their publication was and still is subject to political consideration. (See Silberner, 1949:5). For example, the correspondence between Marx and Engels was "purified" by its social democratic editors, August Bebel and Eduard Bernstein, who eliminated all passages which they believed to be vulgar, including all anti-Semitic slurs. (See Der Briefwechsel zwischen F. Engels and K. Marx, Stuttgart, 1919, 4 volumes.)

The most relevant sources for Marx's attitudes on the "Jewish question" are Zur Judenfrage (1844); Die Klassenkamfe in Frankreich (1850); Der Achtzehnte Brumaire des Louis Bonaparte (1852); articles in the Neue Rheinische Zeitung (1848-1849); Neue Oder-Zeitung (1855); The New York Tribune (1852-1856); and Revolution and Counter-Revolution in Germany in 1848, a collection of articles written by Engels but subscribed to by Marx. Other sources that can be used are:

Marx-Engels Gesamtausgabe, Moscow: Marx-Engels Institute, 1927-1935, seven volumes.

Marx-Engels Gesamtausgabe. Dritte Abteilung. Der Briefwechsel zwischen Marx und Engels, MEKOR, Berlin, 1929-1931, Four volumes.

Mehring, Franz (ed.), Collected Works of Karl Marx and Frederich Engels, Stuttgart, Dietz Nachf, 1902, four volumes.

Karl Marx: Chronik seines Lebens, Moscow: Marx-Engels-Lenin Institute, 1934.

One of the most important and comprehensive analyses to appear in recent years is Julius Carlebach's Karl Marx and the Radical Critique of Judaism (1978) mentioned earlier. I ask readers to use his section on bibliography and notes for other books and articles on the subject.

One popular source that should be avoided because of its many errors, its polemical and unscholarly introduction, and its biased approach is Dagobert D. Runes' Karl Marx: A World Without Jews (1959) mentioned above. An excellent critique of the book can be found in Harap (1959), and a useful but unfair critique of Carlebach's book can be found in Ruchwarger (1979).

References

Bloom, Solomon F., "Karl Marx and the Jews." Jewish
    Social Studies 4 (January, 1942) pp. 3-16.

Dreier, Peter and Jack Nusan Porter, "Jewish Radicalism
    in Transition." Society 12 (Jan.-Feb., 1975) pp.
    34-43.

Deutscher, Tamara, "Unkept Promise" (book review).
    Olam: Jewish Themes and World Issues (London) 3
    (Winter-Spring, 1977) pp. 57-60.

Friedland, W.H., "Book Review." American Journal of
    Sociology 83 (May, 1978) pp. 1551-1552.

Gotlieb, Y.S., "Israel and the Left: Historical and
    Contemporary Theory and Politics." Unpublished
    manuscript (1978).

Laqueur, Walter, "Zionism, the Marxist Critique, and
    the Left." Dissent (December, 1971) pp. 560-574.

Lewin, Kurt, "Self-Hatred Among Jews." pp. 186-200 in
    Resolving Social Conflicts. (New York: Harper and
    Brothers, 1948.) Originally appeared in the
    Contemporary Jewish Record 4:219-232, 1941.

Lichtheim, George, "Socialism and the Jews." Dissent 25
    (July-August, 1968) pp. 314-342.

Liebman, Arthur, Jews and the Left. (New York: John
    Wiley, 1979.)

Lipset, S.M., "The Socialism of Fools: The Left, the
    Jews, and Israel." (New York: Anti-Defamation
    League, 1969.) Also reprinted in S.M. Lipset,
    "The Left, the Jews, and Israel." pp. 375-400 in
    Revolution and Counter-Revolution: Change and
    Persistance in Social Structures. (New York:
    Doubleday-Anchor Books, 1970.)

Padover, Saul K., "The Baptism of Karl Marx's Family."
    Midstream 24 (June-July, 1978) pp. 36-44.

Porter, Jack Nusan and Peter Dreier, (eds.) Jewish Rad-
    icalism: A Selected Anthology. (New York: Grove
    Press 1973.)

Porter, Jack Nusan, (ed.), The Sociology of American
    Jews. (Washington, DC: University Press of
    America, 1978.)

Schappes, Morris, "The Jewish Question and the Left-
    Old and New." Jewish Currents 24 (June, 1970) pp.
    4-13, 29-37.

Silberner, Edmund, "Was Marx an Anti-Semite?" Historic
    Judaica 11 (April, 1949) pp. 3-52.

Wistrich, Robert S., Revolutionary Jews from Marx to
    Trotsky, (New York: Barnes and Noble, 1976).

Additional References

Berlin, Isaiah, The Life and Opinions of Moses Hess,
    (Cambridge: Cambridge University Press, 1959.)

_____, Karl Marx: His Life and Environment,
    (New York and London: Oxford University Press,
    1963), Third Edition.

Carlebach, Julius, Karl Marx and the Radical Critique
    of Judaism, (London and Boston: Routledge and
    Kegan Paul, 1978).

Draper, Hal, Karl Marx's Theory of Revolution: State
    and Bureaucracy, (New York and London: Monthly
    Review Press, 1977), esp. pp. 591-608.

Feuer, Lewis S., "Karl Marx and the Promethean
    Complex," Encounter, December, 1968: pp. 15-32.

Harap, Louis, "Karl Marx and the Jewish Question,"
    Jewish Currents, July-August, 1959, pp. 11-15,
    33-34.

Kunzli, Arnold, Karl Marx: Eine Psychographie, Vienna,
    1966.

Moore, Carlos, "Were Marx and Engels Racists?" Berkeley
    Journal of Sociology 19, 1974-75.

Padover, Saul K., Karl Marx: An Intimate Biography,
    (New York: McGraw-Hill, 1978).

Ruchwarger, Gary, "Marx and the Jewish Question: A Response to Julius Carlebach," Jewish Socialist Critique (Berkeley, California), vol. 1, no. 1, Fall, 1979, pp. 19-38.

Runes, Dagobert D. (ed.), Karl Marx: A World Without Jews (New York: Philosophical Library, 1959).

Chapter 4

The Jewish Presence in Sociology

Ironically, this article, in a previous version, came under a great deal of criticism, since I put a value judgment on the models young Jews had at their disposal in sociology. The most well-known sociologists, it seems, were also the most assimilated or had the most antipathy toward Jews or Judaism; while the proudest Jews were the least known in the field--at least until the 1960s and 1970s. That seemed pretty logical to me. Blacks and others looking for role models in academia found the same problem. I was heavily criticized because I was mixing apples and oranges. It is unimportant, some said, what a scholar feels about his or her religion, nationality, or race. What counts is his or her contribution to knowledge. I don't disagree. I only wanted to make a point about myself as a young Jewish sociologist. I could not find a Jewishly-committed sociologist while I was in graduate school (and that was only in the late 1960s). Somehow, reviewers felt I was unkind to David Reisman, Robert K. Merton, Lewis Coser, and even the memory of Georg Simmel and Emile Durkheim for bringing up such an indelicate subject as their religion. But I have brought it up and I want to explore this "dirty little secret." This version appears here for the first time, though portions of it appeared in the introduction to my The Sociology of American Jews (University Press of America, rev. ed., 1980). I suppose I should have tried to get it published in the American Journal of Sociology or the Jewish Journal of Sociology, but it takes so long and there's so little guarantee of success. In this collection it will appear earlier and just the way I want it.

* * * * *

Introduction

Since the mid-1960s American colleges have seen the rise of what have been called ethnic studies. Spurred on by the growing influence of Third World countries, the New Left, the black activist movements, and Chicano, Indian, feminist, and the "white ethnic" resurgence, Jewish studies has taken its place alongside others. (Spiegel, 1973) These studies can be exemplified by such collections as The Death of White Sociology (Ladner, 1973); Another Voice: Feminist Perspectives on Social Life and Social Science (Millman and Kanter, 1975); Jewish Radicalism: A Selected Anthology (Porter and Dreier, 1973); and similar ones for other minorities.

But Judaism is an ancient religion, as are the Jews a people, and Jewish studies in terms of Biblical studies, Talmudic analyses, and Hebrew literature go back long before the 1960s. Secular universities, as opposed to religious yeshivot, are, however, a new setting for Jewish studies. The purpose of this article is to describe the Jewish role in sociology from about 1900 to 1980. Such a topic could naturally be enlarged into a book or several books, so what follows can only be considered a sweeping overview of the field.

A Note on Terms

A few concepts should be explained at the onset. By Jewish, one means not only a religion but a people, an ethnic group, with a common heritage and a common set of interests. Jews are a sociological as well as a religious category. Furthermore, when I use the term "Jew" or "Jewish" in describing or labeling someone, I make no value judgment about the type of Jew he or she is (how religious or how assimilated, for example). What I mean by the label is that the person has a Jewish background (parents are Jewish, for example) or that he or she is labeled as a Jew by non-Jews. This is a thorny problem and makes even the labeling of a Jew difficult. Is Karl Marx Jewish because his father and mother came from a long line of rabbis? However, his father converted to Lutheranism. Does that make Marx a Jew? What of someone who is a nonpracticing Jew, an assimilated Jew? Is he or she still Jewish? Let us simply say that for the purpose of this paper, anyone with a Jewish parent will be considered as coming from a Jewish background.

I will be discussing the history of the <u>sociology of Jewry</u> in this article. The sociology of Jewry is a subfield of <u>contemporary Jewish studies</u>, which is the study of modern Jewish life but using other methods and disciplines besides sociology--psychology, demography, anthropology, etc. In turn, contemporary Jewish studies is a subsection of the field of Jewish studies, which consists of everything from Biblical and Talmudic studies to Hebrew and Hebrew literature to Jewish history, Israeli politics, and Jewish art and music. I will refer to Jewish studies when discussing this very broad field and to the sociology of Jewry when discussing the subfield of sociology.

Some of the academic and professional problems that affect Jewish studies in general also affect contemporary Jewish studies and the sociology of Jewry, but a few are unique to the latter for the following reason: Jewish studies such as Biblical exegesis, Hebrew language, and Jewish history have been taught on secular college campuses for a long time, but contemporary Jewish studies, like sociology itself, are of relatively recent vintage.

The Growth of Jewish Studies on Secular Campuses

The rise of ethnicity in the 1960s led several scholars to examine the history and growth of Jewish studies in America. (See Jick's excellent collection, 1970; Band, 1966; Jacob Neusner, 1977; Daniel Elazar, 1974, 1978; Sklare, 1974b:1-27, 1974c:151-173; Ritterband and Wechsler, 1979; Jick, 1976; and Porter, 1978:1-4.)

As Elazar (1978:202) points out, Jewish social research began as an offshoot of the scientific study of Jewish history, the so-called <u>Wissenschaft des Judentums</u> movement, the science of Judaism promulgated by such 19th century thinkers as Leopold Zunz, Nahman Krochmal, and Abraham Geiger. While in the past Judaism was studied as an exercise in Jewish piety, now it was to be seen as a scientific mission, an academic and intellectual pursuit. (Sklare, 1974b:4). However, while the <u>Wissenschaft</u> movement was instrumental in laying the foundation for the scientific study of Judaism, it dealt mainly in the past and did not expand into contemporary Jewish studies. Furthermore, the leaders of this movement wished to "summarize the Jewish experience before the Jews disappeared. Most German and Central European Jewish scholars of the mid-nineteenth century saw Judaism on its way out, following on the heels of the demise of the Jewish people as a corporate entity. Hence, they saw it as their contribution to Jewish history and to mankind....to give the Jewish people a decent burial." (Elazar, 1978:202)

The genesis of contemporary Jewish studies would arise from other sources, sources that saw Judaism and Jews as active, ongoing participants in the world, not as "fossils" to be placed in a museum. I would place the origins of contemporary Jewish studies with two movements: the most important one is Zionism, the second is Diaspora nationalism. The first promoted Jewish nationalism and the Hebrew language with a return to a Jewish state in Palestine-Israel; the second was anti-Zionist, but saw a viable Jewish life outside of Israel based on social democracy, secular Judaism, and the use of Yiddish.

Before turning to a major Zionist influence on the sociology of Jewry, I would like to say a few words about the influence of Diaspora nationalism. The major vehicle of the latter was and is the YIVO--Yiddish Scientific Institute, founded in Europe and today housed in New York City. YIVO has long been a repository of social research in Jewish history, institutions, and language. Its journal, the YIVO Annual of Jewish Social Science (founded in 1946), and its Yiddish-language monographs and collections, combined the best of Jewish learning of Eastern Europe with the secular learning of Western Europe and America; the heritage of the yeshiva and the methodology of the university; the traditions of Jewish life in Poland and Lithuania with the needs of Jews in America.[1] Some of the major figures in this group were Max Weinreich, Nathan Reich, Jacob Lestchinsky, Abraham Ain, Jacob Shatzky, Leibush Lehrer, Shlomo Noble, Elias Tcherikower, and Rudolf Glanz. Today, despite the growth of new journals, the YIVO Annual remains a major place for sociologists and other social scientists to publish their results of research in the Jewish field.

As Ritterband and Wechsler (1979:73-76) point out, Jewish learning found its first American home in institutions that modeled themselves on the great German universities of the 19th century. The German model of universities as graduate schools for research was brought to America by a few emigre professors and by Americans who had studied in Europe. Starting with Johns Hopkins University in 1876, a small but growing

-68-

number of colleges began to introduce the field of
Semitics, a major innovation at the time. Some of the
major figures at this time were Thomas C. Murray and,
later, Paul Haupt at Johns Hopkins; Richard J.H.
Gottheil at Columbia University; and Morris Jastrow at
Pennsylvania. In 1897, fifteen academic centers
offered programs in Semitics, but of these only four
(University of Chicago, Columbia, Johns Hopkins, and
Pennsylvania) offered instruction in specifically
Jewish areas (rabbinic and medieval Jewish texts).

A generation after Gottheil and Jastrow, there
appeared several other scholars that were to make
important contributions to Jewish cultural history.
They were Isaac Husik of the University of Pennsylvania, Harry Austryn Wolfson of Harvard University, and
Salo Baron of Columbia University. Coming from pious
traditional homes in Eastern Europe, they migrated to
the United States and concentrated on medieval Jewish
philosophy in the cases of Husik and Wolfson and Jewish
history in the case of Baron. They had to labor for
many years in insecurity until they found a respected
place in the university. (Ritterband and Wechsler,
1979:75)

These men are mentioned even though they are not
sociologists, because they provided some of the few
models in Jewish learning on American universities at a
time when few Jews were in academia. In time this
would change as Jews moved into American society.
Between 1880 and 1920, large numbers of Jews came to
this country, and they moved quickly out of the ghettos
and into the middle class. They took advantage of the
educational opportunities in the "Golden Land" of
America, and large numbers entered schools of higher
education. Other factors that led to the greater
acceptance of Jewish studies were the shift from an
esoteric study of the past to analyses of the totality
of Jewish experience, especially anti-Semitism, ethnic
identity, and contemporary Jewish institutions; the
increased funding of Jewish research on the part of the
Jewish community; and the changing size and character
of higher education in the United States.[2]

These trends were to accelerate after World War II
and especially after 1967. Jospe (1972:i) summarizes
the growth of Jewish studies as follows:

The steady growth of programs of Jewish studies in our colleges and universities during

the past two decades constitutes a development of great significance for Jewish life. The Old Testament and Hebrew had, of course, been taught at Brown, Harvard, Princeton, Yale, and some other institutions of higher learning since their earliest days. However, these studies reflected not an interest in Judaism but the conviction that a knowledge of the Hebrew Bible was indispensable for an understanding of Christianity and the training of Christian clergymen.

The first courses dealing with Jews and Judaism after the biblical period were introduced in the curriculum of an American university only at the end of the nineteenth century. However, the number of institutions offering Judaic studies remained very small, and it was only after the end of World War II that we find a growing awareness and recognition that Jews and Judaism are legitimate subjects of academic study and inquiry. Since then, credit courses in Judaic studies and especially in Hebrew language and literature have been introduced at numerous institutions at which they had not existed before, while others have steadily expanded their Judaica programs and still others are currently exploring ways of introducing new, or expanding existing course offerings.

Among the factors that contributed to this development have been the growing articulation of demands for Jewish studies arising from increased Jewish self-awareness generated by the impact of the Holocaust and the creation of the State of Israel; the democratization of academic policies and admission practices which, together with the increased social mobility and affluence of the Jewish population, led to substantial increases in Jewish enrollment and greater Jewish "visibility" throughout the country; the climate of greater acceptance of Jews and Judaism by the general and academic communities, especially after World War II; the growing recognition and acknowledgement of Hebrew as a living language and of Judaism as an essential component in the fabric of Western civilization deserving of serious academic in-

terest and study; the postwar growth of
specialized area studies and of courses and
departments of religious studies; the growing
readiness of Jewish communities or agencies
to fund such developments; and the greater
receptivity to ethnic studies as a by-product
of the pressures for the introduction of
Black Studies programs.

Jewish studies on secular campuses have increased
sevenfold since World War II. A major study by Arnold
Band (1966) showed sixty one full-time positions in
Jewish studies, about forty accredited colleges and
universities offering fairly adequate training in
undergraduate Jewish studies, and at least twenty five
others offering a variety of courses but no major in
Judaic studies. By 1966, the number of universities
with graduate programs in Jewish studies had grown to
twenty, and in 1980 that figure had more than doubled
to nearly fifty. (See Jick, 1976:194). Courses on some
aspect of Jewish life or Hebrew language are taught at
over 350 colleges and universities in the United States
and Canada, and more than ninety offer undergraduate
majors in Jewish studies. (Meyer, 1979:vii) The growth
has been spectacular. There is hardly a major university or college that does not offer at least one or two
courses in Jewish studies.

While sociology of Jewry courses have also increased during this period, they still make up only a
tiny percentage of all courses in Jewish studies. Out
of some 3,125 courses, only thirty five are sociology
of Jewry courses taught in a sociology/anthropology
department (about one percent) and another forty five
are taught in other departments (history, philosophy,
religion, etc.). Taken together, there are only about
eighty out of some 3,125 courses that deal specifically
with the sociology of Jews (2.5 percent), and even
these courses are usually temporary and sporadic.[3]

Still, Jewish studies have found a secure place in
academia, though growth has leveled off somewhat in the
wake of recent economic problems. On the brighter
side, at over fifty colleges Jewish students have organized "free Jewish universities," and many of them
are quite innovative.[4] The largest is at Boston
University, but almost every major school has courses
taught at the local Hillel Foundation. For example, at
Oberlin College, a live-in center set up by Jewish
students, called Hebrew House, was incorporated into
the credit curriculum.

Important centers of research and teaching have
also emerged in the postwar period, while earlier ones
(for example, the YIVO Institute) have been reinvigor-
ated. In 1959, the Institute of Contemporary Jewry of
the Hebrew University was founded and has carried out
wide-ranging research on Jewish communities throughout
the world. (Davis, 1974) The Philip Lown Center for
Contemporary Jewish Studies where such figures as
Marshall Sklare and Ben Halpern teach has been, since
1963, an important center. (It is located on the campus of Brandeis University.) In September 1969, fifty
professors of Judaica met at the Lown Center to discuss
the state of the field. Out of their deliberations
emerged the Association for Jewish Studies, in which
the sociology of Jewry has become one subsection. By
the year 1974, membership in the Association had grown
to 600, of whom 300 are regular members who hold full-
time academic positions in an area of Jewish studies;
an additional 150 are graduate students in Judaica; and
the rest are faculty members in other disciplines (such
as sociology) who maintain an active interest in Jewish
culture. (Jick, 1976:195) Today, in 1980, the total
membership is over 900. While no sociologist has been
president yet, Marshall Sklare sits on the board of
directors and was one of the co-founders of the Association, and the first president, Leon Jick, has close
relationships to sociology.

Sociologists have, however, their own association.
In 1971, a "Jewish caucus" emerged out of the American
Sociological Association calling itself the Association
for the Sociological Study of Jewry. Mervin Verbit of
Brooklyn College was its first president, followed by
Marshall Sklare, Samuel Klausner, Celia Heller, and
Chaim Waxman. The ASSJ holds regular sessions in con-
junction with ASA or SSSP meetings and publishes a
newsletter plus a journal called Contemporary Jewry: A
Journal of Sociological Inquiry. Membership now stands
at about 400.

A few other groups should also be mentioned. The
Institute for Jewish Policy Analysis was founded about
a decade ago and has been instrumental in transforming
research into useful policy. Other policy and research
centers established in the past few years include the
National Jewish Conference Center and those at Bar-Ilan
University near Tel Aviv and at City College in New
York. There are important research and archival cen-
ters in London (the Weiner Library), Boston (American
Jewish Historical Society), Cincinnati (American Jewish

Archives), Los Angeles (Simon Weisenthal Center), and a few more in Israel and Europe.

Journals naturally play an important role in the field of Jewish studies, and the first in the field of contemporary Jewish studies were not in sociology per se, but in social work because of the many problems faced by Jewish immigrants. The titles themselves reflect these interests: Jewish Charity appeared in the early 1900s but is no longer published today: the Jewish Center was another; and later, in the 1920s and 1930s, there appeared the Jewish School Quarterly and the Jewish Social Service Quarterly (founded in 1924). The latter would later broaden its scope and be re-titled the Journal of Jewish Communal Service (1955-). It is sponsored by the National Conference of Jewish Communal Service and deals with the role of the Jewish professional in social services--educational institutions, Jewish community centers, summer camps, Jewish family and welfare agencies, and similar places.

In 1939, Jewish Social Studies was founded by the Conference on Jewish Relations with Salo Baron, Morris R. Cohen, and Hans Kohn as editors. It included such social scientists as Oscar Janowsky, Maurice Karpf (an important figure in Jewish social work), and Edward Sapir. The journal is still publishing today, but has been overshadowed by newer journals. Still, sociologists such as Nathan Glazer and Marshall Sklare sit on its editorial board today.

In 1946, the YIVO Annual of Jewish Social Science was founded and, as mentioned earlier, played an important role in keeping alive a tradition of research in contemporary Jewish studies. In 1948, American Jewish Archives came into print and contains useful historical information, though few sociologists contribute to it. Judaism, sponsored by the American Jewish Congress, was founded in 1952 with Robert Gordis as its first editor, and its pages have always been open to sociological perspectives.

In the late 1950s, several other journals appeared. In the area of orthodox Jewish life came Jewish Life (1958-); in Holocaust studies came the Yad Vashem Bulletin and Yad Vashem Studies, both published in Jerusalem; and in sociology came an important journal out of England, the Jewish Journal of Sociology (1959-). The latter was founded by Aaron Steinberg, Morris Ginsberg, and Maurice Freedman with Ginsberg as founding editor. In June, 1971, upon Ginsberg's death, Freedman became editor, but tragically, at a young age, Freedman died four years later and his wife, Judith Freedman, became the managing editor in 1975. The journal publishes out of London and contains articles from a wide variety of perspectives. Its contributors are from America, Australia, Israel, Europe, and Great Britain, making it an international sociological journal of Jewish affairs.[5]

A few other journals, both historical and contemporary, should be mentioned. While some are not, strictly speaking, sociology journals, they have all been open to sociologists writing in the field. The oldest historical journal is American Jewish History, first published in 1893 as Publications of the American Jewish Historical Society; the Menorah Journal, an intellectual magazine founded in 1915; Jewish Education, founded in 1928; the American Jewish Yearbook (1899-), a very useful research tool; Jewish Book Annual (1942-); and several others such as the Contemporary Jewish Record, which later became Commentary; Jewish Currents; Midstream; Jewish Frontier (1934-); Jewish Spectator (1935-); Reconstructionist (1934-); and Response (1967-). All of these journals are still publishing.

After a long struggle, the sociology of Jewry and contemporary Jewish studies in general finally had both scholarly journals and associations to call their own. In short, they had an "address" in the discipline of sociology, something they had not had during the past century.

Ruppin and Wirth: Two Founders--Two Opposing Views

Up until the rise of Nazi power in Europe, there were few Jews in American sociology. This issue will be explored later, but suffice it to say that as Cahnman notes (1972: vol. 15:66), as late as the 1930s, only two Jewish sociologists of some importance were on the scene, Samuel Joseph at the predominantly Jewish City College of New York and Louis Wirth of the University of Chicago. (One could perhaps add Samuel Koenig of Brooklyn College to Cahnman's list.) However, in Europe and later out of Israel would emerge a man who could be considered the founder, or at least, the first systematic scholar in the field of the sociology of Jewry: Arthur Ruppin (1876-1943). The contrast between Ruppin and Wirth is important, because the former

-74-

represented an active "survivalist" perspective, while the latter promoted an assimilationist point of view.

Ruppin was born in Prussia and studied law and political economy in Berlin and Halle. In 1902 he graduated from the University of Halle with the degree of doctor of political science. In the following year, he received international reknown by winning the Haeckel Award for his work Darwinismus und Soziologie. He set out to apply scientific sociological methods to the study of Jewish problems, and in 1905 founded the Bureau for Jewish Statistics in Berlin and began publication of the Zeitschrift fur Demographie und Statistik der Juden. This quarterly continued in existence until the advent of the Nazi regime in 1933.

Ruppin continued his legal studies in Germany, but his interest in Zionism led to a trip to Israel in 1907. It was intended to be a short trip, but he remained for nine years, during which time he established and became head of the Palestina-Amt (Palestine office) at Jaffa and became an important figure in early colonialization projects. He later served on the board of the Jewish Agency in Palestine as well as on numerous other organizations and companies. He is considered today an important figure in the history of Zionism and the development of what was to become the modern state of Israel.

Upon the opening of the Hebrew University in Jerusalem in 1925, he became its first lecturer, and later professor, of sociology. His most important works include Die Juden der Gegenwart (1904, 3rd. ed. 1918; English translation, The Jews of Today, 1913); Der Aufbau des Landes Israel (1919); Soziologie der Juden (2 volumes, 1930-1931); The Jews in the Modern World (1934, an abridged English version of the Sozologie der Juden); and The Jewish Fate and Future (1940).

Ruppin's The Jew in the Modern World (1934) reminds one of Park and Burgess's An Introduction to the Science of Sociology published in 1921. Ruppin takes all the major sociological fields (racial-ethnic characteristics, migration patterns, fertility, occupation, income, political institutions, the family, education, intermarriage, the press, the immigrant experience) and applies them to contemporary Jews, not only in the United States, but in England, Russia, and Palestine. In short, it is a very modern sociology

-75-

textbook, one that sociologists would feel very comfortable reading even today.

At about the same time that Ruppin was beginning his teaching career at the Hebrew University, a young graduate student at the University of Chicago, Louis Wirth (1897-1952), completed his doctoral dissertation under Robert Park. This dissertation was later published by the University of Chicago Press and is considered a classic in the field: The Ghetto (1928).

Wirth was born in Gemueden, Germany and emigrated to the United States as a young man. He was the son of Joseph Wirth and Rosalie Lorig. After coming to America in 1911 to join relatives in Omaha, Nebraska, he entered the University of Chicago in 1914, at the age of seventeen, and studied sociology with Robert Park, Ernest Burgess, W.I. Thomas, and Albion Small as well as social psychology with George Herbert Mead. After graduation he was employed for a time in the Bureau of Personal Services of the Jewish Charities of Chicago, serving as the director of the division for delinquent boys.

In 1923 Wirth married Mary Bolton of Paducah, Kentucky. He returned to the University of Chicago and completed his doctorate in sociology in 1925. In this period he taught part time at the University and at the downtown YMCA College. In 1926 he was appointed assistant professor of sociology at the University of Chicago. After teaching at Tulane University from 1928-1930 and spending 1930-1931 in France and Germany on a Social Science Research Council fellowship, he returned to Chicago as an associate professor and spent the rest of his career there.

He served as president of the American Sociological Association in 1946, the first Jew to be elected; and he also became the first president of the International Sociological Association in 1950. He died two years later at the age of fifty five. His principal works were The Ghetto (1928), his preface to the English edition of Karl Mannheim's Ideology and Utopia published in 1936, and many important articles on urbanism, race relations, international affairs, and the history of sociological thought. (From Cahnman, vol. 16, 1972:553-554 and Faris, 1970:160)

But after The Ghetto, Wirth wrote no other books on Jewish subjects, edited no anthologies on Jewish issues, and wrote only a single article in major sociological journals dealing with the Jews. (Wirth, 1943) As Sklare (1974c:161-162) perceptively notes:

> Since Wirth viewed the Jewish community as a dying entity, he did not continue the research which had eventuated in publication of The Ghetto. Rather he proceeded to direct his attention to the need for social planning, for better cities, and for improved understanding between racial groups. Nevertheless, his interest in fighting discrimination and his desire to combat Nazism had the effect of keeping him in touch with Jewish organizations. It also motivated him to write once again on a Jewish topic. Thus during World War II Wirth published an article in the American Journal of Sociology which paid homage to Jewish tenacity in the face of persecution.

While Wirth saw the ghetto as an interesting sociological phenomenon because it represented a prolonged isolation of a people, thus permitting the preservation of a distinct culture in the face of urban conditions which would ordinarily produce rapid assimilation, he also felt that as prejudice diminished, the ghetto would die. It was an anachronism in his eyes. Through intermarriage and assimilation, the Jew would finally be accepted into the general community (if, of course, irrational prejudice decreased or was eliminated). This was Wirth's hope. That is why Marshall Sklare (1974c:160-162; 1974b:13-15) has called Wirth's perspective, assimilationist. Wirth himself married a non-Jewish woman and raised his two daughters in an agnostic environment with only a vague minority ethnic identification. (Marvick, 1964:337)

It is for this reason that Arthur Ruppin, though almost unheard of in sociological circles, could better be called the founder or father of contemporary Jewish studies, not only because he devoted his scholarly career to the sociology of Jewry worldwide, but because he believed in the survival and continuity of the Jewish people. It is possible that had Louis Wirth lived longer and if he had been more influenced by the repercussions of World War II, the Holocaust, and the establishment of the state of Israel, he might have changed his views from the assimilationist perspective to that of survivalist.

Furthermore, it was Ruppin's Zionism that led to a dynamic, "problem-oriented" view of the Jews, and this viewpoint was in essence sociological. How was Zionism the impetus for a more sociological way of looking at the world? First, Zionism sees Jews and Judaism as facing the constant threat of anti-Semitism and assimilation, two quintessential Jewish problems as well as two quintessential sociological issues. Second, through Zionism, that is, the establishment of a sovereign state in Israel where Jews can flock to, these problems can be alleviated and, perhaps, abolished. Zionism also saw the Jewish people not simply as a religion but as a people, a nationality, an ethnic group. In short, according to Zionist theory, all Jews everywhere belong to a particular people, one people with a central homeland in Israel. This converts the Jews into a sociological entity like other ethnic groups.

Furthermore, Zionism sees the Jewish people as a growing, creative, living organism, constantly adapting to forces around them, again a sociological perspective. Arthur Ruppin adapted these classical Zionist views. Louis Wirth, on the other hand, saw the Jews as a dying phenomenon, an anachronism that would eventually assimilate and disappear. Marshall Sklare (1974b:14) succinctly summarizes the differences between Ruppin, the Zionist and survivalist, and Wirth, the non-Zionist and assimilationist:

> The contrast between Arthur Ruppin and Louis Wirth is instructive. One, the founder of contemporary Jewish studies, was a Zionist whose pioneering work is being continued today at the Institute of Contemporary Jewry of the Hebrew University. The other, a non-Zionist if not an anti-Zionist, became the most influential Jew of his time in American sociology and prefigured the present prominence of Jews in American social science.... As a leading authority on urban sociology and minority groups.... Wirth was a consultant to many official bodies and private agencies. However, he made no effort to establish contemporary Jewish studies as a distinctive field of scholarly inquiry.

In the next section, we will see that the themes of survival or assimilation would be a leitmotif throughout the past eighty years. Unlike some other minorities, Jews in America had the choice of either assimilating/blending into American society, leaving behind little or no religious traces, or of survival, growth, and activism.

Survival or Assimilation: A Sociological Mosaic, 1900-1980

The Founding Fathers

Naturally, to do justice to this subject, an entire book could easily be written. However, this section will cover the Jewish presence in sociology over the past eighty years with some insight into the major issues that have confronted the Jewish people in the world (anti-Semitism, Israel, the Holocaust, and cognate areas).

From its very beginnings, there has been a Jewish presence in sociology. Karl Marx, while not a Jew by a strictly religious definition, did come from a Jewish background. His own relationship to Judaism and his subsequent attitude towards Jews were puzzlingly ambivalent and often antagonistic. (Wistrich, 1976; Carlebach, 1978) He wrote little on Jews and felt that in the triumph of communism, all religions, including Judaism, would no longer be necessary. His intellectual and political legacy, of course, attracted many Jews.

When we look at the founding fathers of sociology, we also find Jews in prominent positions. Georg Simmel (1858-1918), Emile Durkheim (1858-1917), and Ludwig Gumplowicz (1838-1909) all came from Jewish back-grounds. Gumplowicz is the least known today, having spent most of his academic life in the provincial University of Graz. His first acquaintance with the field of sociology came through the writings of Comte and Spencer, and his pessimistic form of social Darwinism is manifested in his major works: Race and State (1875), Race Struggle (1883), and Outlines of Sociology (1885). His gloomy life was lightened by a visit by Lester F. Ward and, as a result, Gumplowicz found his way into American sociological journals. (See Timasheff and Theodorson, 1976:47.) He had somewhat of a revival of interest in his work in the 1960s as one of the "founders" of conflict theory.

Georg Simmel was born in Berlin of Jewish parents who later converted to Protestantism. His academic career was slow despite his brilliance. It was not until 1914, four years before his death, that he obtained a full professorship at the University of Strassburg. Part of Simmel's failure was attributable to anti-Semitism prevalent in German universities prior to World War I, but part could be due to the breadth of his interests. Many in German academic circles were scandalized by the way Simmel turned his attention to philosophy, metaphysics, sociolgoy, psychology, esthetics, ethics, and economics. He was not the specialist. Despite his not receiving official academic recognition, he was popular with students and scholars from abroad, among them Robert E. Park, and Park later would translate and publish Simmel's work for American journals and for Park's own textbook on sociology.

While Simmel rarely even mentioned Jews in his writings, there is a mood to his work that betrays the "outsider," sitting alone at parties counting dyads and triads. Simmel's "outsider" status is best depicted in his short essay "The Stranger," a formal concept that is the prototype for the Jew, the eternal middleman. (See Simmel, 1964:402-408.)

Like Simmel, Emile Durkheim also wrote almost nothing on Jews, yet his Jewish background did have some influence on him. Durkheim, like Karl Marx, came from a family of rabbis, yet both rejected orthodoxy and became liberal thinkers. Durkheim was born in Epinal, Lorraine, in the northeastern part of France, and as Timasheff and Theodorson (1976:105) point out, it is likely that his birth in the most nationalistic section of France, his early contacts with the disaster of the Franco-Prussian War, and his identification with the cohesive Jewish community all contributed to his interest in the study of group solidarity. Durkheim was also fond of quoting from Biblical sources of Hebraic law as one of the primitive manifestations of "mechanical solidarity," but went even further: in his book Les Formes Elementaires de la Vie Religieuse, he showed that religion itself was a social phenomenon of the first order, a deification of the solidarity of past, present and future generations. (Cahnman, 1972:64) The themes of group solidarity, collective conscience, and sacred symbolization were easily obtained from Durkheim's Jewish heritage.

Cahnman (1972:65) also goes on to make an interesting point about Durkheim's followers. More than any other European sociologist, Durkheim formed a school of

thought, and although most of his <u>first</u> generation
disciples were Jews, few of them were sociologists!
One could mention here Maurice Halbwachs, primarily a
demographer; Marcel Mauss, Durkheim's son-in-law and
his successor as editor of the <u>L'Annee Sociologique</u>
(founded in 1896); Lucien Levy-Bruehl and his son Henry
Levy-Bruehl; and Marc Bloch, an economic historian.
Essentially, the Durkheimian school consisted of an
anthropological and ethnographical approach. However,
a later, second generation of students in France
included such sociologists (and Jews) as Raymond Aron,
Georges Gurvitch, and Georges Friedmann. Prominent
American interpreters of Durkheim (as well as of
Simmel, Weber, Mannheim, and Toennies) included such
sociologists as Louis Wirth, Kurt Wolff, Harry Alpert,
Reinhard Bendix, Lewis Coser, and Werner Cahnman.

A fascinating and illuminating book could be written on the relationships between sociologists and other
thinkers in <u>fin de siecle</u> Vienna, Berlin, and Paris.
Sociologists did not live in a vacuum, and for this
essay, if one looks at the Jewish "connection" between
Jewish sociologists and other Jewish thinkers of their
time, one finds some interesting intersections. Simmel, for example, was a personal friend of the great
Jewish theologian Martin Buber, and Buber's "I-Thou"
theology was influenced by Simmel's work on dyads and
triads. Simmel and Buber both emphasized that the primal goal of the human world was dialogue, dialogue
among relationships. While Simmel discussed dialogues
among dyads and groups, Buber included a dyadic or
group relationship with God.

Durkheim, too, had an influence on an important
Jewish thinker--Mordechai Kaplan, founder of Reconstructionist Judaism. Kaplan was deeply impressed with
<u>The Elementary Forms of Religious Life</u>, because it re-
futed the classic conception of religion as an individual phenomenon that spread to the group. Kaplan was
searching for a theoretical base that would see religion as social and reflective of collective realities.
Reconstructionist Judaism, the smallest of the Jewish
denominations, exists to this very day and is based
upon the Durkheimian model of religious life.

Ludwig Gumplowicz also had an interesting Jewish
connection. In 1899, he had a brief correspondence
with Theodore Herzl, the founder of modern political
Zionism. However, Gumplowicz thought that Herzl was a
dreamer and that the historical foundation for Zionism

was totally wrong. Still, he admitted that Herzl could be correct about the need for a Jewish homeland, and he asked Herzl not to label him an anti-Zionist. Herzl later proved to be the correct one. (Cahnman, 1958: 165-180)

These few examples show that a dissertation could be written on the impact of secular sociologists on Jewish religious and political thinkers, and it is an area that has been rarely touched upon in the literature.

Pre-World War II America

As was noted earlier, there were few Jewish sociologists active before World War II, aside from Louis Wirth and one or two others. Among the founding fathers of American sociology, there were none at all. As Table 1 shows, before 1939 there were no presidents of the American Sociological Association or the Eastern Sociological Society who were Jewish, black, or women. It was only after World War II that their numbers would increase, but even then quite slowly in the late 1940s and 1950s, with larger numbers in the 1960s and 1970s.

It is not entirely clear why Jews were late in entering sociology in large numbers. Werner Cahnman (1972, vol. 15:66) has, however, a provocative theory that may explain it. When one compares the situation with Jews in the field of anthropology, one sees a great many Jewish anthropologists: the founding father of cultural anthropology, Franz Boas, and next to him Edward Sapir were both German-Jewish immigrants. In the second generation, Jews are prominently represented by such students of Boas as A.A. Goldenweiser, Robert Lowie, Paul Radin, and L. Spier, all of them Austrian, Polish, or Russian immigrants, as well as the American-born Ruth Benedict and Melville J. Herskovitz. Why so many early Jewish anthropologists and so few Jewish sociologists?

Cahnman feels that in academic circles it was fine when foreign-born scholars concerned themselves with remote cultures such as the Crow, Klamath, and Winnebago Indians, but for "sensitive" issues such as U.S. history, literature, and sociology, it was better that American-born-and-bred scholars did the work. Foreigners, it was felt, might "contaminate" the research and teaching of these fields. This was especially true for American literature where it was felt that no Jewish,

-82-

TABLE 1

Number of Jewish, Black, and Women Presidents in the American Sociological Association and the Eastern Sociological Society

	American Sociological Association (ASA) (Founded in 1905) N=75 presidents			Eastern Sociological Society (ESS) (Founded in 1930) N=50 presidents		
	Jews	Blacks	Women	Jews	Blacks	Women
1905-1929	0	0	0	---	---	---
1930-1939	0	0	0	0	0	0
1940-1949	1	1	0	0	1	1
1950-1959	1	0	1	0	1	2*
1960-1969	3	0	0	4	0	0
1970-1980	3	0	1	3	2	4
Totals	8	1	2	7	3	7
Percentage	11%	1%	3%	14%	6%	14%

* Jessie Bernard, a Jewish woman, was elected president of the ESS in 1950. That made her the first Jewish president, but the second woman. I counted her as a woman in this case.

Percentages were rounded off.

Italian, or other immigrant scholar (or even son or daughter of immigrants) could properly teach such a subject.

Cahnman also indicts radical progressives such as Henry Pratt Fairchild, Edward A. Ross, and Robert Faris, who reminded immigrants that as "guests" in America they must adapt themselves to their hosts if they wished to be accepted as "equals," and he emphasized that "this attutude amounted to a formidable psychological barrier for aspiring Jewish intellectuals" to enter the field of sociology. (Cahnman, 1972:66)

There is no question that such "elitism" caused some early sociologists to hold negative views towards immigrants, Jews, Catholics, and blacks. As Richard Hofstadter (1955) in his book <u>Social Darwinism in American Thought</u> points out: Darwinian individualism, whether for individual or imperialist uses, is always a possibility in a competitive society like America. Social Darwinism, even outright racism, affected social thinkers like Madison Grant and Lothrop Stoddard and led to the imposition of new immigration laws in the early 1920s that halted or slowed to a trickle the immigration of Jews, Italians, Asian-Americans, and others. These laws had a profound effect on Jews in <u>Europe</u> as well as in America. In 1933, when Hitler came to power, he set in motion legislation which, by 1939, would seal in the Jews of Europe. With no country to take them in and America's strict quotas filled, they perished in Nazi concentration camps and ghettos. Thus, the legacy of Social Darwinism led not simply to discrimination against Jews, but eventually to genocide in Europe.[6]

Cahnman's provocative thesis must be tested further by historical research, but there were other reasons for the lack of Jews in sociology in the early years of American sociology. First, before 1880, there were few Jews in America, but between 1880 and 1910, large numbers of Jewish immigrants from Eastern Europe flooded American shores. Most of these Jews were too poor and uneducated to think about college educations for themselves. However, their children, the second generation, quickly moved out of the ghettos, many going on to higher education. However, business, government positions, and social work, rather than university teaching, were more popular choices. Mobility was faster in business than in academia. Anti-Semitism within higher education led to numerical quotas that limited the number of Jews in private colleges such as Harvard and Yale before the 1930s. These quotas would be lifted after World War II, and the numbers of Jews entering college and, therefore, into academic careers would dramatically increase. Jews, up to World War II, were more likely to have been the subjects of sociological research on social problems than scholars engaging in such research themselves. (See Stein, 1956: 3-98.) One must confront, nevertheless, Cahnman's assertion that elitism and anti-Semitism played an important role in barring many Jews from a career in sociology in the early part of this century. His thesis must be seriously considered when one compares the field of sociology to anthropology.

The Frankfurt School

The rise of Nazism led to an important wave of migration from Germany, Austria, Hungary, and Italy in the 1930s, a small but intellectually powerful migration of the first magnitude encompassing not only scientists, musicians, writers, and artists but psychologists, sociologists, and philosophers. In this wave, of course, came many Jews fleeing Europe, Jews who were to make an important contribution to sociology.

Among these immigrants was a group which had founded the Institut fuer Sozialforschung, the so-called Frankfurt School, led by Theodor Adorno and Max Horkheimer, but also including Herbert Marcuse and Erich Fromm. Others who played a role in the Institut's endeavors as members, journal contributors, friends, or enemies were Hannah Arendt, Raymond Aron, Bruno Bettelheim, Gershom Scholem, Bertolt Brecht, Siegfried Kracauer, Paul Lazarsfeld, Georg Lukacs, Karl Mannheim, Wilhelm Reich, Leo Lowenthal, and Paul Tillich. (See Buck-Morss, 1977:xi and Jay, 1973.) Most of them came to America in the 1930s, and all of them, except Tillich and Brecht, were Jews.

The Frankfurt School rejected both dogmatic, party-bound Russian Marxism and nonideological American positivism. Its "negative dialectic" was a blend of Freud and Marx, aesthetics and social science, art and politics. Many of these illustrious men and women would later make a profound impact on American intellectual life. Furthermore, Adorno, Lowenthal, Bettelheim, Arendt, and Fromm would later make important contributions to our understanding of fascism and anti-Semitism.

The Holocaust: Anti-Semitism at its Peak

Aside from the establishment of the state of Israel, no other event has influenced the sociology and psychology of Jews as has the Nazi Holocaust and the entire issue of anti-Semitism. The years prior to, during, and after World War II saw large numbers of works by sociologists on the subject of anti-Semitism and fascism.

This period of research, starting in the 1930s, has been described by Marshall Sklare (1974d:363) and Daniel Elazar (1978:203) as the era of anti-anti-Semitism research. The Jewish community decided that it needed more sophisticated knowledge about who the anti-Semites were, where they were located, why certain situations were more prone than others to generate anti-Semitism, and which groups were more likely to be anti-Semitic. Jewish community relations agencies wanted facts at their disposal in order to carry out their work. Since sociology had long been interested in prejudice and social distance among groups, a marriage was made, and it is not surprising that some of the earliest work by sociologists during and after the war was on anti-Semitism.

The first anthology on the subject edited and, for the most part, written by sociologists was Isacque Graeber and Steuart Henderson Britt's Jews in a Gentile World: The Problem of Anti-Semitism (1942). The contributors were an interesting group: J.O. Hertzler and Talcott Parsons on the sociology of anti-Semitism; Jessie Bernard, Samuel Koenig, and Leonard Bloom (later to be changed to Broom) on the sociology of American Jewish communities; Everett Stonequist and Carl Mayer on Jewish marginality; and Jacob Lestchinsky and Miriam Beard on the economic position of the Jews in America. The book is today considered a classic in the sociology of anti-Semitism.

But there were other important books on the subject that should also be mentioned: Anti-Semitism Historically and Critically Examined by Hugo Valentin (1936); The Jewish Problem by Louis Golding (1938); Questions and Answers Concerning the Jew by the Anti-Defamation League (1942); Must Men Hate? by Sigmund Livingston (1944); Anti-Semitism: A Social Disease edited by Ernst Simmel (1946) with a preface by Gordon W. Allport and contributions by several members of the Frankfurt School--Max Horkheimer, Theodor Adorno, and

-86-

Else Frenkel-Brunswik; An Enemy of the People: Anti-Semitism by James Parkes (1946); A Mask for Privilege: Anti-Semitism in America by Carey McWilliams (1948); Hitler's Professors: The Part of Scholarship in Germany's Crimes Against the Jewish People by the director of the YIVO-Yiddish Scientific Institute, Max Weinreich (1946). An influential social psychologist of Jewish background, Kurt Lewin, also contributed to the subject with his classic statements on Jewish self-hatred and on raising a Jewish child, both written in the early 1940s. (Lewin, 1948:169-200.)

The classic study of anti-Semitism is, of course, The Authoritarian Personality by Theodor W. Adorno, et al (1950). This study was one of several in a series called "Studies in Prejudice" sponsored by the American Jewish Committee, the University of California Berkeley Public Opinion Study, and the Institute of Social Research, then at Columbia University in exile from its original home in Frankfurt am Main. Others in this series included Bruno Bettelheim and Morris Janowitz Dynamics of Prejudice (1950); Nathan W. Ackerman and Marie Jahoda Anti-Semitism and Emotional Disorder (1950); and Leo Lowenthal and Norbert Guterman Prophets of Deceit (1949).

With such a heritage to follow, twenty years later the Anti-Defamation League together with the Survey Research Center of the University of CaliforniaBerkeley launched another series of works on antiSemitism called "Patterns of American Prejudice." These important works included: Christian Beliefs and Anti-Semitism by Charles Y. Glock and Rodney Stark (1966); The Apathetic Majority: A Study Based on Public Responses to the Eichmann Trial by Charles Y. Glock, Gertrude J. Selznick, and Joe Spaeth (1966); Protest and Prejudice: A Study of Belief in the Black Community by Gary T. Marx (1967); and The Tenacity of Prejudice: Anti-Semitism in Contemporary America by Gertrude J. Selznick and Stephen Steinberg (1969). There are several other volumes as well in this series. Between the first series in the 1949-1950 period and the second series in the 1966-1970 period emerged another book that investigated whether anti-Semitism had declined in America--Jews in the Mind of America by Charles Herbert Stember, et al (1966) which contained contributions by such sociologists as Dennis Wrong, Robin Williams, Marshall Sklare, Ben Halpern, Robert Gutman, Thomas O'Dea, Thomas Pettigrew, and Benjamin Ringer.

Because of the tenacity of this "eternal hatred," we should see even more studies on anti-Semitism, neo-Nazism, and fascism in the future.[7]

Post-World War II America

After World War II, Jews found themselves in increased numbers within sociology. The latest figures by Lipset and Ladd (1971:95) show that approximately 13 percent, or about 1,800, of the 14,000 sociologists in America and Canada are of Jewish background. While this figure is roughly four times the percentage of Jews in America (about 2.9 percent of the U.S. population), there are other fields with an even higher percentage of academics who are Jews--psychology (16.5); bio-chemistry (21); law (25); social work (16); and anthropology (14).

However, despite their 13 percent, the influence of sociologists with Jewish backgrounds goes beyond their actual numbers. For example, in the years 1967-68, 25 percent of the editors and advisory editors of the American Sociological Review and the American Journal of Sociology, the two most prestigious journals in American sociology, were of Jewish origins. To show this growth further, as Table 1 notes, before Louis Wirth's election in 1946, there were no ASA presidents of Jewish origin. Since Wirth, seven of thirty-three presidents, or 21 percent, were of Jewish descent. These included Robert K. Merton, Paul F. Lazarsfeld, Philip M. Hauser, Arnold M. Rose, Reinhard Bendix, Peter M. Blau, and Lewis A. Coser. If one also included those who ran for ASA president but lost, one could add Nathan Glazer, Raymond Mack, and S.M. Miller.

While the percentage of ASA presidents of Jewish origin (11 percent) is about the same as the percentage of Jews in the ASA (13 percent), the percentage of Jewish presidents of the Society for the Study of Social Problems (founded in 1952) is over three times their percentage in the ASA--forty-three percent. Almost half of the SSSP presidents have been of Jewish origin! (See Tables 2 and 3.)

Lipset and Ladd (1971) have shown that 75 percent of Jewish academicians characterize their politics as either "liberal" or "left" in contrast to 42 percent of the Protestants; furthermore, 12 percent of Jewish faculty consider themselves "left" as opposed to only 4 percent of Protestant faculty. This "left-liberal"

TABLE 2

Number of Jews, Blacks, and Women
Elected to the Presidency of the
Society for the Study of Social Problems
(SSSP) (Founded in 1952)

	Jews	Blacks	Women
1952-1959	1	0	1
1960-1969	7	0	1*
1970-1980	4	0	3**
Totals	12	0	5
Percentage	43%	0%	18%

* Here too, Jessie Bernard, a Jewish woman, was
counted as a woman.

** Rose Laub Coser and Jacqueline Wiseman were
counted as women.

Note: This, of course, would raise the total
number of Jews to fifteen, or 54 percent of the
total number of presidents if these women were
counted as Jews and not women.

Percentages were rounded off.

TABLE 3

Percentage of Jewish, Black, and Women Presidents
in the ASA, ESS, and SSSP, up to 1980

	Jews	Blacks	Women
ASA (N=75)	11%	1%	3%
ESS (N=50)	14%	6%	14%
SSSP (N=28)	43%	0%	18%
Total (N=153 presidents)	18%(27)	3%(4)	9%(14)

Percentages were rounded off.

perspective is prominent among Jewish sociologists, especially within an organization that was founded with the express purpose of combining sociological inquiry and progressive social involvement. Within such an environment, one would, of course, find many liberals and left-liberals, and naturally, it would also attract a great many Jews. Thus, it is no surprise to find many SSSP presidents of Jewish origins, people like Alvin Gouldner, S.M. Miller, Bernard Beck, Howard S. Becker, Lewis Coser, Rose Coser, and Arnold Rose.

However, it must be emphasized that to be labeled as Jewish it does not follow that the Jewish religion or the Jewish people are prominent in either the research of the person or in his or her lifestyle. To many, if not most, Jewish sociologists, their Judaism is irrelevant to their role as sociologist. Lipset and Ladd (1971:110) found in their sample of 5,907 Jewish academics that only 32 percent identified themselves as "deeply or moderately religious" while 68 percent saw themselves as "largely indifferent" or "opposed" to religion. Allan Mazur (1971), in a study of Jewish social scientists in three major universities in Boston, found that Jewish identity was considerably weaker among such social scientists when compared to the general Boston Jewish community. While 38 percent of the social scientists had a Gentile spouse, this was true for only 7 percent of the Jewish Bostonians; while only 13 percent of the academics belonged to at least one Jewish organization, 50 percent of the Boston Jews belonged; and while only 27 percent of the social scientists attend High Holiday services, 77 percent of the Bostonians attended. (See Sklare, 1974c:156.) Norman Friedman (1971, 1969) also arrived at similar conclusions about the lack of religiosity among Jewish academics, and what holds for academics in general can with reasonable certainty hold for Jewish sociologists.

The reason for this is that the sociologist tends to see Jewish studies as being in conflict with his or her professional identity. (Sklare, in Jick, 1970: 64-65) Such Jews wished to be seen as American intellectuals rather than Jewish sociologists. The universalism of the discipline and of academia were more important than the particularism of the ethnic/ religious group. In an often quoted selection, Lipset (1963:163) succinctly analyzes this tension:

> The failure of Jewish social scientists to engage in research on the Jews reflects their

desire to be perceived as American rather than Jewish intellectuals. To write in depth about the Jewish community would seemingly expose them to being identified as 'Jewish Jews', as individuals who are too preoccupied with an ethnic identity, and who lack the universalistic orientation prized by social scientists and American intellectuals generally.

This is the way early Jewish sociologists such as Simmel and Durkheim felt as well. It is also the way other minority academics (women, blacks, AsianAmericans felt about their engagement with "minority" research. This would all change, and radically so, in the late 1960s, but in the immediate postwar period of the 1940s and 1950s, there were few sociologists, Jewish or otherwise, involved in research on Jewish issues.

But there were some, and they laid the groundwork for the resurgence of ethnicity which would come later. In fact, while the majority of social scientists were busy in other areas, small pockets of people were keeping the tradition of research on Jews alive through the 1950s; Alvin Chenkin in demography, the YIVO people in ethnography and linguistics, and Marshall Sklare in various areas of Jewish life.

Sklare, who is considered the dean of postwar sociologists of Jewry, worked at the American Jewish Committee where he carried out his famous "Lakeville" studies of a Jewish community in the tradition of the Lynds and Warner. He also compiled the first postwar anthology on the sociology of Jewry called The Jews: Social Patterns of an American Group (1958). His other interests included intermarriage, communal structures, and a study of Conservative Judaism (1955, later edition 1972). Sklare called the 1950s period that of the "critical intellectual" (1974c:162-165) or the "alienated intellectual" (1974d:363). This period was marked by the sociologist who wished to retain his or her Jewish identity but who at the same time felt alienated from the general Jewish community. This period should be contrasted with the prewar era which was marked by the "assimilated intellectual" best personified by Louis Wirth. (Sklare, 1974c:162)

The next period was to see a rejection of the assimilationist and the alienated-intellectual perspectives, and, once again, Israel would be the touchstone for these charges.

Post-1967: New Religious and Political Trends

The year 1967 was a turning point in American and world Jewry. The surprisingly decisive victory by the Israelis in the Six-Day War set in motion a great many trends. First, it gave Jews throughout the world increased pride, perhaps vicariously, in "Jewish might"--Israel is, and by extension all Jews were, not a people to be trifled with. Surrounded by enemies that far outnumbered it in tanks and soldiers, Israel soundly and swiftly defeated the Arabs with no help from anyone. At the same time, the rising radical left, black, and Third World movements were beginning their actions, and Israel was soon labeled an "imperialist," even "fascist" state. Anti-Zionism brought back memories of anti-Semitism, and at times the two were interwoven. For many Jews in the left, this contradiction led, as it often does, to a new movement of Jews--the so-called radical Jewish movement with its countercultural side, similar to the American counterculture of the 1960s. (See Porter and Dreier, 1973; Dreier and Porter, 1975; Sleeper and Mintz, 1971.)

The radical movements also set into motion the resurgence of ethnicity on campus and, with it, "ethnic studies." If blacks, women, and Chicanos could have their studies, why not Jewish students? And, as was pointed out earlier, Jewish studies saw a sudden spurt in the late 1960s which continued up until the late 1970s. All minority groups made gains during this period, but Jews, no longer considered a minority group under affirmative action, grew somewhat defensive, and with the sobering October 1973 war in the Middle East, this defensiveness and conservatism increased.

While Sklare (1974c:165-171) ends his typology of Jewish perspectives with the "survivalist" period of the 1960s, I would add one more: the activist perspective of the post-1967 era which combined Jewish scholarship, Jewish survival, and Jewish progressive action. Several people active in the radical Jewish movement/counterculture of the late 1960s and early 1970s were also active in sociology: Jack Nusan Porter; Steven M. Cohen, a sociologist from Queen's College, and Stephen Cohen, a student of Robert Bales and now a CCNY social psychologist.

The post-1967 era also heightened interest in Jewish "sub-communities" such as the Jewish poor, black

Jews, Jewish women, and Orthodox Jews (Lavender, 1977); in fact, Orthodoxy had somewhat of a revival of intellectual interest on the part of such younger social scientists as Samuel Heilmann, William Helmreich, David Glanz, Chaim Waxman, and Charles Leibman. This by itself might show how far the sociological study of Jewry had come when not only discussing Orthodox Judaism, but actually being an Orthodox Jew in sociology and doing research in the area could be as acceptable to both prominent publishing houses and to conference organizers as social theory and methods.

There was also new interest in religious behavior generally; in sex roles and the family; in the synagogue and its alternatives, chavurot, Jewish fellowships; in Jewish education; in new political analyses; in black-Jewish relations; in nostalgia for the past; and for new evaluations of the present, especially a more mature relationship with Israel and toward the Holocaust. (See Fein, 1979.)

While books by Irving Howe (1976) and Arthur Leibman (1979) explored the turbulent and sometimes radical immigrant past, new interpretations and studies of Diaspora-Israel relations were necessary. (See for example, Peretz, 1967; Goldscheider, 1974, and Waskow, 1978:252-258.) While in the past, studies by Americans have been mostly of kibbutz life, we should see more sophisticated analyses of Israeli society and of Israeli-Arab relations in the future.

It is difficult to conclude this ongoing and dynamic process of research on Jewish life. Let us simply say that while Jewish studies have found a fairly secure niche in academia, the sociology of Jewry is still only taught on a sporadic basis. Ethnic studies in general and studies of the Holocaust, of the sociology of Jewish life, or of Israeli society in particular as found in sociology departments, are not so secure. Contemporary Jewish studies, like black or women's studies, are fragile institutions, and in economically depressed times they have to fight to survive. So it is ironic that while the sociology of Jewry has enjoyed a vigorous growth, and while the Jewish presence in sociology, in 1980, the 75th anniversary of the American Sociological Association, is stronger than at any time in history, the future of the field is still precarious. Only the continued vigilance and energy of concerned scholars, journals, and organizations can assure that the sociology of Jewry will not disappear as a field of inquiry because no field is ever assured of immortality.

Notes

1. Long before there was to emerge specifically Jewish sociological associations, the YIVO-Yiddish Scientific Institute organized symposia and monographs on the sociology of Jews. One of the most interesting of these symposia was published in the YIVO Annual of Jewish Social Science, Volume IV, in 1949. It included contributions by such eminent sociologists as Florian Znaniecki, Pauline Young, Kurt Wolff, Leo Srole, Sophia Robison, Robert MacIver, Uriah Zevi Engelman, Samuel Flowerman, Maurice Davie, Daniel Bell, Nathan Glazer, Frank Hankins, Donald Young and Morris Ginsberg. Alvin Johnson of the New School for Social Research criticized the assembly for using the word forms "Jewish Research" or "Jewish Social Research," because he would never think of reading an article or book on "Catholic...or Episcopalian Research." He feared what he called "splinter social science" which might "geneologize" or glorify ancestral situations. "...I don't want to see any barriers between you (the Jews) and me," he emphasized. (See Lurie and Weinreich, 1949:173.)

2. For a more comprehensive history of Jewish studies on American campuses, see the article by Ritterband and Wechsler (1979).

3. The number of courses is based on the latest and best compilation of Jewish studies at American and Canadian universities edited by Samuel Z. Fishman and Judyth R. Saypol (1979) of the B'nai Brith Hillel Foundations with the help of the Association for Jewish Studies.

4. Such "free universities" included many courses that more traditional departments would not allow into their curriculum: such as "Judaism, War, and Conscientious Objection," "Jewish Mysticism, Chassidism, and Radical Theology," "Zionism and World Liberation," "The Oppression of Jewish Women," "Marxism, Anarchism, and Judaism," "Jewish Cooking," and "Homosexuality and Judaism." After

being "tested" at these free universities, aspects of them, or at times entire courses, later found themselves into the university curriculum.

5. The Jewish Journal of Sociology was brought into being in order to provide "serious writing on Jewish social affairs." As its first editorial (dated April 1959) stated: "There are few opportunities at present for publishing academic and scientific papers on the sociology of the Jews; the purpose of the Journal is to expand (such) opportunities....(and) we hope that the very existence of the Journal....will encourage scholars to turn their attention to Jewish topics. The (journal) cannot become a permanent institution unless it rests on a broad foundation of research and systematic thinking." The journal was open to all, not only social scientists, and its audience, while mainly academic, was any concerned reader who would like to make a "rational appraisal of Jewish questions."

6. We need more research on the impact that sociologists had on the immigration laws of the early 1920s; for example, which sociologists were in favor of such restrictions and which opposed them. In general, we need a revisionist analysis based upon primary historical data on the influence of Social Darwinism on American sociologists and on American minority groups.

7. A provocative analysis of the ADL studies is Dawidowicz (1970:36-43). In it, the author questions whether the "narrow" social survey research approach can truly measure anti-Semitism.

References

Ackerman, Nathan W. and Jahoda, Marie, <u>Anti-Semitism</u>
  <u>and Emotional Disorder: A Psychoanalytic Inter</u>
  <u>pretation</u>, (New York: Harper and Brothers, 1950.)

Adorno, Theodor W., et al., <u>The Authoritarian Person</u>
  <u>ality</u>, (New York: Harper and Brothers, 1950.)

Anti-Defamation League of B'nai Brith, <u>Questions and</u>
  <u>Answers Concerning the Jew</u>, (Chicago: ADL of B'nai
  Brith, 1942.)

Band, Arnold, "Jewish Studies in American Liberal Arts
  Colleges and Universities," <u>American Jewish Year</u>
  <u>book</u>, Vol. 67, New York, 1966, pp. 3-30.

Bettelheim, Bruno and Janowitz, Morris, <u>Dynamics of</u>
  <u>Prejudice</u>, (New York: Harper and Brothers, 1950.)

Buck-Morss, Susan, <u>The Origins of Negative Dialectics:</u>
  <u>Theodor W. Adorno, Walter Benjamin, and the</u>
  <u>Frankfurt Institute</u>, (New York: The Free Press,
  1977.)

Cahnman, Werner, "Scholar and Visionary: The Corres
  pondence Between Herzl and Ludwig Gumplowicz,"
  <u>Herzl Year Book</u>, Vol. 1, 1958, pp. 165-180.

_____, "Sociology," <u>Encyclopedia Judaica</u>,
  Jerusalem: Keter, Vol. 15, 1972, pp. 62-69.

Carlebach, Julius, <u>Karl Marx and the Radical Critique</u>
  <u>of Judaism</u>, (London and Boston: Routledge & Kegan
  Paul, 1978.)

Davis, Moshe, "From the Vantage of Jerusalem," <u>America</u>
  <u>Jewish Historical Quarterly</u>, Vol. 63, No. 4, June
  1974, pp. 313-333.

Dawidowicz, Lucy, "Can Anti-Semitism be Measured?"
  <u>Commentary</u>, Vol. 50, No. 1, July 1970, pp. 36-43.

Dreier, Peter and Porter, Jack Nusan, "Jewish Radical
  ism in Transition", <u>Society</u>, Vol. 12, No. 2,
  January-February, 1975, pp. 34-43.

Elazar, Daniel, "Contemporary Jewish Civilization on
  the American Campus," editor, symposium, <u>American</u>

Jewish Historical Quarterly, Vol. 63, No. 4, June
1974.

_____, "What We Know and What We Need to Know
About the Status of Jewish Social Research,"
Journal of Jewish Communal Service, Vol. 54, No.
3, Spring 1978, pp. 200-209.

Faris, R.E.L., *Chicago Sociology, 1920-1932*, (Chicago:
University of Chicago Press. 1970.)

Fein, Helen, *Accounting for Genocide*, (New York: The
Free Press, 1979.)

Fishman, Samuel Z. and Saypol, Judith R. (eds.), *Jewish
Studies at American and Canadian Universities: An
Academic Catalog*, (Washington, DC: B'nai Brith
Hillel Foundations and the Association for Jewish
Studies, 1979.)

Friedman, Norman, "The Problem of the 'Runaway Jewish
Intellectuals': Social Definition and Sociological
Perspective," *Jewish Social Studies*, Vol. 31,
No. 1, Jan. 1969, pp. 3-19.

_____, "Jewish or Professional Identity? The
Priorization in Academic Situations," *Sociological
Analysis*, Vol. 32, No. 3, Fall 1971, pp. 149-157.

Glock, Charles Y. and Stark, Rodney, *Christian Beliefs
and Anti-Semitism*, (New York: Harper and Row,
1966.)

Glock, Charles Y. et al, *The Apathetic Majority: A
Study Based on Public Responses to the Eichmann
Trial*, (New York: Harper and Row, 1966.)

Golding, Louis, *The Jewish Problem*, Harmondsworth,
(England: Penguin Books, 1938.)

Goldscheider, Calvin, "American Aliya: Sociological and
Demographic Perspectives" in Marshall Sklare (ed.)
The Jew in American Society, (New York: Behrman
House, 1974), pp. 337-384.

Graeber, Isaque and Britt, Steuart Henderson (eds.),
*Jews in a Gentile World: The Problem of Anti-
Semitism*, (New York: Macmillan Company, 1942.)

Hofstadter, Richard, *Social Darwinism in American
Thought*, (New York: Knopf, 1955.)

Howe, Irving, World of Our Fathers, (New York: Simon and Shuster, 1976.)

Jay, Martin, The Dialectical Imagination: A History of the Frankfurt School and the Institute of Social Research 1923-1950, (Boston: Little, Brown, 1973.)

Jick, Leon (ed.), The Teaching of Judaica in American Universities, (New York: KTAV Publishing House, 1970.)

_____, "Judaica in American Universities", Encyclopedia Judaica Yearbook, 1975/76, (Jerusalem: Keter Publishing House, 1976), pp. 193-197.

Jospe, Alfred (ed.), Jewish Studies in American Colleges and Universities: A Catalogue, (Washington, DC: B'nai Brith Hillel Foundations, 1972.)

Ladner, Joyce (ed.), The Death of White Sociology, (New York: Random House-Vintage Books, 1973.)

Lavender, Abraham D. (ed.), A Coat of Many Colors: Jewish Subcommunities in the United States, (Westport, CT: Greenwood Press, 1977.)

Leibman, Arthur, Jews and the Left, (New York: John Wiley, 1979.)

Lewin, Kurt, Resolving Social Conflicts, Gertrud Weiss Lewin, (ed.) (New York: Harper and Brothers, 1948.)

Lipset, S.M., "The American Jewish Community in a Comparative Context," The Jewish Journal of Sociology, Vol. V, No. 2, December 1963, pp. 157-166.

Lipset, S.M. and Ladd, Everett C., "Jewish Academics in the United States: Their Achievements, Culture and Politics," American Jewish Year Book, Vol. 72, 1971, pp. 89-128.

Livingston, Sigmund, Must Men Hate?, (New York: Harper and Brothers, 1944.)

Lowenthal, Leo and Guterman, Norbert, Prophets of Deceit: A Study of the Techniques of the American Agitator, (New York: Harper and Brothers, 1949.)

Lurie, Harry L. and Weinreich, Max, (eds.), "Jewish
    Social Research in America: Status and Prospects,
    A Symposium", YIVO Annual of Jewish Social
    Science, Vol. IV, 1949, pp. 147-310.

Marvick, Elizabeth Wirth, "Louis Wirth: A Biographic
    Memorandum," in Louis Wirth: On Cities and Social
    Life, Albert J. Reiss, Jr. (ed.), (Chicago:
    University of Chicago Press, 1964.)

Marx, Gary, Protest and Prejudice: A Study of Belief in
    the Black Community, (New York: Harper and Row,
    1967.)

Mazur, Allen, "The Socialization of Jews into the
    Academic Subculture," in The Professors, Charles
    H. Anderson and John D. Murray, (eds.) (Cambridge,
    Massachusetts: Schenkman Publishing Company,
    1971,) pp. 265-287.

McWilliams, Carey, A Mask for Privilege: Anti-Semitism
    in America, (Boston: Little, Brown, 1948.)

Meyer, Michael, "Introduction" to Samuel Z. Fishman and
    Judyth R. Saypol, op. cit., 1979, pp. vii-viii.

Millman, Marcia and Kanter, Rosabeth Moss (eds.),
    Another Voice: Feminist Perspectives on Social
    Life and Social Science, (New York: Doubleday/
    Anchor Books, 1975.)

Neusner, Jacob, The Academic Study of Judaism: Essays
    and Reflections, Second Series, (New York: KTAV,
    1977.)

Parkes, James, An Enemy of the People: Anti-Semitism,
    (New York: Penguin Books, 1946.)

Peretz, Martin, "The American Left and Israel,"
    Commentary, Vol. 44, No. 5, November, 1967, pp.
    27-34.

Porter, Jack Nusan and Dreier, Peter, (eds.), Jewish
    Radicalism: A Selected Anthology, (New York: Grove
    Press, 1973.)

Porter, Jack Nusan (ed.), The Sociology of American
    Jews (rev. ed.), (Washington, DC: University Press
    of America, 1980.)

_____, The Jew as Outsider, Contemporary and Historical Perspectives, (Washington, DC: University Press of America, 1981.)

Ritterband, Paul and Wechsler, Harold S., "Judaica in American Colleges and Universities," Encyclopedia Judaica Yearbook 1977/78, (Jerusalem: Keter, 1979,) pp. 73-77.

Ruppin, Arthur, The Jews in the Modern World, (London: Macmillan and Co., 1934.)

Simmel, Ernst (ed.), Anti-Semitism: A Social Disease, (New York: International Universities Press, 1946.)

Simmel, Georg, The Sociology of Georg Simmel, tr., ed., and with an introduction by Kurt H. Wolff, (Glencoe, Illionois: The Free Press, 1955.)

Sklare, Marshall, Conservative Judaism, (Glencoe, Illinois: The Free Press, 1955.)

_____, The Jews: Social Patterns of an American Group, (Glencoe, Illinois: The Free Press, 1958.)

_____, (ed.), The Jewish Community in America, (New York: Behrman House, 1974a.)

_____, (ed.), The Jew in American Society, (New York: Behrman House, 1974b.)

_____, "The Jew in American Sociological Thought," Ethnicity, Vol. 1, 1974c, pp. 151-173.

_____, "Problems in the Teaching of Contem porary Contemporary Jewish Studies," American Jewish Historical Quarterly, Vol. 63, No. 4, June 1974d, pp. 361-368.

Selznick, Gertrude J. and Steinberg, Steven, The Tenacity of Prejudice: Anti-Semitism in Contemporary America, (New York: Harper and Row, 1969.)

Sleeper, James A. and Mintz, Alan L. (eds.), The New Jews, (New York: Vintage Books, 1971.)

Spiegel, Irving, "Study Finds a Marked Increase in Jewish Studies in 10 Years," New York Times, Sunday, August 26, 1973.

Stein, Herman D., "Jewish Social Work in the United
    States, 1654-1954," American Jewish Yearbook, Vol.
    57, 1956, pp. 3-98.

Stember, Charles Herbert et al., Jews in the Mind
    of America, (New York: Basic Books, 1966.)

Timasheff, Nicholas S. and Theodorson, George A.,
    Sociological Theory: Its Nature and Growth, 4th
    ed., (New York: Random House, 1976.)

Valentin, Hugo, Anti-Semitism: Historically and
    Critically Examined, (New York: Viking Press,
    1936.)

Waskow, Arthur, "Beyond Idolatry: Towards a Trans
    national Alternative," in Jack Nusan Porter (ed.)
    The Sociology of American Jews, op. cit., 1978
    edition, pp. 252-258.

Weinrich, Max, Hitler's Professors: The Part of
    Scholarship in Germany's Crimes Against the
    Jewish People, (New York: YIVO, 1946.)

Wirth, Louis, The Ghetto, (Chicago: The University of
    Chicago Press, 1928.)

_____, "Education for Survival: The Jews,"
    American Journal of Sociology, Vol. 68, No. 6, May
    1943, pp. 682-691.

Wistrich, Robert S., Revolutionary Jews from Marx to
    Trotsky, (New York: Harper and Row/Barnes and
    Noble, 1976.)

Appendix A

Major Textbooks and Anthologies
in the Sociology of Jewry

The following is a list of major textbooks and
anthologies in the field of the sociology of Jewry.
The first attempt to assemble information on the whole
range of Jewish life in America--historical, military,
governmental, religious, and associational was Isaac
Markens The Hebrews in America (New York, 1888; reprinted 1978). The huge migration of the Jews at the
turn of the century led to several other books: Maurice
Fishberg, The Jews: A Study of Race and Environment
(1911), an early classic from an anthropological perspective; Samuel Joseph Jewish Immigration to the
United States from 1881-1910 (New York, 1914; reprinted
1978), a history of Jewish immigration from Russia,
Roumania, and Austro-Hungary to the United States; and
Arthur Ruppin's The Jews of Today (1913) and later The
Jews in the Modern World (1934). Another interesting
book that should be mentioned before we enter the 1930s
is A.A. Roback's Jewish Influence in Modern Thought
(1929). Published in Cambridge, Massachusetts, it is a
500-page compendium of how Jews and Judaism influenced
modern philosophical and psychological thought.

In the 1930s and 1940s, aside from the Ruppin
books, we have works by Horace Kallen such as Judaism
at Bay, published in 1932, which are really socio-
philosophical essays on Zionism, anti-Semitism, and
Jewish-Christian relations; Maurice J. Karpf's Jewish
Community Organization in the United States (1938), a
brief but comprehensive description of organizational
Jewish life written by a noted Jewish social worker and
agency director; Ben M. Edidin Jewish Community Life
in America (1947), a similar book but directed at high
school students; plus one of the first anthologies on
Jewish life, Oscar I. Janowsky's The American Jew: A
Composite Portrait (1942). The Graeber and Britt book
discussed earlier, Jews in a Gentile World (1942), was
also published during World War II in response to
Jewish persecution. Uriah Zevi Engelman, Director of
Research at the Association for Jewish Education in New
York and a contributor to the American Journal of
Sociology, wrote a sociological and economic account of
Jewish life in his The Rise of the Jew in the Western
World (1944; reprinted 1978).

The 1950s and early 1960s increased the flow of books in the field, and the contributions became more sophisticated as more scholars turned their attention to Jewish issues. The first sociological anthology on Jews appeared in 1958 and was edited by Marshall Sklare. 1957 saw the publication of Nathan Glazer's well-received American Judaism, now in a second edition (1972). Ben Halpern, in 1956, published a short introducpeared in this period were: Robert Morris and Michael Freund, Trends and Issues in Jewish Social Welfare in the United States, 1899-1958 (1966); Oscar I. Janowsky (with an updated version of his earlier book called The American Jew: A Reappraisal (1964); and a well-edited, lively reader by sociologist Peter I. Rose The Ghetto and Beyond: Essays on Jewish Life in America (1969), a popular classroom anthology.

Other important texts and general works in the 1960s included an often overlooked book by the labor Zionist thinker C. Bezalel Sherman The Jew Within American Society (1961); the Sidney Goldstein and Calvin Goldscheider book Jewish Americans: Three Generations in a Jewish Community (1968); and a controversial little book by Ernest Van den Haag The Jewish Mystique (1969).

The 1970s reflected the growth in Jewish studies across the nation and many more texts were published. Marshall Sklare continued his prolific ways with America's Jews (1971), and updated his 1958 anthology with two companion books, The Jew in American Society and The Jewish Community in America (both 1974). A survey called the Jewish Family (1971), edited by Benjamin Schlesinger was also published around this time.

New and sometimes provocative textbooks, anthologies, and overviews of contemporary Jewish life were to emerge in the 1970s: Daniel Elazar Community and Polity (1976); Gerald S. Strober's American Jews: Community in Crisis (1974); Abraham D. Lavender's A Coat of Many Colors; Jewish Subcommunities in the United States (1977); and from a British perspective, Stephen Sharot Judaism: A Sociology (1976).

Will Maslow's short booklet proved to be a useful textbook, The Structure and Functioning of the American Jewish Community (1974). Charles Liebman's The Ambivalent American Jew (1973) and Jacob Neusner's

American Judaism: Adventure in Modernity (1972) also
were popular classroom books, standing alongside their
other prolific contributions. The David Sidorsky
anthology The Future of the Jewish Community (1973) and
Nathan Glazer and Daniel Moynihan's Beyond the Melting
Pot (1970) should also be mentioned as important books
in the 1970s. Finally, the first radical anthology on
American Jews was published in 1978: Jack Nusan
Porter's The Sociology of American Jews: A Critical
Anthology, a sociological companion piece to his
earlier anthology with Peter Dreier called Jewish
Radicalism: A Selected Anthology (1973).

    Regarding general works on Israel and Israel-
Diaspora relations, here too we should mention the
following books, knowing that we could easily expand
the list tenfold. One of the most useful and enduring
anthologies of Zionist philosophies is Arthur Hertzberg
The Zionist Idea (1959; reprinted 1972). A unique
socialist-Zionist and sociological analysis of Jewish
life is Allon Gal Socialist-Zionism: Theory and Issues
in Contemporary Jewish Nationalism (1973). A provocative book that appeared immediately before the 1967
Six-Day War was written by the French sociologist from
the Sorbonne, Georges Friedmann, The End of the Jewish
People? (1965). S.N. Eisenstadt's numerous works on
youth, Israeli society, and comparative world institutions should also be mentioned here. The indefatigable
Moshe Davis has edited and written many books in this
area and one can be noted here: World Jewry and the
State of Israel (1977); as well as another post-1973
"Yom Kippur War" Anthology, Israel T. Naamani and David
Rudavsky Israel: Its Politics and Philosophy (1974).
Based on these preliminary anthologies, we should see
some constructive textbooks appearing on the sociology
of Israel/Diaspora relations in the 1980s. (These
textbooks are not listed in the reference section.)

Appendix B

Major Research Organizations and Centers on Jewry
(Listed in order of founding)

American Jewish Historical Society (1892)

Bureau of Jewish Statistics and Research of the
    American Jewish Committee (1907)

Bureau of Jewish Social Research (1917; combined with
    the Council of Jewish Federations and Welfare
    Funds in 1935)

YIVO--Yiddish Scientific Institute (1925 in Vilna,
    Poland; moved to New York City in 1940)

American Academy for Jewish Research (1930)

Conference on Jewish Relations (1933)

Commission on Community Interrelations of the American
    Jewish Congress (1944)

Department for Scientific Study of Anti-Semitism of the
    American Jewish Committee (1944)

Scientific Research Division of the American Jewish
    Committee (late 1940s)

Institute for Contemporary Jewry, Hebrew University
    (1959)

Philip Lown Center for Contemporary Jewish Studies,
    Brandeis University (1963)

Institute for Jewish Policy Analysis (1972)

National Jewish Conference Center, and several others
    (1970s)

Appendix C

A Note on the Number of Jewish, Black and Women Presidents of the ASA, ESS, and SSSP

As was mentioned in the context of the paper, Jews, blacks and women were slow in being allowed into positions of power in the major American professional associations in sociology. Taking the American Sociological Association first (often called the ASA), the first Jew, Louis Wirth, was not elected until 1946. He was followed the following year by the first black, E. Franklin Frazier, also of the University of Chicago. A few years after Frazier, in 1951, the first woman was elected, Dorothy Swaine Thomas. In 1957, the second person of Jewish descent, Robert K. Merton, was elected. Thus, up until 1960, after fifty five years, the ASA had only elected one woman, one black, and two Jews.

Things picked up in the 1960s slightly for Jews with Paul Lazarsfeld, Philip Hauser, and Arnold Rose as ASA presidents. There were no blacks or women elected. In the 1970s, again three more Jews were elected (Reinhard Bendix, Peter Blau, and Lewis Coser), one woman (Mirra Komarovsky), and no blacks. Thus, despite the influential presence of Jews in sociology, they are not at all overrepresented in the presidency of the ASA. This is in stark contrast with the Society for the Study of Social Problems (SSSP), a group that attracts generally liberal and left-liberal sociologists, as well as the Eastern Sociological Society (ESS) which has also been much more sensitive over the years to elected minority representatives.

The ESS, founded in 1930, elected its first black in 1944, again E. Franklin Frazier; followed by its first woman the following year, Gladys Bryson. In 1950 it elected its second woman and first person of Jewish descent, Jessie Bernard. In 1952, it elected its second black, Ira De A. Reid. In 1954, its third woman, Mirra Komarovsky, was elected. After Ira De A. Reid, Blacks would have to wait over twenty years to see another of their race in this position: Charles V. Willie in 1974. (President-elect for 1981, by the way, is another black, James Blackwell.) Thus, over the fifty years, only four blacks have been elected, if we include Blackwell. My chart (see Table 1) stops in 1980 and thus has only three blacks.

-106-

In the 1960s, Jews and women did better, but for women, the 1960s were disappointing; there were no women elected to the ESS presidency during that decade. During the 1970s, things picked up and four were elected. As for Jews, the first president after Jessie Bernard was Alex Inkeles in 1960, and this was followed by six others throughout the 1960s and 1970s, concluding with Milton Gordon in 1978.

As Tables 2 and 3 show, the SSSP has by far been the most open to minority representation. Since 1952, 43 percent of the SSSP presidents come from a Jewish background, starting with Arnold M. Rose in 1955-56 and culminating with Bernard Beck and Jacqueline Wiseman in the late 1970s. For women it has also been higher than the ESS and ASA: 18 percent of the SSSP presidents were women. Ironically, the SSSP failed to elect a black president until 1980-1981, when again, James E. Blackwell of the University of Massachusetts-Boston was elected.

Chapter 5

The Jewish Comic

This should probably be the funniest essay in the book, but it may be the saddest and that would be appropriate for the theme of Jewish comic. Comedians usually bring sad tidings despite the gay wrappings. This essay is a reflection of my abiding interest both in show business and in Lenny Bruce. Bruce, especially, was a folk hero to me long before he was crucified. He has also been the epitome of the Jewish rebel, taking his place alongside d.a. levy, Jerry Rubin, Abbie Hoffman and Allen Ginsberg, among others. Students today tend to get nervous when they hear his records. They sense the bitterness, even the hatred. They don't see the rollicking good times, the side-splitting put-downs, and the funny impersonations. My generation saw that part of Lenny Bruce; perhaps all the present generation sees is the moral messages. Bruce was not just a philosopher nor a martyr--he was a funny guy. Today's audiences would have been tough to please, and maybe Bruce could not have adjusted his act to them. No one will ever know. This essay is the best tribute I could make to a very humorous, very talented, but very confused and stubborn Jew. It has never appeared in print before.

* * * * *

The comic is probably the most "rebellious" and most "dangerous" of all entertainers, and the Jewish comic best epitomizes the Jewish rebel. As theologian John Dart has observed: "The absurdities of life fascinate and stimulate both philosophers and comics." (Dart, 1977:588) Sociologist Ralf Dahrendorf has called the intellectual the "fool" of society. One can judge the humanity of a society by how it treats its fools--and its comics.

Historically, the jester, the fool, the buffoon has played a unique role in society. He was allowed a freedom of expression denied most others. By way of humor, the clown or comic could covertly convey taboo messages, uncover hidden fears and prejudices, and unmask the veiled structures of society. As sociologist William Bruce Cameron (1967:94) noted: "If you know what people joke about, you can guess what worries them." And what seems to worry people most is sex, race relations, religion, and politics.

Why do societies allow comics, jokesters, punsters, and clowns to exist? One reason may be that the price one pays to uphold public decorum is high and almost impossible to do at times. The comic is allowed, within a well-defined setting, to lower the stiffness of decorum. The oppressed are allowed to laugh, and the oppressor is allowed to laugh with them. Each, in his own way, finds relief in humor.

Sigmund Freud in his classic study, <u>Jokes and Their Relation to the Unconscious</u> (1903), broke open the underlining meaning of jokes. They were, like dreams and fairy tales, slips of the tongue, symbolic representations of deep-rooted fears, apprehensions, and suppressed desires. Such "covert culture" as jokes, forms of address, and myths can tell the scientist a great deal about the social structure and the social relationships within a society. Freud, it should be added, was a great admirer of Jewish jokes, most of which originated from Galicia and other Eastern European regions. (See Cuddihy, 1974 and Grollman, 1965.) In what is probably the best article on Judaism and comic art, Albert Goldman (1976:18-24) notes that "Jewish" and "comic" go together like "Irish" and "cop," "Chinese" and "laundry," and "Italian" and "tenor." From Freud's day on, Jews have raised the art of comedy to higher and higher levels. The list of American and British comics from Jewish backgrounds is endless. It goes from the earliest years of vaudeville, from Weber and Fields and slapstick (slap<u>shtick</u>) to the silent movies of Charlie Chaplin and Ben <u>Blue</u>, on to radio with Ed Wynn, Eddie Cantor, and Jack Benny, to the talkies and the Marx and Ritz Brothers to Phil Silvers, Red Buttons, Bert Lahr, and Zero Mostel. It continues with nightclub comics like Joe E. Lewis, Henny Youngman, Georgie Jessel, and Buddy Hackett, to television stars like Milton Berle, Sid Caesar, Howard Morris, Carl Reiner, and Mel Brooks, and on to the modern comic-philosophers such as Lenny Bruce, Mort

Sahl, Shelley Berman, Woody Allen, Nichols and May, David Steinberg, Robert Klein, Ed Bluestone, and a host of others.

The relationship between Jewish humor and generational background is an intriguing one and has been noted by both Goldman and by Irving Howe (1976:556573). Jewish humor has come around full circle from first to second to third generation. Each generation's humor and type of comic reflected the fears and freedoms of assimilation in America. In short, the humor ot the first generation of immigrant American Jews who spilled out into the streets of the Lower East Side was honest, raucous, bawdy, and wholly unself-conscious. The "street" itself was the great educator. As Howe emphasizes, it was within the prostkeit of the street that the youngster learned and turned to crime or to entertainment. The "street" became the first place to perform for the likes of Al Jolson, Eddie Cantor, Sophie Tucker, Fanny Brice, George Burns, Mae West (she was part Jewish) and others now either dead or the elder statesmen of show business.

The second generation, however, that is the generation up until the 1950s according to Goldman (1976:18), hid its Jewish identity. The same comics and entertainers who would utilize Jewish humor in their acts in the '20s began to eliminate or disguise it throughout the '30s, '40s, and '50s. There were still large numbers of Jewish comics, but never a Jewish joke! They changed their names from Jerome Levitch to Jerry Lewis, from David Kaminsky to Danny Kaye, from Murray Janofsky to Jan Murray. As Goldman puckishly writes (1976:18):

> Look at how they tacked cute little pigtails on their names: Joe-y, Dan-ny, Sand-y, Len-ny, Hen-ny; at how they studied announcers' diction so that they shouldn't nasalize, dentalize, glottal stop, and fall into that yeshiva-student singsong; nose jobs because people wanted to see a nice gentile face--no more beaks and popeyes; quiet, 'tasty' clothes; cigarettes instead of cigars; flat-finished tuxedos instead of shiny mohairs. Why, some of those Jewish comics rubbed out so many Jewish features from their faces....they wound up looking as if they had been molded in the same factory that makes Barbie dolls. 'Ladies and Gentle-

men, the networks are proud to present Bob
Blank! He isn't Jewish--but then he isn't
human either.'

Goldman, of course, exaggerates. He does admit
that on occasion these Jewish comics, at a Friars
"Roast" or a B'nai Brith banquet or up in the Cat-
skills, would relax and invoke their Jewish identity by
using Yiddishisms and Jewish humor as if to say--"<u>Ich
bin oich a Yid</u>--I'm a Jew too." Goldman points to Jack
Benny and Charlie Chaplin as two good examples of
"white-washed" Jewish comedians. Chaplin in particular
was at pains to deny or minimize his Jewish origins
while at the same time develping his art to the point
that his "Little Fellow" was simply a universal equivalent of the Jewish <u>schlemiel</u>. The same with the
Brothers Marx. Their humor according to Goldman was
Jewish farce <u>manque</u>. Their subversive and rude mockery
of bourgeoise pretensions were perfect examples of the
Jewish rebels in comic drag.

Irving Howe, in his perceptive analysis of Jewish
entertainers in <u>World of Our Fathers</u> (1976:556-573),
observes that the first generation Jewish immigrant
parents at the turn of the century, like so many immigrants, wanted their children to grow up to become
manufacturers, accountants, and doctors. They wanted
them "to make it" in America. But there were some kids
who dreamed of "breaking into" vaudeville and comic
acts. To some parents this may have been analogous to
becoming a pimp or a criminal. The entertainment world
was then seen as verging on the amoral or, at the
least, as an unstable choice of occupation--"better he
should have been a businessman."

Howe, however, points out that there were models
for these Jewish kids. Historically, there was the
<u>badkhn</u> back in the <u>shtetl</u>--the jester and clown who
enlivened weddings and parties. There was also the
predominance of Jews in the theatrical business, on
Broadway, in Yiddish theater, and in the movies (as
directors, producers, agents, and owners). The drive
to succeed in this "golden land" was a powerful
propellent. Some went into business; some into the
university; and some into entertainment. As Howe puts
it (1976:558): "What the intellectually ambitious Jews
looked for in the schools, others were finding in the
streets." It was in the streets that many of the early
great comics learned their trade, from Eddie Cantor to
George Burns to Fannie Brice.

In the first two decades of the century there was a singularly unself-consciousness among American racial and ethnic groups. This was manifested, for example, in song titles that today would not only cause deep embarrassment but would certainly stir up racial animosity. To wit: "Sadie Salome;" "Oh! How That German Could Love;" "Colored Romeos;" "Yiddishe Eyes;" "Yiddle On Your Fiddle (Play Some Ragtime);" "Goodbye, Becky Cohen;" "Nathan, Nathan, Tell Me Vot Are You Vaitin', Nathan." Sophie Tucker was billed as the "World-Renowned Coon Shouter" or in a more refined title, the "Manipulator of Coon Melodies." Later she would become just as famous for her rendition of "My Yiddishe Mama."

These early comics at once were both sentimental and defensive about their Jewish identity. Jewish comics, like birds of a feather, often flocked together. They felt comfortable among their own kind. Yet they were at times sensitive or defensive about some of their "Yiddish" habits. It was said that Eddie Cantor took a great deal of ribbing from Will Rogers and W.C. Fields because he would not eat pork or ham. Nevertheless, these comics were seldom self-conscious about their Yiddish dialect humor. (Howe, 1976:565)

With the rise of Hitler and Nazism and the increasingly isolationist position of the United States came a process of "de-Semitization" in the popular arts. Jews felt it best to keep a low profile both sociologically and in the field of humor. As Howe states: "The Jewish comedians fell upon hard days; everyone was so touchy...." (1976:567) By 1944, there was such a whitewash that the Jew almost disappeared from American fiction, stage, and movies. Again, "non-Jewish" Jews like Jack Benny and Charlie Chaplin were the epitome of this new style of "Jewish" comic.

This trend continued after the war was over and into the McCarthy period and Eisenhower quietis. But later a kind of philo-Semitism gradually emerged. To be Jewish was "in." It was no longer necessary to be either careful or defensive, and the sons and daughters and grandsons and granddaughters of immigrants shpritzed one-liners again in a crazy mishmash of English and Yiddish. (See Howe, 1976:568-569; Goldman, 1976:22-24.) The Jew emerged as a kind of Everyman. With television, comics like Buddy Hackett, Sid Caesar, and Milton Berle used Yiddish like an "insiders" code. After a period of worldwide anti-Semitism and defensiveness, the new Jewish comics of the postwar years gave vent to the pent-up anger and frustration churning inside them and let loose. This breakthrough reached a turning point with the advent of Lenny Bruce. He was to push Yiddishkeit full into the faces of the goyim and the devil go hang, and not only Yiddishkeit but everything--all the hypocritical masks of society were shoved right into its craw. It was a revolutionary force but ultimately self-destructive. The parallel of the revolutionary politics of the 1960s to Bruce's humor is chilling. Both led to "suicide-trips" in the pursuit of destroying the sacred idols of bourgeoise society. They "demolished" society's mores and in the end destroyed themselves.

Lenny Bruce was the cultural rebel par excellent. As Albert Goldman put it: "Lenny Bruce was a comic genius who revolutionized his art by insisting that the tightly impacted humor of the New York ghetto be made the common property of the American people. Driven by the twin screws of talent and chutzpah, Lenny blasted into the open the golden veins of comedy that for many years had lain hidden behind tons of shame and self-consciousness and fear of self-assertion." (Goldman, 1976:22; also see Goldman, 1974; Hentoff, 1974; Bruce, 1966; and Cohen, 1967.)

Bruce led the vanguard of radical ethnic comics. The door had been blown open by the student, black, and countercultural upheavals of the '60s and again the comic only reflected his times. Bruce's humor was not polite--it was irritating, electric, and, yes, vulgar. If J.M. Cuddihy's theory (1974) is correct, then Bruce is a good example of the sensitive Jew who could no longer stomach the refinement of Christian society. He had to be prost and he was going to be more prost (vulgar) than any comic before (and after) him. As Howe writes: "Having stored up a bellyful of Jewish humiliation, Bruce cast it back onto his audiences. The laughter he won was a nervous laughter, tingling with masochism....Humor of this kind bears a heavy weight of destruction; in Jewish hands, more likely self-destruction, for it proceeds from a brilliance that corrodes the world faster than, even in imagination, it can remake it." (1976:573)

Bruce's humor was obsessed with Yiddishisms of the most vulgar and striking kind: schmuck, goyishe punim, emmis, schlep, schtarker, haisser, schtup. He mingled his insider Yiddish with bantering to his jazz back-up men, again mixing jazz terms with the black idiom and over and over emphasizing that he, his musician friends, and his fellow blacks were "outsiders" schpritzing on straight, white, WASP/Catholic, uptight society. His stand-up routines have often been compared to jazz improvisations. He was, in fact, the comic analog to the jazz soloist.

To Bruce, the world was divided between Jews and Goyim (non-Jews), yet something rings false here. There is confusion. He married out of the faith. His knowledge of Judaism was scanty and at times inaccurate. He retold and reconstituted Jewish stereotypes as well as any anti-Semite. And in many ways, he was as moral and as bourgeois as anyone he condemned. He was, in short, a confused Jew. But he was also a genius at making socio-psychological insights. Bruce, in short, was a great sociologist.

> Now I neologize Jewish and goyish. Dig. I'm Jewish. Count Basie's Jewish. Ray Charles is Jewish. Eddie Cantor is goyish. B'nai Brith is goyish; Hadassah, Jewish. Marine Corps--heavy goyim, dangerous. Koolaid is goyish. All Drake's Cakes are goyish. Pumpernickel is Jewish....Fruit salad is Jewish. Lime jello is goyish. Lime soda is very goyish....Balls are goyish. Titties are Jewish. Mouths are Jewish. All Italians are Jewish...."
>
> (Cohen, 1967:41-42).

* * *

> ....as beautifully liberal as any Jewish mother is--she'll march in any parade--yet, let the daughter bring home a nice, respectable Filipino son-in-law, with a nice, long, black foreskin and a gold tooth-- "Ma, this is my new husband. I met him in college."
>
> "Ahhhhhhhhhh! Ahhhhhhhhhh!"
>
> That's all. Yeah.
>
> (Cohen, 1967:37)

* * *

> "....And I really searched it out, why we pay the dues. Why do you keep breaking our balls for this crime?"

"Why, Jew, because you skirt the issue. You
blame it on Roman soldiers."

"Alright. I'll clear the air once and for
all, and confess. Yes, we did it. I did it,
my family. I found a note in my basement.
It said:"

    "We killed him.
      signed,
        Morty."

"And a lot of people say to me,"

"Why did you kill Christ?"

"I dunno....it was one of those parties, got
out of hand, you know.

We killed him because he didn't want to
become a doctor, that's why we killed him."
(Cohen, 1967:40-41)

* * *

... Now the Jew gets into show business.
And, he writes motion pictures, he's making
the images--he has the film industry knocked
up--he controls it!   And the Jew naturally
writes what he thinks is pretty, what he
thinks is ugly--and it's <u>amazing</u>, but you
never see one Jewish bad guy in the movies.
Not ever a Jewish villain.   Gregory Peck,
Paul Muni--haha! It's wonderful! Who's the
bad guy? The <u>goyim</u>! The Irish!

And you see a lot of pictures about Christ--a
ton of religious pictures, in the most
respectful position. And the reason that is,
I'm sure, it's the way the Jew's saying, "I'm
sorry." That's where it's at. (Original
emphasis).
(Cohen, 1967:50-51)

    The death of Lenny Bruce may have been the begin-
ning of the end for Jewish prominence in American
culture. The fad, as Albert Goldman observed, was
coming to an end. New ethnic stars were on the hori-
zon, learning from Jewish elder statesmen, but going
their own way: Richard Pryor, J.J. Walker, and Freddie

Prinze. But all contemporary comics must pay their
respect to Lenny Bruce: Irish-American comics like
George Carlin; Jewish comics like David Steinberg and
Robert Klein; even Japanese, Spanish, and WASP
comedians.

        Jewish eminence in the field will continue, but it
seems that its peak has already passed. Looking back,
an intriguing question still remains: why did so many
Jews become comics? As for blacks and other struggling
minorities, entertainment like sports had been an
easier road to success, or in fact one of the few roads
to success. Second, J.M. Cuddihy (1974) may be correct
about comics, that their attack against Christian and
Jewish gentility was their means of breaking out of the
ghetto. Their rebellion can best be understood as an
uncontrollable urge to shatter the image of edelkeit
(refinement). Yet, for some, their marginality and
anger remained even after they had "made it." Their
"outsider" status as Jews had given them a unique win-
dow on the world. As anthropologist Edmund Carpenter
has said: "A fish will be the last to discover water."
One must stand back from the environment in order to
really "see" it. Furthermore, both Jews and comics are
sensitive to hypocrisy and oppression. Minority groups
tend to use humor in two ways: as a form of tension-
relief and as a way to create in-group solidarity.
Finally, there is the ever-present, ever-necessary need
to be paranoid. Jewish paranoia is enough, but when a
society's paranoia reflects the paranoia of its Jews,
the Jew may be in trouble. As Goldman (1976:24)
concludes: "The word 'paranoid' is on everyone's lips
today. Precisely! What greater evidence of the paranoia of the average American could be found than the
fact that he identifies so glibly with the Jew?" Such
identification is good; it has led to hero-worship of
Jewish media icons--but this uniqueness can also lead
to Auschwitz. And this reminds me of what Elie Weisel
said when someone asked him what they should build over
the torn-down death camps, and his reply: a circus with
plenty of clowns, jesters....and comics.

References

Bruce, Lenny, How To Talk Dirty and Influence People, (Chicago: Playboy Press, 1966.)

Cameron, Wm. Bruce, "The Sociology of Humor and Vice-Versa," in his Informal Sociology, (New York: Random House, 1967) pp. 79-94.

Cohen, John, The Essential Lenny Bruce, (New York: Ballantine Books, 1967.)

Cuddihy, John Murray, The Ordeal of Civility, (New York: Basic Books, 1974.)

Dart, John, "Woody Allen, Theologian," The Christian Century, Vol. 94, No. 22, June 22-29, 1977, pp. 585-589.

Freud, Sigmund, Jokes and Their Relation to the Unconscious, (New York: W.W. Norton Company, 1963.)

Goldman, Albert, Ladies and Gentlemen, Lenny Bruce!!, (New York:Random House and Ballantine Books, 1974.)

_____, "Jewish Comics," Moment, Vol. 1, No. 6, January 1976, pp. 18-24.

Grollman, Earl, Judaism in Sigmund Freud's World, (New York: Bloch Publishing House, 1965.)

Hentoff, Nat, "Dancing on the Grave: Everybody's Doing Lenny's Act," College Monthly, October 1974, pp. 27-31.

Howe, Irving, World of Our Fathers, (New York: Simon and Shuster, 1976.)

Additional Material

Several magazines have had special sections or issues devoted to Jews in Hollywood and in the entertainment world. For example, the Times of Israel (published in Los Angeles), Issue No. 12, Vol. 1, October 1975, Joyce and Alan Sugarman, "Will the Real Jews Please Stand Up!" pp. 11-14; Chai (published in Baltimore), Vol. 2, No. 1, Sept.-Oct. 1975, Judy Bachrach, "Why TV's Jews Aren't Real," and "Joan Rivers: On Being a Jew and Other Things," pp. 7-8 and 20-23; a special issue of Davka (Los Angeles--UCLA Hillel Foundation), Vol. 5, No. 3, Fall 1975 on "The Hollywood Jew" with articles by Tom Tugend, Howard Suber, Herbert G. Luft, Eric Goldman, David Dotort, William Cutter, Barry Gordon, and David Colloff. Also see the Newsweek section on "The New Stand-Up Comics," April 21, 1975, pp. 87-92.

Chapter 6

The Jewish Poet

This is perhaps the most personal of the essays in this book. Written in the dead of night and with a white-heat intensity, it conveys better than any scholarly analysis the bitterness and frustration of the 1960s. I saw d.a. levy (he always wrote in small caps, even his name) as the epitome of the alienated artist. His alienation as Jew was also intertwined with his role as poet, and he painfully points this out in two of his most moving poems--"new year" and "poem to michael solomon." "Michael Solomon" (a pseudonym for Richard Wishnetsky) himself could also have been portrayed in these pages--as an example of a man so frustrated with the utter futility of life that he shot and killed his rabbi (the renowned Morris Adler) and himself in his Detroit synagogue in the middle of Sabbath services. It was an act so outrageous and so helpless that it temporarily paralyzed the minds of social scientists attempting to understand such anomie. A book has appeared by T.V. LoCicero called Murder in the Synagogue, (Englewood Cliffs, NJ, Prentice-Hall, 1970) which chronicles the life and death of "Michael Solomon" and, in so doing, presents insights into the suicide of d.a. levy as well. This article originally appeared in the January, 1975 issue of Jewish Currents under the title of "d.a. levy: the life, death, and poetry of an american jewboy" and is reprinted with the permission of their editorial board. I toyed with the idea of making this essay more "objective" and less emotional, but have decided to keep its original tone because it can never be captured again. I no longer am that angry and I would not write such a piece today. It would be much gentler.

* * * * *

> "When I'm dead, you ought to give more attention
> to live poets."
>
> (d.a. levy)

d.a. (Darryl Allen) levy was a "poetpublisher-editor" who lived a short fast bittersweet life and then shot himself to death in his Cleveland apartment on November 24, 1968. There were people who said he might have taken over the mantle of Allen Ginsberg if only he had lived longer, but....

levy was among the many "new left" poets that emerged out of the '60s. He takes his place alongside Diane di Prima, Jane Stembridge, Todd Gitlin, Michael Rossman, Don Lee, Nikki Giovanni, and others, black and white, who have placed art and literature at the disposal of the people, for the liberation of the oppressed.

levy, like so many artists, was deeply influenced by older "gurus" of the left: Paul Goodman, Allen Ginsberg, Gary Snyder, and Alan Watts.

He was born in Cleveland in October, 1942 (a Scorpian), grew up, decided to commit suicide at seventeen, changed his mind and began to read and write; graduated in 1960 from James Ford Rhodes High School, didn't have the money for college, joined the navy, spent seven months and three days there, talked his way out, returned to Cleveland, became the charismatic personality behind Cleveland's avant-garde in and around the University Circle area, was mocked, hounded, and arrested the final years of his life. His father, Joseph Levy, was a shoe salesman; his mother was a Christian.

In Cleveland, he edited the Marijuana Quarterly and The Buddhist Third Class Junk Mail Oracle, wrote a lot of poetry, inspired ukanhavyrfuckincitibak,[1] and helped a lot of poets.

Morris Edelson, editor of the Madison, Wisconsin paper, Quixote, poet, a good friend to writers, and a kind of Max Brod to levy's Kafka, wrote the following in a short intro to one of levy's collections--Private No Parking. (See the mini-bibliography at the end for more books by and about levy.)

...,(levy) was invited in 1968 by Quixote to spend some time in Madison.

he came, slept at Grace and Dave Wagner's, visited some Freshman English classes and Comparative Literature Department meetings,[2] gave a non-reading, and taught/ didn't teach a class: it was a Free University class in telepathy, d.a. never went but the class met anyway, thinking he was trying to tell them something. he was.

after the month in Madison, d.a. went back to Cleveland--some say he killed himself, others say the pigs did it because they had sent him up before for reading his poetry to people. TO THAT SENTENCE HIS ATTITUDE WAS ONE OF DEFIANCE NOT SELF-PITY. Yours?

levy becomes now a memory, a target, an energy....levy's death released his poems for a lot of people--I liked them a lot better when he was alive.

A cult has sprung up in the past five years since his death. Death as the final success. Like Lenny Bruce, most people didn't appreciate levy until he died. He didn't make it as big as Bruce or Marilyn Monroe or Janis Joplin or Jimi Hendrix. They haven't written a play or a book about his life yet, but they may.

America, without question, is a little crazy and a little different. In Russia, they take poets and writers much more seriously than here. There, if they don't dig what you're doin', they send you to Siberia, or shoot you, or put you in a mental asylum. Here they give you five minutes on the Johnny Carson show....if you're not too much of a threat to the State. If you are, they arrest you and drain your time/resources/ energy with trials, outrageous bail, writs, appeals, etc., and then you're usually acquitted and set "free."

If that doesn't work, they make you turn inward and kill yourself. Do the job yourself; it's less trouble for the State.

Like Baudelaire, Joyce, D.H. Lawrence, and Andre Gide, levy too was harrassed. Throughout 1966 and 1967, his arrest and trial made him a cause celebre in Cleveland. On November 28, 1966, the Cuyahoga County Grand Jury secretly indicted levy on charges of "publishing and disseminating obscene literature," which carried a fine of $200-$2000 and 1-7 years in jail, or both. He eluded the police for a few weeks, but finally gave himself up. He was released on parole and eventually the charges were dropped. levy was a symbol for the entire counterculture-drug-psychedelic world that Cleveland's "moral entrepreneurs" wanted to demolish. The obscenity charges were only a ruse. They carried more hard-core magazines in the porno stores near the Asphodel Bookstore (where levy worked) that were more "pornographic" than anything levy ever wrote. Those porno stores weren't touched by the police. People like Allen Ginsberg, Tuli Kupfenberg, and the Fugs came to Cleveland to raise bail and hell.

* * * * *

Some say levy's final act of suicide defined Cleveland....and defied it. It might have, but I don't glorify or romanticize suicide. I don't mean to moralize, but suicide is against God's law and against Jewish law. There must be a good reason for that. There are a lot of "death trips" around and the 1960s produced even more: speed, smack, revolutionary suicide, personal suicide. Little insidious trips: overwork, overworry, overeating, overbreathing. If we look closely, we all have them; everything we do that's no good for us kills us a little.

For levy, life got to be too much, too thick and heavy, too frightening and too powerful, or maybe it was more simple: he committed an act of free will. He saw a fucked-up world and then just dropped out. But he died long before he died. He lived death; he felt death; he carried death around with him. It was his steady companion.

> ... it is always a question of
> finding a way to die
> that is acceptable to the
> mass media
> so the people can hear you
> when you insist that your
> death was their failure to provide
> you   withameaningful life."[3]

What is it that turns off so many people to America? (Like Listerine, I love it and hate it.... twice a day.) But not the poor or the working class-- they seem to love America, to glory in it. They're the real patriots. No, I mean the affluent, suburban, well-educated white kids--Jewish, Protestant, or

-124-

Catholic. One of the things that turns their rage out and then inward is a tremendous feeling of frustration, disappointment, and a naive expectation that America is somehow different--the gap between creed and deed.... and then the lies, bullshit and more lies.

Our teachers (parents, presidents, senators, mayors, etc.) lied to us. Columbus didn't "discover" America; George Washington was a slave driver; Betsy Ross never existed; Benjamin Franklin was a double-agent; Abe Lincoln wasn't too happy about freein' "his niggers" for if he could have, he would have liked to have kept the country united and the blacks as slaves; FDR didn't lift a finger for the Jews; Eisenhower was a twerp whose greatest talent was not getting America involved in a war; Jack Kennedy (o'holy Kennedy) was the man responsible for the Bay of Pigs and the oppression of Castro; his brother Ted is an irresponsible driver who should be in jail for negligence and involuntary manslaughter; and Nixon, dear Nixon, would have sold his own momma to get re-elected. Will the high-school civics books mention Watergate? My Lai? Chicago?

What the '60s did to me, to you, to levy, and to everyone of our generation (and others) was to destroy our heroes, our history, and (to some degree) our hopes. We've now got to start again (this time with patience); for some, like levy, the trip was too much, so he split, but he left us a bit of his vision.

Our disillusionment blinded us from a fact: our "leaders" are human; scandal and corruption is business as usual. America has a great p.r. job to live up to but it hasn't always done it. The working class knows this: they aren't astounded by Watergate; they know all political leaders are on the take. To them, in short, leaders may be corrupt and incompetent (and still human), but basically the country is good and democratic and noble.

For the political and cultural "left," the entire system, not simply its leaders, has to be scrapped and replaced with some kind of (as yet undefined) noncompetitive, nonexploitative socialist state.

Probably, levy saw such contradictions and barriers for a proletarian revolution because his vision owes as much (maybe more) to Paul Reps, Alan Watts, and Phillip Kapleau as to Karl Marx or Chairman Mao.

Mike Kaplan, once an SDS leader, now a Hillel counselor at the University of Wisconsin--Milwaukee (radical politics is becoming theologized) knew levy and said this about him:

> I was impressed with the man. He was a very
> sensitive guy. He had a personal vision, but
> he wasn't trapped in it....and other people
> could see it too. He wasn't an obscure poet,
> or so private that no one could understand
> him. He truly meshed the personal with the
> political.

But levy was criticized by the New Left for being "decadent" and not concerned enough with the proper working class ideological dogma. It was a common attack, one that Abbie Hoffman, Jerry Rubin, and John Sinclair also had to put up with. The Yippies tried to bridge the gap between the drug-oriented/inner-consciousness/ hippie faction and the non-drug/ community-organizing/Marxist-radical faction. I don't know if they succeeded. levy stayed on his own track without necessarily putting down either.

Morris Edelson probably laid it down better than anyone:[4]

> He was a lovable guy and he didn't claim to
> be the revolution or the greatest, as did
> some young poets he knew....But the revolu-
> tion was on his mind, the state of the nation
> was his concern, his poetry had big topics
> and a large, honest way of looking at things.
> An article in the Maoist "Literature and
> Ideology" first issue criticizes him at
> length for not being a Marxist and for think-
> ing that inner consciousness could affect
> power structures. d.a. didn't have their
> steady, simple faith, being caught more in
> the ugliness and death all around him, cut
> off from his own. tradition by the grotesque
> travesty it had become in America. He did
> feel that the country was his enemy in an
> immediate sense, and, being acute, he put
> little faith in long-term strategies and
> planning that went by the book. So his poems
> may not sound consistent--they speak of a new
> consciousness, which we have associated with
> the hippie line, and they speak of sabotage,
> which we think is usually anarchistic. They

-126-

point beyond life in several places, and the narrow Marxist here can say they are decadent. But d.a.'s need was for an immediate sense of overcoming the shit and hell of life, and vague references to the future and rising revolutionary consciousness weren't enough for him.

To me, d.a. was not a political message-bearer so much as a teller of stories that were true up to the moral. He told clearly, with wit and anger, the experiences of his generation, of himself as right in the middle of the forces bearing on his country. Politically he was valuable because he put it better than others (no claim that he was in control of everything or above it or outside it) and because he was involved in trying to attack the oppression that threatens everyone. His example of courage and persistence inspired people.

levy's poems were terse and muscular and specific. He didn't play games nor did he prattle about his integrity. His Madison work interested me because it not only included the description of oppression and the desire for love that his other work had, but it commented on the efforts groups here were making in an attempt to change society. We need that dimension of comment on our work; we need a public poet who is unprotected by a grant or an official status, whose attention goes beyond lousy self-consciousness into description and attack. levy did this better than others and his poems will survive the anthologies and the editing and the belated recognition that Random House or somebody else is going to give them.

A moody, curly dark-haired, shy, thin, worried, restless, pale, nervous man, levy was constantly searching for THE WAY out of the maze. His poetry was a form of self-analysis. To change society, change yourself first. To be a radical is to grasp the matter by the root. Now the root of man/womankind is man/womankind itself, and the real meaning of revolution is not so much a change in management but a change in man/woman.

-127-

This is what ive been
trying to say - if you
attack the structure -
the system - the establishment
you attack yourself

KNOW THIS!
& attack if you must
challenge yourself externally

but if you want a revolution
return to your childhood
& kick out the bottom ....

this is not a game
your childhood
is the foundation
of the system ....

if you want a revolution
do it "together"
but don't get trapped in
words or systems

people are people
no matter what politics
color or words they use
& they all have children
buried in their head

if you want a revolution
grow a new mind
& do it quietly
if you can ....[5]

Though he was into a search for inner consciousness and other maps, still he was wary, wary especially
of the "phoney psychedelic advertisements" of California poets, mystics, and sensitivity leaders who came
East bearing gifts.

he came here
just like a tourist
is this the best
california has to offer? ....

i had to tell him
we didn't need
his undeveloped love
images ....

```
california, don't send
your myths to us

your dream mecca
is a whorehouse
painted with phoney
psychedelic advertisements

we have a different game
still undefined, we spend
our mornings wandering the
soft hills of Ohio
looking for the
hidden words
that grow here
without the help of
your artificial
inner sunlight.6
```

levy spent his whole life in Cleveland except for a month or so in Madison. He had a Midwestern simplicity; he lacked the light sunlit optimism of the West; he lacked the academic cool of the New England and New York writer/poet. The coasts got the media play, but Cleveland was different; it had different problems, a different lifestyle than Berkeley or Boston. levy decided to stay in that city, a city that most people think isn't worth shit, just a ramp off of I-90.

There was a Yippie-like thrust to his poetry, for he was trying on different hats, finding new ways to protest, fun but deadly serious ways to show life's absurdity and still keep from having the cops and the system come down on his head too hard.

```
Last week I threw 75 university ashtrays
into the lake - sailed them high into the air
like clay pigeons Pow Pow

sealed ten parking meters with Elmers glue
and tonight some hippy will call me a creep
and the r(R)adicals will try to rake my
conscience with words about war

the system is going to fall I'm sure
next week I'm putting plaster of paris
in the toilets of city hall
I'm just making sure it doesn't fall on me.

There must be a million ways to protest a   war
economy other than getting your head
```

beaten to dust for television audiences
I don't let the pigs get between me and
the enemy anymore

In my pocket 100 student subscriptions
to Time Magazine and 100 unknown addresses
there must be a million of us who drop tacks
in official parking lots - let them have
their special reserved spaces.....[7]

The allusions and the tactics seem dated today,
but the questions levy (and the left) raised are, to
use the language of Watergate, still operable. People
may wear a suit and tie, but they must still listen to
an inner voice: do it as best as you can (you may fail
at times) but DON'T GET CO-OPTED.

you might call me a hypocrite, but inside
I know who my enemy is and I know who
protects him.
I don't smoke pot or talk against the system
I'm just helping it along
the mysterious road of suicide.[8]

But in the end, levy was not pushing a "heavy"
trip on anyone. As Morris Edelson pointed out, levy,
like Elie Weisel, was a teller of tales. If they ring
true and touch you, so much the better.

note:

peace & awareness
like two small birds
trying to leave the planet
because they are tired of dying

im not advocating anything[9]

I don't want to leave the impression that all of
levy's poetry was bitter or angry or polemical--it
wasn't. He was capable of some beautiful tender lyri-
cal moments:

Once at Edgewater Park
I sat on the breakwall
& unbuttoned a young girls
blouse -

her bra was white like the
snow of the himalayas
& her mouth was full of flowers

the first time i balled
was on Memorial Day

it was something else[10]

Last O

oh

d.a. levy was a religious poet on a religious
search. As an outsider, as the wandering Jew, he could
see what others had overlooked. As a Jewish rebel par
excellence, he felt cut off from mainstream Judaism,
wanted to return, was repelled, and began to seek other
old/new paths toward self-realization, mostly from the
eastern religions. He was part of a long line of
rebels/heretics from Jesus to Spinoza to Marx to Kafka
to Lenny Bruce.

im a levy of the levites
yet in cleveland
i have painted myself
        celtic-blue
& am feeling
something like an outlaw
the druids give me soup
& think im a lama[11]

His "outsider" status was centered on the fact
that levy was the offspring of an intermarriage. (His
wife, too, I believe, was not Jewish.) His mother was
a Christian, his father a Jew. Though technically,
according to the Orthodox halacha, levy was not a Jew,
still his Jewishness mattered to him. He had a "Jewish
heart."

i am a levy of the levites
and last week
a fanatic jew in the heights[12] called me a
halfbreed
because my mother was a christian

i am a levy of the levites
& last week a rabbi
thought i was kidding

when i told him
i was interested in judaism

god i think yr sense
of humor is sad

-131-

```
        & perhaps you are also
        feeling something
        like an outlaw

        god i am wondering
        for how many years
        have the jews
        exiled you
        while they busied themselves
        with survival13
```

Like a true Hasid, levy took his prayers and
supplications straight to God, with no distracting
middleman. Yet deep in his heart, he felt that even
God was not listening and that the Messiah was not
coming. This lack of faith was levy's fatal flaw.
(Nihilism and resignation are not the way.) Yet, his
vision was prophetic and accurate; he clearly saw the
dilemmas of being a Jew in America. In his three most
"Jewish" poems--"new year," "poem to michael
solomon,"14 and "sitting on a bench near TSQuare" he
brings these cries out.

```
        they want to pay $2 at the box office
        & call it faith
        walk out if its a bad movie ....

        .... their holy cities
        will not stand if built with
        american money & the real jews
        here cannot walk into a temple
        without vomiting15

        .... & now i wonder how many jews are
        destroyed in this country each year
        my father with his lonely eyes
        trying to return home
        only to have the american god of money
        slapped in his face16
```

Where is God? What does He want? What does He
want of us? levy asked the right questions. Rather
than find a rebbe (not a rabbi) and study; rather than
find others, a community, and search on, he was among
these very people he mentions in his poems, those Jews
who were "destroyed." Rather than rebuild, he
destroyed himself, thus finishing the job that American
society and the Jewish community had started.

                    * * * * *

A mini-bibliography

I wish to thank Morris Edelson for his kind help--all of it long distance, but still nevertheless, extremely beneficial, both in background and bibliographic information; also Jon Reilly of the Madison Coop Book Store and Mike Kaplan of Milwaukee.

ukanhavyrfuckincitibak: d.a. levy: a Tribute to the Man, an Anthology of his Poetry, is the best collection of levy's work, collected and edited by rjs, published by t.l. kryss, Ghost Press, P.O. Box 91415, Cleveland, Ohio 44101. No price, no date, but I believe it's 1969, a limited edition of 1000 copies. It contains great gobs of his poetry, tributes by Charles Bukowski, Douglas Blazek, and other friends and admirers, odds and ends like newspaper clippings of his busts and trials, his "concrete" poetry plus a good bibliography of his farflung outpouring. A difficult book to find--the Lamont Library at Harvard University has a copy; check other major libraries.

His poetry has appeared in Quixote and Connections (Madison, Wisconsin), Radical America (Boston), The Buddhist Third Class Junk Mail Oracle (levy's paper in Cleveland), as well as Response, Davka, Jewish Currents, among others. His poetry seems to be popping up everywhere and anywhere.

Morris Edelson has begun to copyright it in order to stop the major publishers from ripping off levy's poetry for major profits for themselves; but the copyright is not aimed at struggling "underground" presses. levy's view was simply: "all copyrot rejected by author." Non-exploitative journals are, of course, free to publish his poems and donate whatever they can.

Some of levy's collections are:

Private No Parking, published by Quixote, Morris Edelson (ed.), 933 Spaight St., Madison, Wisconsin 53703. ($1.00)

To Be a Discrepancy in Cleveland, published by Radical America, 1878 Massachusetts Ave., Cambridge, Massachusetts 02140. (No price indicated but about a dollar.)

Madison and Suburban Monastery Death Poems, (Madison poems written in Madison; suburban,

written in Cleveland) published, edited, printed
and collated at the Condom House
Division of Quixote Press, January-March 1969 at
the above address for Quixote.   Second edition
printed   partially   by   RPM   printshop,   1255
Williamson Street, Madison, Wisconsin.   Should be
ordered from Quixote; send a couple of dollars for
the poems; an essay, a biblio graphy by Edelson,
and various collages and "concrete" poems.   Only
500 copies were printed and are nearly all sold
out; the best places to look are major libraries.

Tombstone as a Lonely Charm (50¢) and Songs for
Dead Children   (25¢)   are   distributed   by   WIND
Catalog, P.O. Box 243, Madison, Wisconsin, phone:
(608)   251-5717.   But   they   aren't   too   reliable.
Try Quixote or the best library in town.

Prose: On poetry in the wholesale education &
culture system.   Milwaukee: Gunrunner Press, 1968.

Tune in today for tomorrow's episode: Stone
Sarcophagus, Madison: Radical America, 1966, 24
pp., illustrated.

Tombstone as a Lonely Charm, Sacremento: Runcible
Spoon, 1967, 12 pp.

Zen Concrete, Vancouver (?), B.C. Blewointment
press, 1968.

Nearly all the anthologies of modern contemporary
poetry that I've seen never mention levy.   Some of his
poems,   however,   have   been   reprinted   in   Todd Gitlin
(ed.) Campfires of the Resistance: Poetry from the
Movement, Indianapolis, Indiana: Bobbs-Merrill, 1971,
pp. 179-186, ($3.95 paper) and "new year" was reprinted
in Jack Nusan Porter and Peter Dreier (eds.) Jewish
Radicalism, New York: Grove Press, 1973, pp. 126-130.
($2.45 paperback).

What is not too well known was that levy also did
collages that are literally beyond description.   They
have to be seen.   Done in dadaist tradition, their purpose was to push the boundary of sensibility in art/
literature to the point of absurdity and then to start
afresh, because America has that wonderful knack for
killing words.   levy called it "an experiment in
destructive writing."   It was a form of surrealistic
subversion in the manner of Andre Breton and Antonin
Artaud.

He also did "concrete" prose, which were bits or words and whorls and designs, that again defy simple description. Two examples are the above packet that Quixote put out, and The Tibetan Stroboscope, collaged in Cleveland, published by Quixote (address above) and printed by the RP, Printing Coop (address also above). It says 35¢ on the cover, but send a dollar donation to Quixote. It may be out of print by now.

Notes

1. This is his "magnum opus", his collected works and a tribute by others (though it doesn't contain all his poetry and collages), and sells, I hear, for $20.00. (See mini-bibliography.)

2. At the University of Wisconsin.

3. "It's a matter of presentation," Madison and Suburban Monastery Death Poems, 1968.

4. From Edelson's introduction to Madison and Suburban Monastery Death Poems, 1968.

5. "Tombstone as a Lonely Charm," from To be a Discrepancy in Cleveland: Poems by d.a. levy, 1968, pp. 33-34.

6. "BLIND MYTH doing a death dance ON GROUND ZERO (for Willie)" from To be a Discrepancy in Cleveland, 1968, pp. 37-38.

7. "Letter from an Invisible Greek", from Private No Parking, 1968.

8. Ibid.

9. Suburban Monastery Death Poem, 1968

10. Ibid.

11. "sitting on a bench near TSQuare," ibid., p. 11

12. Cleveland Heights, Ohio

13. sitting on a bench near TSQuare", op. cit., pp. 11 and 12.

14. Michael Solomon was a young brilliant crazy Jewish fellow who on the Sabbath in a Detroit synagogue, killed his rabbi, the well-known and respected Rabbi Morris Adler, and then killed himself on the bimah, the central "stage" of the synagogue.

15. "poem to michael solomon", op. cit., p. 13.

16. "new year", op. cit., p. 16.

-136-

Part II
Minorities Within a Minority

Chapter 7

The Jewish Homosexual

The burst of gay liberation in the 1960s led to a rediscovery of past heroes. One of those "lost" figures is Magnus Hirschfeld, a man that Allen Young calls the "zeyde" (Yiddish for grandfather) of gay liberation. Young is not off the mark. A long-forgotten martyr has been found and resurrected. This essay deals less with the Jewish homosexual than with one particular homosexual, Magnus Hirschfeld, a German sexual researcher who was hounded by the Nazis for being a Jew, a pacifist, a socialist, an intellectual, a political activist, and, perhaps most of all, a homosexual and transvestite. As with Rosa Sonneschein in the next essay, I am fascinated by neglected historical figures. Why are they overlooked? One reason could be a combination of historical and personality factors-- the timing of one's work, its distribution, and one's relationships to other intellectual movers and shakers. But it seems to me that another factor is perhaps more salient: their minority status. Rosa Sonneschein was a woman; Magnus Hirschfeld was a homosexual.

Another reason for my interest in Hirschfeld is my fascination with the sexual politics of the Third Reich and its curious relationship to homosexuality, given that many early Brownshirts and SS were gay themselves. As we move from Wilhelminian to Weimar to Nazi Germany, we can follow the tortuous route of homosexual movements and attitudes, and Hirschfeld lived through that period. His life was one part of that story. The entire history of homosexual "genocide" has yet to be written.

* * * * *

The gay liberation movement is really a splinter of many sub-movements, just as the women's, black, or Chicano movements have their various permutations. The gay movement too has its "lavender left" on one side; its more moderate, even conservative, elements on the other. One part of this movement that is often over-looked is the Jewish gay liberation movement. Like their counterparts among Catholics and Protestants, the Jewish gay groups have been struggling for both social and theological acceptance with only minor success. Jewish gays will probably never be totally accepted by the rabbinate (especially Orthodox rabbis) and the Jewish community, but they are being heard and we will be hearing more about them.

The Jewish gay movement sprung from the loins of the student, feminist, and leftist movements of a decade and a half ago. Since then it has become an international movement with gay religious congregations in more than ten cities in the United States and Canada as well as in Israel, France, England, and Australia. In July of 1979, it held its fourth International Conference of Gay and Lesbian Jews in Israel. Their reception was marked by coolness and outright disgust. There were threats and intimidations by the Israeli Rabbinate. Earlier, an attempt to donate more than 900 trees to the Jewish National Fund and have a suitable plaque erected was refused by Israeli officials if either the word "gay" or "lesbian" was included. Only a neutral "closeted" name was deemed acceptable.[1]

This was in marked contrast to the fifth International Conference held in San Francisco in August, 1980 which was warmly welcomed. The conference drew participants from six foreign countries including Israel and from all sections of the United States. For the first time an equal number of men and women participated. There were also several teenagers and people in their 50's and 60's, plus a wide range of religious and political viewpoints. Over forty workshops were held addressing most areas of gay and Jewish life: Sabbath programming, female spirituality, the Middle East, and personal issues such as relationships with friends and lovers, with non-Jews, and with members of the community "oppressed" because of age, physical difference, or handicap.[2]

One anonymous Jewish homosexual from San Francisco tells how he became involved in small, informal groups comprised of mostly gay men who were Jewish who somehow

wanted to combine these two aspects of their lives.
Activities were primarily social, with some outreach to
the "straight" Jewish community as well as High Holyday
and Passover services.[3] He comments:

> As time progressed several of us felt the
> need for a more organized and religiously
> oriented Jewish-gay organization. In 1977,
> together with a stockbroker and a school
> teacher, I helped found Congregation Sha'ar
> Zahav ("Golden Gate" in Hebrew, a nice pun on
> S.F.). It rapidly became apparent that
> Sha'ar Zahav was filling a real need. Since
> that time, (it) has grown to 140 members, has
> an average attendance at Friday night
> services of 75 and has a full program of
> activities in addition to religious services.
> The Congregation has a rabbi--Rabbi Allen
> Bennett, an openly gay rabbi--and publishes a
> monthly newsletter--the Jewish Gaily
> Forward....[4] (emphasis in the original).

Sha'ar Zahav joins such other Jewish congrega-
tions/groups as Am Tikvah ("Nation of Hope") in Boston
and Beth Chayim Chadashim ("House of New Lives") in Los
Angeles. The latter is officially a member of the
Union of American Hebrew Congregations (Reform Jews).
What their members want is to be accepted as full, not
flawed, Jews. They will not accept the label of
sinner, deviant, or degenerate. To them, being gay is
normal. They want to live as complete Jews without
compromising their psychosexual nature.[5]

* * * * *

Every movement needs its heroes, and the Jewish
and general gay movement has one in the figure of
Magnus Hirschfeld. Hirschfeld should not have been so
quickly forgotten. He must take his proper role in the
history of sexual research, right alongside Richard von
Krafft-Ebing (1840-1902), Havelock Ellis (1859-1939),
Sigmund Freud (1856-1939), and later pioneers such as
Alfred Kinsey (1894-1956) and Masters and Johnson.
Hirschfeld (1868-1935), however, died in exile, and is
today forgotten. As one biographer lamented:

> ....Hirschfeld's works on homosexuality would
> seem to hold automatically a place as the
> most truly authoritative of the works of the
> great sexologists. Yet his major homosexual

works have not been translated into English, and those sexologists opposed to his 'innate homosexuality' views assert that his own alleged homosexuality disqualified him from objectivity and credibility. This seems rather like saying that a naval officer with long service on submarines is much less qualified to write about submarine warfare than a naval officer who has never been down in a submarine.[6]

Hirschfeld will probably be most remembered not for his theories of homosexual development but for his sociological research and political activism. He interviewed thousands of homosexuals and lesbians, and, therefore, his firsthand knowledge of the field was pioneering, ultimately laying the scientific groundwork for later sexologists such as Kinsey and his associates, as well as numerous other social scientists, medical investigators, and survey researchers. And his political activism attracted the best minds in Europe, many of them Jewish. Who was this quiet, warm-hearted, courageous man, affectionately referred to by many homosexuals as "Auntie Magnesia," and why was he hated and feared by the Nazi regime?[7]

He was born in Kolberg, Germany on the Baltic coast, the third of three sons of a prominent Jewish doctor, Hermann Hirschfeld. Determined from an early age to be a physician, Hirschfeld was also greatly attracted to philosophy and languages and, at fifteen, published an erudite essay in a Berlin weekly on a proposed universal language. He attended schools in Breslau and Strasburg and completed his medical training at the University of Munich.

He wished to travel a bit before settling down and embarked on a world tour in the 1890s, an occupation that was to be an important and regular part of his life. Similar to Kinsey, Hirschfeld had a good comparative grasp of crosscultural sexual mores. In 1893 he visited the World's Fair in Chicago and then traveled throughout America, Africa, and the Orient, returning to Europe via North Africa, Spain, and Italy. In 1894 he began his career as a general practitioner in Magdeburg, moving in 1896 to Charlottenburg where he practiced medicine until 1909. He was a specialist in nervous and psychic maladies. From 1910 on, he practiced as a neurologist in Berlin, where he founded a workers' health insurance institution which was widely imitated.

The trial of Oscar Wilde and the suicide of a patient on the eve of his marriage triggered Hirschfeld's lifelong devotion to sexology in general and homosexuality in particular, perhaps also causing him to examine his own sexual and emotional inclinations more honestly.[8] In 1896, he anonymously published the first of many sexological works, Sappho und Socrates, in which he defended the view that the homosexual urge, like the heterosexual, is the result of a "certain in-born goal-striving constitution, influenced by glands of internal secretion." This biochemical interpretation was rejected by later theorists and replaced by a socio-sexual, developmental and environmental perspective, but recently biological analyses have come back in vogue. It might well be that Hirschfeld was correct. However, the causes of homosexuality, and what he called "intermediate sexual stages" (sexuelle zwischenstufen), namely transvestites and hermaphrodites, are indeed complex.

In 1897, he founded a political action group called the Scientific-Humanitarian Committee and gained immediate publicity for it by drawing up a petition to the Reichstag for the repeal of Section 175 of the German Criminal Code, the section dealing with homosexual offenses. With a feeling for statistics and polls much ahead of his time, he prepared, in 1900, a "psychobiological questionnaire" with 130 questions which was ultimately filled out by more than 10,000 men and women. It is alleged that Hirschfeld talked with over 30,000 men and women who unburdened themselves of their troubles and maladjustments. This figure is exaggerated, but the good doctor was no doubt an excellent listener.

With this impressive application of the principles of science to the study of human sexuality, Hirschfeld rapidly established a reputation as the most knowledgeable and undogmatic of doctors specializing in sexual problems. In 1903, he published The Uranian Person and, the following year, Berlin's Drittes Gsschlect (Berlin's Third Sex) which provided an unprecedented amount of well-informed "inside" material on matters homosexual.

The term "Uranian" was first coined by a great pioneer of the gay liberation movement, a man who lived even before Hirschfeld, Karl Heinrich Ulrichs (1825-1895). It was Ulrich who developed many original ideas about homosexuality and constantly attempted to enlist homosexuals in the fight for freedom and liberation, but his words fell on deaf ears. He was much ahead of his time on these matters. He coined the term Urning from the god Uranus in Plato's Symposium to denote a homosexual, a distinct type of human being. While he was neglected by most gays during his lifetime, he was visited by the well-known writer John Addington Symonds and, after Ulrichs'death, Hirschfeld (in 1909) and other gays made a pilgrimage to his grave.[9]

In 1908, with the collaboration of other leading sexologists, Hirschfeld founded his Journal of Sexual Science, and in 1909, for matters more specifically homosexual, his Jahrbuch fur Sexuelle Zwischenstufen (Yearbook for Intermediate Sexual Stages) which from 1909-1923 produced one of the richest collections of homosexual studies of all time in history, literature, art, music, and psychology. Somewhat similar were the Quarterly Reports of the Scientific-Humanitarian Committee. The Committee also served as a publisher of books, such as the collected works of the pioneer homosexual judge and pamphleteer, Karl Heinrichs Ulrichs, mentioned earlier.

By 1900 Hirschfeld was giving heavily attended lectures on such subjects as "Love and Life" and "The Nature of the Human Personality" throughout Germany. His stature had grown to such a point that he was called upon as an expert witness in many sexual and political trials and scandals.[10] In 1913, Hirschfeld joined with Dr. Iwan Bloch and Dr. Heinrich Koerber to form the Medical Society for Sexual Science and Eugenics, and, in 1914, he published his masterwork, Homosexualitat des Mannes und des Weibes, which was expanded into a two-volume edition in 1920 and formed the most comprehensive and knowledgeable book to date on the subject.

In 1918, he launched his most ambitious project. Acquiring the beautiful mansion of Prince Hatzfeld, the former German ambassador to France, he set up his Medical Society which now became the world-renowned Institute for Sexual Science with a range of activities equalled by few others anywhere. The Institute, which in 1919 was taken over by the Prussian government as the Magnus Hirschfeld Foundation, acquired a library of about 20,000 volumes, a collection of about 35,000 pictures from all over the world, and served as world headquarters for specialists in the field.

Its Marriage Consultation Department, free in most cases, was the first of its kind in Germany and was soon followed by many imitations there and around the world, offering a physical and psychological examination for the prospective couple to determine their suitability, as well as advice on problems such as birth control, frigidity, and impotence. Once a week there was a so-called "Question Evening" where anyone could deposit a written question in a box for discussion, a program that brought large crowds to the Institute's auditorium. Its Sexual-Forensic Department dealt with "moral delinquencies" (child abuse, exhibitionism, etc.) and any robberies, assaults, murders, and homocides with a sexual connection, often providing expert testimony at many trials which were usually helpful to the accused homosexual or defendant. The Institute also conducted biological studies on blood, sperm, and other fluids.

The scientific discoveries of Hirschfeld and his followers added urgency to the question of sexual reform, and so, in 1921 he convened an international congress, followed by later congresses in Copenhagen, London (under the chairmanship of the famous English sexologist, Dr. Norman Haire), and Vienna. A World League for Sexual Reform was formed, under the honorary presidency of Havelock Ellis, to work toward the realization of Hirschfeld's humanitarian ideas regarding homosexual rights, birth control, abortion, and other issues.

When the Nazis came to power, Dr. Hirschfeld was doomed on every count--as a Jew, as a pacifist, as a socialist, as an advocate of women's rights, as an anti-racist lecturer, and as a homosexual. He was everything the Nazis despised, and his humanitarianism was the antithesis of everything they stood for. His meetings were terrorized, and he himself was beaten up and sent to the hospital with a fractured skull. At the end of 1931 he went to New York at the invitation of the German-American Medical Society to deliver a series of lectures, and he never again returned to his mother country of Germany. After traveling through the United States, he went to Japan, China, Java, Ceylon, India, Egypt, Palestine, Syria, Lebanon, and Greece delivering lectures in halls and universities in the major cities of these lands. Much sexual-ethnological material collected on the way was shipped to the Institute.

Advised by friends of the danger of returning to Germany, Hirschfeld settled for a while in Vienna and then in Switzerland. He was writing his autobiography, The World Journey of a Sexologist, (Die Weltreise eines Sexualforscher), when he learned that on May 6, 1933 the Nazis had pillaged his Institute and burned most of his books and collections. His own property was confiscated on the grounds that he was "undeutsch" (un-German) and that his work was "antagonistic to the spirit of the state."[11] His Institute was officially closed and reopened to house, with a bitter twist of fate, the National Socialistic Juristic Union, the Institute for Research in Judaism, and other offices. It is also alleged that Hirschfeld saw the destruction of his Institute with his own eyes while in a movie theater watching a documentary newsreel.

Hirschfeld next settled in Paris where he founded a more modest Institute of Sexual Science, using the remnants of the Berlin showplace that had been salvaged by friends. Active to the end despite ill health, he died in Nice on May 14, 1935 at age sixty-seven.

His major works are still to be translated into English and include: Sexualpathologie (three volumes, 1917-20, 1921-28), Geschlechtkunde (five volumes, 1925-30), Die Transvestiten (1910), Geschlecht und Verbrechen (1930), Geschlechtsanomalien und Perversionen (1938), and other works.

* * * * *

Hirschfeld was one of tens of thousands of homosexuals persecuted under the Nazi regime. If he had returned to Germany, there is no doubt that he would have been incarcerated in one of several concentration camps reserved for Jews, homosexuals, criminals, gypsies, Jehovah Witnesses, and political prisoners. There he would have worn a double emblem, the pink triangle denoting homosexuality and the yellow patch for Jew. With this double stigma, this frail little man would not have lasted long under the extreme conditions of the "death camps." Yet it is ironic that it was not the Nazis who dealt his work a death blow but later scholars who ignored his numerous contributions. Today, the work of Magnus Hirschfeld is being looked at again, and students, criminologists, judges, social workers, probation officers, physicians, and educators will once again have the opportunity to learn from a man who pioneered in so many fields.

Notes

1.   Anonymous, "Worldwide Gay Jewry, Five Years Together", Sh'ma: A Journal of Jewish Responsibility, 11/201, November 14, 1980.

2.   Maggid, Aliza, "Gay Jews Form World Congress," Genesis 2, Vol. 12, No. 3, November, 1980, p. 6.

3.   Anonymous, op. cit., p. 6.

4.   Ibid., p. 6.

5.   Ibid., p. 7.

6.   Garde, Noel I., Jonathan to Gide: The Homosexual in History, (New York: Nosbooks, copyright, Vantage Press, 1969), p. 677.

7.   I have based my history of Hirschfeld's life on the following secondary sources. As more data becomes available from German archival sources, primary data should add even more knowledge. See Noel I. Garde, op. cit., pp. 674-677, Victor Robinson (ed.), Encyclopedia Sexualis: A Comprehensive Encyclopedia- Dictionary of the Sexual Sciences, (New York: Dingwall-Rock, 1936); Foreward to Magnus Hirschfeld, Sexual Anomalies: The Origins, Nature and Treatment of Sexual Disorders, (New York: Emerson Books, Inc., 1956), pp. vii-xv; and John Lauritsen and David Thorstad, The Early Homosexual Rights Movement, 1864-1935, (New York: Times Change Press, 1974), pp. 9-29, 41-43, 73-76.

8.   See Noel I. Garde, op. cit., p. 674 and his entry on Oscar Wilde as well. It is interesting to note that a man who would later support his work, Martin Buber, was also deeply affected by the suicide of a friend who wished to discuss a problem. Buber did not have time to help his friend, and his guilt over the matter led him to write I and Thou, his most famous work.

9.   Lauritsen and Thorstad, op. cit., p. 73.

10. See Noel I. Garde, op. cit., p. 675, especially about the trial of Prince Philip Zu Eulenberg-Hertefeld, pp. 679-683.

11. See Noel I. Garde, op. cit., p. 677 and Lauritsen and Thorstad, op. cit., p. 75.

References

Bullough, Vern L., Homosexuality: A History, (New York: Meridian/New American Library, 1979.)

Ellis, Albert and Abarbanel, Albert (eds.), The Ency clopedia of Sexual Behavior, (New York: Hawthorn Books, Inc., 1967.) See especially the sections on homosexuality by Donald Webster Cory, pp. 485-493; sex reform movements by Robert Wood, pp. 956-966; sexual research institutes by Wardell B. Pomeroy and Hedwig Leser, pp. 967-975; and sexual life in Europe by Conrad Van Emde Boas, pp. 373 383.

Friedlander, Benedict, Die Liebe Platons in Lichte der Modernen Biologie, (Treptow bei Berlin: Bernhard Zack, 1909.)

_____, Renaissance des Eros Uranios, (Berlin: Otto Lehmann, 1904.) Friedlander should be studied as an early opponent of Hirschfeld's scientific views on the origin of homosexuality. Friedlander, speaking from within the gay community, saw Hirschfeld's position as too dogmatic, too conservative, and totally incorrect. He thought Hirschfeld offered a "beggarly and degrading" position to the heterosexual world. His criticism was analogous to a black militant confronting his "Uncle Tom" soul brother.

Garde, Noel I., Jonathan to Gide: The Homosexual in History, (New York: Nosbooks, 1969.) With an earlier 1964 copyright held by Vantage Press. See especially pp. 674-677 on the life of Hirschfeld which I have drawn heavily upon. Gide, in turn, drew upon Victor Robinson (ed.), Encyclopedia Sexualis, pp. 317-332. This fascinating book is actually a "Who's Who" of homosexuals throughout history. Some of his entries are provocative and even questionable (i.e., George Washington and Napolean Bonaparte), since Garde implies that asexual or sexual apathy among his entries quali-fies as homosexual. Still, a very useful handbook and very well researched and written.

Heger, Heinz, **The Man with the Pink Triangle**, (Boston:
   Alyson Publications, 1980.) Translated and with a
   good introduction by David Fernbach. The German
   publisher was Merlin-Verlag in Hamburg. This is a
   moving personal memoir of one young 22-year-old
   homosexual caught up in the Nazi dragnet of homosexuals and his experiences in the Sachsenhausen
   and Flossenburg concentration camps. Highly
   recommended. One of the few accounts of that time
   and place in English.

Hirschfeld, Magnus, Homosexualitat des Mannes und des
   Weibes, two volumes, (Berlin: Louis Marcus Verlag,
   1920.)

_____, Sappho und Socrates, 1896. His
   first book.

_____, Berlin's Drittes Geschlecht,
   (Berlin and Leipzig: Verlag Hermann Seeman, 1904.)

_____, Die Transvestiten, 1910, 1925.

_____, Sexualpathologie, three volumes,
   1917-20, 1921-28.

_____, Geschlecht und Verbrechen, (Leipzig
   and Vienna: Verlag fur Sexualwissenschaft,
   Schneider and Co., 1930.)

_____, Die Weltreise eines Sexualforscher,
   (Brugg: Bozberg Verlag, 1933.)

_____, Geschlechts anomalien und Perver
   sionen, (Frankfurt A/M and Stockholm: Nordische
   Verlagsgesellschaft, 1938.)

_____, Sex in Human Relationships, (London
   and Redhill: Atheneum, 1935.) With an introduction
   by Norman Haire.

_____, Men and Women, (New York: G.P.
   Putnam, 1935.)

_____, Sexual Anomalies, (New York: Random
   House, 1942.) Another version was reprinted in
   New York: Emerson Books, Inc., 1948 and revised
   edition, 1956 with an introduction by an anonymous
   student of Hirschfeld that sheds some light on his
   psychosexual theories but is altogether too
   fawning of the master.

Hodann, Max, <u>Sex Life in Europe</u>, (New York: Julian Press, 1932.)

Lauritsen, John and David Thorstad, <u>The Early Homo sexual Rights Movement (1864-1935)</u>, (New York: Times Change Press, 1974.) One of the finest short histories of its kind and regretfully not widely circulated. Excellent discussion of Magnus Hirschfeld's life and theories (pp. 9-29, 41-43, 73-76) plus those of his contemporaries in the homosexual movement. Contains a very useful bibliography.

Lautman, Rudiger and Erhard Vismar, <u>Pink Triangle: The Social History of Anti-Homosexual Persecution in Nazi Germany</u>, unpublished mss (1979). Lautman is a professor at the University of Bremen and this is a tightly written social history of anti-homosexual legislation and persecution during the Nazi regime.

Pederson, Lyn, "The Ordeal of Prince Eulenberg", <u>One</u> magazine, October-November and December, 1956. This is a Los Angeles gay journal containing an account of the trial of Prince Philip Zu Eulenberg Hertefeld (1847-1921), a German statesman who was engaged in a homosexual scandal. Hirschfeld testified in his behalf at the trial.

Peyrefitte, Roger, <u>The Exile of Capri</u>, (London: Secker and Warburg, 1961.) Foreward by Jean Cocteau. This is a novelized biography of Jacques d'Adelsward-Fersen, an exiled French minor poet and novelist with many famous gay friends. Contains many dropped names.

Reade, Brian (ed.) <u>Sexual Heretics</u>, (New York:Coward McCann, 1971.) Documents the phenomenal growth of a gay literary underground in the late 19th century in England and other parts of Europe whose writers were influenced by Walt Whitman and Edward Carpenter.

Robinson, Victor (ed.) <u>Encyclopedia Sexualis</u>, (New York: Dingwall-Rock, 1936.) See the article on homosexuality written by Hirschfeld, pp. 317-332.

Steakley, Jim, series of articles on homosexuals and the Third Reich, <u>Body Politic</u> (Toronto), Numbers 9, 10, 11, 1974.

Symonds, John Addington, A Problem in Modern Ethics, (London: privately printed, 1896.)

_____, A Problem in Greek Ethics, (London: privately printed, 1901.)

Young, Allen, "Magnus Hirschfeld: Gay Liberation's Zeyde," in Chutzpah: A Jewish Liberation Anthology, (San Francisco: New Glide Publications, 1977), pp. 158-160. A short article showing Hirschfeld's Jewish "roots," based mostly on the research of Jim Steakley and John Lauritsen and David Thorstad, op. cit.

* * * * *

Conference Proceedings, Institute Reports, Journals

World League for Sexual Reform (Congress Proceedings): Berlin 1921; Copenhagen 1928; London 1929; and Vienna 1930; Founded in 1921.

International Congress for Sexual Reform, Proceedings.

The Scientific-Humanitarian Committee (founded in 1897 by Magnus Hirschfeld and lasting for 35 years until 1932). It published a yearbook, Jahrbuch fur Sexuelle Zwischenstufen, which appeared more or less regularly both as a yearly and a quarterly from 1909-1923. Also published were the Quarterly Reports of the Committee plus pamphlets and books. For example, a book about homosexuality called What People Should Know About the Third Sex (1903) with an abridged version appearing in 1923 called The Problem of Sexual Inversion. A movie was also made on the subject but has never been found.

Institute for Sexual Science (1919), most of its archives were destroyed by the Nazis.

Magnus Hirschfeld Foundation for Sexual Research (1918).

See also obituaries in the New York Herald Tribune and New York Times after his death May 14, 1935, for more biography.

The "Hirschfeld Scrapbook," a collection of handbills, minutes of meetings, posters, documents, etc. was

-151-

miraculously saved from the Nazi regime by Hirschfeld's colleague from Hamburg, Dr. Carl Th. Hoefft
and today can be found in the repository of the
Institute for Sex Research at Indiana University
in Bloomington, Indiana (the so-called Kinsey
Institute).

Chapter 8

The Jewish Woman

This is really the story of one Jewish woman rather than Jewish women in general, but from this one woman we may learn some of the pain and frustration that accompanies all talented and ambitious women. This is the most historical of the essays in the book, dealing as it does with a woman editor and journalist who established a unique journal over eighty years ago: Rosa Sonneschein and The American Jewess--the first independent English-language women's journal in America. Ms. Sonneschein was a woman ahead of her time, and for this she paid a high price. My interest in her and her journal was kindled almost by accident while rummaging through the card files of the Brandeis University library. By chance I came across a heading with the name of the journal. It intrigued me. The name itself was most unusual--so dramatic, so chutz-padic. I decided to investigate, and I'm glad I did. The covers and the layout were almost sensual, so beautiful they could put to shame any modern magazine. The journal lasted only four years, 1895-1899, but those were momentous years, and the magazine reflected them. Ms. Sonneschein lived a long but unhappy life except for those four glorious years. I would have loved to have met her, and I think most readers would have also. This essay is a revised version of an article which originally appeared in American Jewish History (vol. 68, no. 1, Sept. 1978) and is reprinted by permission. It is a corrected version of the original.

My thanks to David Loth, Paula Doress, and Dr. Yitzhak Noy for their kind help in writing this article; to Maurice Tuchman and the library staff of Hebrew College in Boston; and to the library staff of Brandeis University where copies of The American Jewess were first discovered by the author.

* * * * *

The year 1967 has become a watershed year in
American Jewish history.[1] In the years that followed
the sudden and victorious war between Arabs and
Israelis, there emerged an entire series of Jewish
social movements: student, countercultural, religious,
neo-Bundist, neo-Revisionist Zionist, socialistZionist,
and feminist.[2] During the process of any nascent
social movement, there is also an educational task: to
rediscover a "usuable past," to unearth heroes and
heroines from that past, and to revise and/or
reincorporate present historical accounts in order to
include those segments of history that have been lost,
stolen, or overlooked.

Nowhere is this more apparent than in the reawak-
ening of the women's rights movements of the past
decade. Many of the leaders and theoreticians of the
feminist movement have been Jews--Susan Brownmiller,
Dr. Phyllis Chesler, Andrea Dworkin, Shulamith
Firestone, Betty Friedan, Robin Morgan, Barbara Seaman
--or part-Jewish like Germaine Greer and Gloria
Steinem.[3] However, since 1967, Jewish women, influenced by the general feminist movement, have begun to
form their own "consciousness-raising groups," discussion groups, speakers' bureaus, and women's minyans.
The Jewish Feminist Organization was founded in 1974.[4]
Several conferences on women's role within Judaism and
on Jewish male-female sex roles have also been held in
the early 1970s. Publications are proliferating:
several women's histories and anthologies have emerged,
and a new journal Lilith was founded in 1976.[5] This
movement, even of this writing, shows no sign of abate-
ment but is pushing ahead in such areas as the role of
women in the rabbinate, within the synagogue, the
Jewish philanthropies, the Jewish defense and social
organizations, community responsibility, education, and
volunteer work.

As noted, part of this "liberation" is the rediscovery of a usuable past, and this present article is
based on the life and work of a nearly-forgotten Jewish
reformer and Zionist sympathizer, Rosa Sonneschein, and
the journal she founded and edited--The American
Jewess. Because every generation often feels that it
is the "first," one finds statements such as: "Lilith,
the first and only independent magazine for Jewish
women, began publishing in June (1976) with a respec-
table number of charter subscriptions and newsstand
sales."[6]

Such a statement is false, but the actual history of Jewish women in America has only recently been made available to Jewish youth and young adults. The American Jewess was the first Jewish women's journal edited by women (or really by one woman) that was independent of any organizational or religious ties. It may not have been as "radical" as present-day feminist magazines, but in its time, it was considered quite a novel and even a "radical" journal. Though it was the first Jewish women's journal edited by women, it was not the first Jewish journal for women in America. This honor goes to a German-language paper founded in 1855, edited by Rabbi Isaac Meyer Wise and called Die Deborah. Thus, The American Jewess was the first English-language journal independently edited by women.

Calling itself "The Only Publication in the World Devoted to the Interests of Jewish Women," The American Jewess had a short but lively life. The first issue, Vol. 1, No. 1, appeared in April, 1895 and four years later in August, 1899 it stopped publishing, never to surface again. This journal, one of the first to appeal specifically to "Hebrew women," had an audacious and successful beginning, winning accolades from such diverse papers as the Reform Advocate, the Chicago Staats-Zeitung, the Milwaukee Journal, and the Times-Herald. It was also a very attractive magazine, devoted to "social, religious, and literary subjects," with beautiful portrait pictures, woodcuts, and engravings. The title cover of the inaugural issue was of a comely "Princess of Judah" playing a Biblical harp.

The years leading up to and surrounding the launching of this journal were formative ones politically and culturally, both with regard to the struggle for equality for women and the proliferation of journals and books discussing both feminist as well as other political issues. In the 1880s and 1890s, record numbers of immigrants reached the shores of America. Men, women, and children flooded the labor market, and the disparity between rich and poor grew. The labor movement at first was not enthusiastic about organizing women, but some women organized unions themselves. Augusta Lewis organized the Typographers Union of New York and Kate Mullaney formed the Troy (N.Y.) Laundry Workers Union. This same period saw the rise of department stores, opening up many jobs for women as store clerks. Working conditions were abominable, with many women working from eight in the morning to twelve midnight, six days a week, with only a few minutes for lunch and no chairs to sit on. On occasion, some wealthy women organized consumer boycotts of stores which refused to improve conditions. Reformers such as Florence Kelley attempted to institute labor laws to protect working women and children, while "muckrakers" such as Ida Tarbell brought national attention to the abusers of large businesses.

In 1884, Ellen H.S. Richards, the first woman admitted to MIT, studied and later taught chemistry and developed the field of home economics, believing that science should serve women in the home. She was also among the first to investigate food additives. In 1889, Jane Addams opened Hull House in Chicago as a social settlement house to help the new immigrants adjust to a new land and deal with the problems of poverty. This social settlement house movement provided playgrounds, nurseries, sewing and cooking classes, and health care. In 1890, the two major suffrage movements, the National Women's Suffrage Association, founded in 1869 by Elizabeth Cady Stanton and Susan B. Anthony, and the American Women's Suffrage Association, a more conservative, break-away group founded in the same year by Julia Ward Howe and Lucy Stone, both finally merged into the National American Women's Suffrage Association with Mrs. Stanton as president. They prepared for what would be the eventual victory of women in 1920 when Congress would pass the right to vote amendment for women.[7]

In 1895, the same year that The American Jewess was first published, Lillian Wald opened her Henry Street Settlement House in New York City where she devoted the next forty years of her life as a public health worker. Lillian Wald was Jewish, one of many German-Jewish women involved with the social movements of the times. Rosa Sonneschein was influenced by all of this activity. Her desire to launch a journal for Jewish women to inform them of the major Jewish and non-Jewish issues of the era seems an almost natural reaction. The Jewish press was proliferating: In 1883, Emma Lazarus's sonnet The New Colussus was published. In 1885, the same year that Reform rabbis adopted the "Pittsburgh Platform" in their formulation of Reform principles, the Yiddishe Tageblatt, the first Yiddish daily in the world, was founded. (Such journals were referred to later by German Jews as the "jargon press.") In 1888, the Jewish Publication Society of America was established. In 1889, the Central Conference of American Rabbis was constituted.

In 1890, **Die Freie Arbeiter Shtimme** and **Die Arbeiter Zeitung** joined a growing line of Jewish workers' publications. In 1892, the American Jewish Historical Society was founded and **Die Zukunft**, a Yiddish literary review, was launched. In 1894, the **Union Prayer Book** standardized Reform ritual and prayer, and the **Abendblatt**, a popular Yiddish evening paper, appeared on newsstands. And the next year, **The American Jewess** came off the press. During the four years of its tenure, the **Jewess** was "rivaled" by the appearance of the **Forverts--the Jewish Daily Forward** in 1897. That same year, the CCAR came out with a statement totally disapproving of any attempt for the establishment of a Jewish state. In the same year, Rosa Sonneschein attended the First Zionist Congress in Basel in 1897 as an observer and returned sympathetic to the Zionist cause. In 1898, the Federation of American Zionists (later the Zionist Organization of America) was organized in response to the Basel conference.[8]

Rosa Sonneschein was caught up in the swirl of these social, cultural and religious movements, actually in the crosscurrents of these movements, and her life is a tragic case because of it. Born in Hungary on March 12, 1847, she came out of a distinguished family. Her father, Dr. H.B. Fassel, was one of the most renowned rabbis in Europe and was decorated by four emperors for his scholarly work and honored by the Academy of Science in Vienna which also published his work. She was soon to become a prominent figure in literary circles and served as a special correspondent for several St. Louis and Chicago newspapers while attending the Paris Exposition. She later married Rabbi Solomon Hirsch Sonneschein in 1864. He was born in Hungary on June 24, 1839, educated at the University of Hamburg and Jena, and was a practicing rabbi in Prague, New York, at Temple Israel in St. Louis, and at Temple B'nai Yeshurun in Des Moines, Iowa. He was a contributor to numerous German and English periodicals for more than forty years. He was also a very close friend of Isaac Meyer Wise. He died on October 3, 1908. His wife Rosa outlived him by twenty-four years, dying in 1932.

One would think that with so much in common they would have had a happy marriage, both coming from similar backgrounds and both being writers. But this was not Rosa's fate. Rabbi Sonneschein belonged to an extreme Reform group and was totally and unalterably opposed to Zionism. They had four children--two of whom predeceased their parents. "It became ideologically and physically a barren union. Perhaps the grim happenings of her day-to-day life drove her to her literary labors."[9] This is the view of Jewish historian Anita Libman Lebeson. Lebeson concentrates on the tension over Zionism between Rosa and her husband, but there was a more important issue, a personal issue that was soon to become a national social problem: the liberation of the woman from her home. (Rosa Sonneschein got along poorly with her husband due to personal reasons--his drinking and adulterous affairs, for example.)

The idea for the magazine originated with this one woman, Rosa Sonneschein, but early support came from the National Council for Jewish Women which had been founded in America in 1893. Many of the early contributors to the journal were from this organization. But the year 1893 was an important one for Rosa Sonneschein in another way.

Before one mentions that event, one should note that many men were threatened by their wives going off to conferences and symposia alone, leaving husband and children behind. Rebekah Bettleheim Kohut, wife of the prominent Rabbi Alexander Kohut, tells the painful story of how, at the last moment, she could not face the guilt-provoking disapproval of her husband, and thereby decided not to go to Chicago to present a paper at the First Congress of Jewish women held in 1893 as part of the Chicago World Fair.[10] Presumably, Rosa's husband also was against his wife's going, but she went in any case. If she had not, we may not have had The American Jewess at all.

During the Chicago Exposition and World's Fair (the so-called Columbian Exposition of 1893), she read a paper before the Press Congress and announced that the time had come to establish a literary journal for Jewish women, a journal that would "connect with the cord of mutual interest the sisters dwelling throughout the length and breadth of the country." This theme of "sisterhood" was restated in the opening editorial of the first issue:

> We invite all to follow us to the goal of universal sisterhood. We need diligent workers and warm friends....Every Jewess in America ought to assist us as best she can, either with word or pen....Every home, be it

humble or proud, can afford to take this magazine; every Jew and Gentile, man and woman of literary ability is invited to contribute to its columns; every child is welcome to join us to build up a journal worthy of American Judaism.
                                    vol. 1, no. 1, April 1895

Such ringing words have the clarion call of a political rally, but the magazine was much more literary than political. It contained poems, historical sketches, short stories, and articles on fashion, music, art, and the care of children. Nearly all of them were written by women, such as Kate Chopin, Elizabeth C. Cardoza, Rebekah Kohut, Hannah Solomon, plus someone with a most "patriotic" name--Sadie American, an early leader of the National Council for Jewish Women.

The first issue was fifty five pages long with ten pages of advertising. The ads themselves were fascinating and included a few that most feminist journals today would never carry: corsets, malt extract, footwear, jewelry, diamond rings, bicycles, cosmetics, wines, investment securities, and restaurants and banks in Chicago and St. Louis where the editorial offices were located. The office moved to New York in April, 1896 and in the process the company changed its name from the Rosa Sonneschein Company to the American Jewess Company with offices at 185 East Broadway on the Lower East Side of New York City.

The magazine prospered due to its novelty and the zeal of its editor, claiming 29,000 subscribers. One of its last issues (May, 1899) was eighty pages long with only seven pages of advertising, and the ads had by this time become definitely haute couture: liqueurs, fancy chocolates, corsets again, a Great Book series, tapestries, and health spas (the famous Garrod Spa where the "Lithia Water are the Favorites (sic)"). The journal was not expensive by today's standards--one dollar a year for the monthly, and ten cents an issue, but as the ads reflect, the subscribers were certainly upper-middle to upper-class German and Sephardic Jews, not the poorer working class Eastern European Jews who crowded into the urban ghettos of the North.

The years 1895-1899 were tumultuous ones for world Jewry. Upheaval in Europe sent hundreds of thousands of Jews to America's "goldeneh medinah" (golden land of

-159-

opportunity). Growing anti-Semitism in France culminated in the Dreyfus Trial which in turn influenced the founder of political Zionism, Theodore Herzl. The first Zionist Convention was held in Basel in 1897. The women's suffrage movement was in ascendance, while the political muckrakers and reformers of the Progressive Era and the noblesse oblige of the upper classes toward the poor and oppressed were swirling currents at the time, all of them affecting The American Jewess.

And all these events were covered in the magazine. Articles on Herzl (a personal friend of Rosa) and on the Dreyfus Trial appear. Israel Zangwill, the well-known exponent of the "melting pot" theory of assimilation and Max Nordau, second to Herzl in Zionist leadership, wrote for the journal, as did Isaac Meyer Wise, Baron F. James de Rothschild, Stephen Wise, Mary Antin, Emma Lazarus, and Benjamin Disraeli. In short, the most famous Jewish personalities of the time wrote for this women's magazine.

The first issue contained an article by Emil G. Hirsch on "The Modern Jewess" ("The last decades of the nineteenth century will probably live in history as the age of woman's emancipation," he proudly proclaimed); Louise Mannheimer painted a literary portrait of a nearly forgotten Jewish writer Nahida Remy, author of an equally forgotten classic called Jewish Woman; and Dr. Adolph Moses contributed an admirable piece called "The Position of Woman in America."

Later issues contained a wealth of practical, as well as aesthetic, information, that is, articles such as "Women as Breadwinners," "Jews in the Army," and a somewhat racialistic piece by Friedrich Kolbenheyer on "Jewish Blood." His thesis was that "Jewish blood was good and pure: look at all the handsome (German) Jews and Jewesses and all the intelligent minds among the Chosen People." His article appeared with a picture of three Jewish women from Cleveland (the Mesdames Wolf, Weil, and Seligman) and the caption underneath read: "Some Handsome Types of American Jewesses."

The American Jewess also contained book reviews, a children's story department, hints on how to write a business letter and a description of the latest styles in kitchen fashion.

This exceptional journal, however, came to an untimely end, and there are lessons to be learned even

from its demise. There was no doubt that it had financial troubles. It was in many ways the creation of <u>one</u>
woman, and it was literally years ahead of its time in
some ways, but the problem went deeper and would still
be relevant today. For how many Jews would even today,
in our more enlightened times, subscribe to a magazine
that unabashedly called itself <u>The American Jewess</u>? It
would be on the newsstands or unfurled by the mailman
on one's front steps for all to see--that one was a
Jew, a Jewish woman, and proud of it. Many subscribers
might be ashamed, and that was exactly what happened
eighty years ago. In the words of Mrs. Sonneschein in
a final valedictory (August, 1899) to her readers:

> We thought that so-called "enlightened" Jews
> would support literature, but we were mis-
> taken. Most of them are ashamed to have
> their neighbors and letter carriers know that
> they are interested in Jewish affairs. We
> have often admired the pluck and candor of
> the "barbaric Russian" Jew, who spreads his
> Yiddish paper before him on the street car,
> in the ferryboat, or in the park....It is a
> travesty on culture that interest in Jewish
> affairs and Jewish literature should be found
> only in the brain of the "uncouth" Ghetto
> Jew, while the minds of our "cultivated" and
> "emancipated" Jews should be bent on getting
> as far away from Jewish affairs as possible.

This poignant paragraph tells us many things.
First, it shows the conflict between German and Eastern
European Jews; secondly, it shows the pride and natur-
alness of the Russian and Polish Jews; and thirdly, it
shows the assimilationist tendencies of the German
Jews. Their being ashamed of their Jewishness in some
instances verged on the point of self-denial of their
religio-ethnic label.

Mrs. Sonneschein concludes her valedictory with
these bitter, yet somewhat prophetic, words:

> It is this condition that makes the lot of
> English Jewish journalism so precarious; it
> is that which makes the jargon (sic) press
> ....so prosperous. This....is....our sad
> experience with <u>The American Jewess</u>. We are
> thoroughly acquainted with the whole English-
> Jewish journalistic field, and we know that
> there is hardly a Jewish weekly published in

English in this country that would make a
profitable investment....No one has ever made
a fortune in (this) field....

And thus concluded one of the most remarkable
journals in American Jewish history, the first English-
language journal edited by women for women. As Lebeson
notes, it was with deep sorrow that Rosa Sonneschein
announced that the "periodical had passed out of her
hands."[11] In 1899, publication ceased, and when her
magazine died, it was almost as if its editor "died,"
too. She did nothing noteworthy for the rest of her
life, and her name was forgotten even by her associates. She died at the age of eighty-five on March 5,
1932 in St. Louis. She is buried in Har Sinai Cemetery
in St. Louis, and her literary remains repose in a
warehouse somewhere in the city.[12] Her biography has
yet to be written.

One should end this unhappy life story with a
eulogy of sorts, and the following words probably do
justice to Rosa Sonneschein:

One could wish to have known her--this woman
of grit and valor and endless personal tra-
gedy and exuberant talents and indefatigable
labors for her people. Yet she is forgotten,
almost totally unknown, as if she had never
lived, or, having lived, had had her name
erased by the tides of time and history. To
have rediscovered her even briefly is a great
privilege. To recall her, to keep her memory
green, is her due.[13]

Notes

1. Sociologist Nathan Glazer in his book **American Judaism** (Chicago: 1972) devotes an entirely new chapter to his new edition called "Epilogue: The Year 1967 and its Meaning, 1956-1972", and he boldly states that one year stands out as a dividing line for Jews in the United States since 1956 and that year is 1967.

2. The rise and impact of the Jewish student and countercultural movement of the late 1960s has been documented in several books and articles including: Jack Nusan Porter and Peter Dreier, eds., **Jewish Radicalism: A Selected Anthology** (New York: 1973); James A. Sleeper and Alan L. Mintz, eds., **The New Jews** (New York: 1971); Mordechai Chertoff, ed., **The New Left and the Jews** (New York: 1971); Louis Schub, ed., **The New Left and Israel** (Los Angeles: 1971); Jacob Neusner, ed., **Contemporary Judaic Fellowship in Theory and in Practice** (New York: 1973); and Richard Siegel, Michael Strassfeld, and Sharon Strassfeld, eds., **The Jewish Catalog: A Do-It-Yourself Kit** (Philadelphia: 1973); plus such articles as Jack Nusan Porter, "Jewish Student Activism," **Jewish Currents** 24 (May, 1970), pp. 28-34; Sara Feinstein, "A New Jewish Voice on Campus," **Dimensions in American Judaism** 4 (Winter, 1970), pp. 4-11; and Peter Dreier and Jack Nusan Porter, "Jewish Radicalism in Transition," **Society** (formerly **Transaction**) 12 (January-February, 1975), 34-43.

3. See Aviva Cantor, "Is Feminism Good for the Jews?," **The Jewish Advocate**, Boston, (Thursday, October 7, 1976), p. 10.

4. **Ibid.**

5. A fine anthology, and there are several others in progress as well, is Elizabeth Koltun, ed., **The Jewish Woman: New Perspectives** (New York: 1976). It contains an excellent bibliography. Another book, a revisionist history of Jewish women in America is Charlotte Baum, Paula Hyman, and Sonya Michel, **The Jewish Woman in America** (New York: 1976). It is interesting to compare this book

with one written in a more traditional style,
Anita Libman Lebeson, Recall to Life: Jewish
Women in American History (New York: 1970); Porter
and Dreier, op. cit., and Siegel, Strassfeld, and
Strassfeld, op. cit., also contain sections on
Jewish women. One should also consult such coun-
tercultural Jewish journals as Response, Davka,
and, of course, Lilith.

6. Aviva Cantor, op. cit., p. 10, emphasis added.

7. For an especially good history of women's rights
in this country, see Eleanor Flexner, Century of
Struggle: The Women's Rights Movement in the
United States (New York: 1973).

8. This outline is based on "A Cultural Chronology of
American Jewry," (New York: American Jewish Press
Association and the Tarbuth Foundation for the
Advancement of Hebrew Culture, 1976.)

9. Lebeson, op. cit., p. 229. Lebeson's account of
Rosa Sonnenschein is based on the research of
Jacob Zausmer, Be-ikve ha-dor (New York: 1957), in
the section on American observers and delegates to
the First Zionist Congress in 1897, pp. 130-152.
The portion on Ms. Sonnenschein (some sources use
the name Sonneschein) is on pages 148-152.
Lebeson and Zausmer state that she was not a
political Zionist or a member of Hovevei Zion, an
early Zionist organization, but was quite
sympathetic. She traveled widely and got to know
some of the early European leaders of Zionism.
Both Herzl and Nordau influenced her thinking. On
an impulse she wrote to Herzl, and he answered her
on May 8, 1897. Along with twelve other women,
her picture can be found on an official photograph
of all delegates and observers at the Congress.
See Lebeson, op. cit., pp. 228-233.

10. This unhappy tale is told in Rebekah Kohut, My
Portion (New York: 1925), pp. 180-182, and retold
in Charlotte Baum, Paula Hyman, and Sonya Michel,
op. cit., pp. 34-36. Baum, et al also discuss
Rosa Sonneschein but fail to place her journal in
the unique position that it deserves. They also,
unfairly, I believe, gloss over her life, her
contributions, and her journal, which they demean
as being too "bourgeois" for their tastes.
Relatively speaking, I think they are too critical
of the journal.

11. Lebeson, *op*. *cit*., p. 230.

12. *Ibid*., p. 230.

13. *Ibid*., p. 233.

Chapter 9

The Jewish Young Adult

This essay emerged as an intellectual excursion undertaken to not only illuminate a corner of society, but also to understand myself better. It was written at a stage in my life when I was single and trying to understand both the general society's and the Jewish community's seeming lack of interest in, or desire to help, the single young adult. Everything in this article, with the exception of some minor comments, can apply to any single adult in an urban setting regardless of religious affiliation. "Singlehood" is not only a stage in life but singles themselves, at least younger singles, could even be considered a social class. They have common interests, common frustrations, and common characteristics. This essay first appeared under the title "Jewish Singles," in _Midstream_, vol. 21, no. 10, December, 1975, pp. 35-43 and is reprinted by permission of the editors and the Theodor Herzl Foundation of New York. It created quite a stir when it appeared. On the positive side, as with the plight of the Jewish poor, it opened up a new area of concern for Jewish and secular social welfare agencies, and it was widely praised by many Jewish singles. On the negative side, it was criticized by some Jewish countercultural groups who felt that I had wrongly placed them in the same category as "swinging singles." These reactions appear in the notes at the end of the article.

* * * * *

Until fairly recently, children were considered miniature adults, small in size perhaps, but with the potential for a rapidly developing maturity. In medieval tapestries or, later, in the paintings of

Gainsborough and Van Dyck, boys and girls are dressed like adults, replicas of their parents. For most of the history of mankind, there was no extended child-hood; even adolescence was condensed. One married at an early age, usually in one's mid to late teens and almost immediately became a member of adult society as a spouse and parent. Being unmarried was a serious break with tradition, particularly for women. Remain-ing single was an option available only to nuns, priests, prostitutes, or the mentally unfit.

However, the Industrial Revolution of the 19th and 20th Centuries and the concomitant changes from an agricultural to a technological society brought in its wake a number of revolutionary changes in family structure--patriarchal authority diminished; women acquired new rights and powers, including control over conception; children became more independent; school, the peer group, and the mass media became major social-izing elements; and religious sanctions and family pressures became more ineffectual. The spectre of over-population and the rise of affluence reduced family size; some even questioned the need for having children at all, or even of getting married.

Increased education and extensive career training led to a prolonged period of dependency on parents. Adolescence was now a new stage in life that was becoming more and more extended. This stage would be followed by other dependent stages: the student stage and the post-student, young adult stage.

If the 1950s were personified by the teenage rebel (the "juvenile delinquent," say, as portrayed by James Dean and Marlon Brando), and if the 1960s were per-sonified by the student rebel, now with a cause (as portrayed by Dustin Hoffman, Jon Voight, and Elliot Gould), then the 1970s might best be characterized by the post-college, young single adult.

Singlehood as such has developed into a particular stage of life, with its own values, goals, rewards, associations, gathering places, and heroes. As indivi-duals marry later in life and divorce more frequently, singlehood or single parenthood will no longer be seen as deviant, but as an alternative to marriage and thus will become ever more important for society to under-stand and accept. What we seem to have today is what Yale psychiatrist Robert Jay Lifton calls "Protean Man and Woman," extending into one's late 30s and beyond.

This lifestyle can be characterized by an endless series of "experiments," some shallow, some profound, that delve into all aspects of human experience-social, sexual, political, educational, aesthetic, and economic. This stage is marked by rootlessness and ennui, yet it also quests for stability, commitment, and love.

Erik Erikson, in Childhood and Society describes eight stages in the life cycle of the the human being-- two of which are of concern here--stages five and six. Stage five consists of tensions of identity and role confusion and covers the ages from twelve to eighteen. Young people in the turbulent climate of Western societies have a more difficult time forming identities than their counterparts in more stable societies. It is this conflict over identity that is the major cause of anxiety and neurosis. This role confusion continues into the next stage, stage six, which covers the period of young adulthood, roughly the ages from eighteen to thirty five.

This latter period revolves around the problem of intimacy versus isolation. Intimacy is the ability to share with another person without fear of losing one's self in the process. Inability to form this bond may lead to feelings of being totally alone in the world. This problem is terribly important to young adults and sets the basis for the sometimes desperate, even comical, search for a partner, or, in a common cliche, for a "relationship."

One of the sadder aspects of urban living is that people must resort to impersonal ways of meeting each other. Our culture has come a long way from the days of the shadchan, the community matchmaker. The following items are ads taken from two Boston newspapers, the Phoenix and the Real Paper which cater to a city where 54 percent of the population is single, formerly married, or widowed. Ads similar to these appear in many journals--the Village Voice in New York, the Los Angeles Free Press, and the highbrow New York Review of Books. Not that most singles meet this way, but these newspapers do reach thousands of young adults; a few will link up after reading such ads. Some might call such ads "sad" or "weird" (in some cases they are), but they are certainly attempts at adjusting to the sixth stage of psychosexual development--the overwhelming need to escape isolation:

Nubile girls, 14-40, sought by Jewish male,
35. Be my sexual playmate. Financially
rewarding. Good food, theater, and money.
State needs. Box 0000.
The Real Paper, October 3, 1973

Big beautiful Jewish brunette about to jump
off bridge--hate bars, ads like this one--
there MUST be attractive, intelligent,
educated, and "together" men, 26-38 in this
city, or is everyone a reject or fruitcake?
I am 25, 5'10", educated, sensual, etc.
Reply fast!....splash, gurgle. Box 0000.
The Phoenix, March 4, 1975

A recent cover story in Newsweek magazine painted
a rosy picture of singles frolicking at the swimming
pool of their singles' apartment-complex--and a pros-
perous one for the entrepreneurs that prey on them.
The public image of the "swinging single" is false.
Loneliness, the bete noire of our civilization, is a
universal problem to which singles are especially
prone.

George F. Gilder, author of Naked Nomads, maintains that the failure of the singles' ideal is a major
sociological fact of the last decade. Yet, understanding this failure can lead to a greater comprehension of
the real potentialities and limits of men and women,
the real possibilities of freedom, the real needs for
dependency and responsibility.

Jewish singles represent one of the great untapped
resources of the Jewish community. A great deal of
interest is being shown by Jewish organizations in
reaching them. In the late '60s and early '70s, it was
the Jewish student that was the focal point of intensive programming; today, with the campuses quiet, the
post-college "young adult" Jew is being sought after.
In other words, it is the 1960s Jewish student, now
older and more mature, that is of interest. How committed is this group to Judaism? to the Jewish people?
to Israel?

Jewish young adults are a diverse group--never
married and formerly married; part-time students, full-
time graduate students, working people; Orthodox,
Conservative, Reform, atheist, and alienated singles;
Zionists and non-Zionists; Jewishly-committed and
uncommitted; the intermarried as well as the converted;

-170-

the "straight" and the "gay" single. While the graduate student may have some affiliation with the local
college Hillel House and the Orthodox single will have
a much greater connection to his or her local shul, the
Jewish young adult who is neither student nor religious
is out there, floating around, oblivious to the fact
that Jewish organizations are worried about him or her.

From Sunday Schools to Golden Age Clubs, the
Jewish community has institutions that cater to the
needs of its constituents. However, a quantum gap
exists with regard to programs for the Jewish young
adult and, especially, the Jewish single adult.

This segment of the Jewish community, because of
its transiency and its lack of organizational affiliation, is difficult to organize. Single young adults
are often far from their own communities; they are isolated from their families; they are in the process of
selecting a career; they must decide whether or not to
choose a mate; they are looking for a community to live
in; and they are deciding whether or not to find some
kind of religious commitment.

The members of this sprawling, diffuse group will
rarely associate with a synagogue or community center.
They will rarely become involved with Jewish Federa-
tions or other philanthropic groups; they will rarely
join the ZOA, the B'nai B'rith, the American Jewish
Committee, or Hadassah, and if they do, it will usually
be later, only after they marry and have children, not
before.

Because they are found as individuals, not through
organizations, fresh approaches must be discovered to
reach them. Community social workers and organizational leaders who deal with singles must be given a
free hand in order to attempt these new approaches.
This will mean a reorientation of traditional techniques of attracting young adults.

One hears a great deal today of the "break-up" of
the Jewish family. Divorce rates and intermarriage are
running neck and neck and approaching a one-in-three
ratio. The key question for Jewish social organizers
is how to bring Jewish singles together and thus
counteract the inroads of assimilation, intermarriage,
and other forms of religious disorganization.

There seem to be four "ideal types" of Jews: the
religiously committed, the secularly committed, the
quasi-committed, the uncommitted or assimilated.

These groups are not discrete aggregates; they are a spectrum of Jewish involvement. One could liken them to the concentric zones of a circle, with the religiously committed in the innermost center of the circle, the secularly committed in the next circle of involvement with Jewish affairs though on a secular rather than a religious basis, and the last two groups as the outermost concentric circles.

The religiously committed are quite heterogeneous; they will spurn most secular Jewish programming just as the assimilated will. The religious group is composed of the Orthodox, the neo-Orthodox, the Hasidic, and the non-Hasidic sects. They rank high in terms of Jewish education, Jewish involvement, Jewish commitment, and Jewish identity.

The first group is very independent. It has its own community, its own shuls, its own lifestyle. Members of this group tend to marry and bear children at an early age. Their courtship patterns lead directly to marriage, and the Jewish cycle of holidays and festivities, weddings and bar-mitzvahs, yeshivot and shadchanim, all provide numerous ways to overcome the single way of life. Singlehood and sexual relations outside of marriage are frowned upon; pressures to conform are intense.

A small number of singles (and marrieds) in the other categories have become attracted to this group, and their numbers are growing. There is some disaffection and reverse movement from the Orthodox group to the secularly committed group, but very rarely into the others.

Jules, age twenty seven, a single, Orthodox Jewish activist and instructor at a college in Boston, had this to say about his identity and his relationship to secular Jewish organizations:

> To me, Judaism is a traditional existentialism that combines reverence for an essential heritage and deep moral responsibility. As an Orthodox Jew, I try to be faithful to this duality through religious consciousness and political activism. While my personal commitment to these ideals is strong, I find that many Orthodox religious institutions do not put them into practice in an effective and sincere way. It also disappoints me that

non-Orthodox institutions likewise fail in these areas, but the failure of Orthodox institutions is a double disappointment, and one which I feel turns off many young people. Jewish community centers and Hillel foundations are necessary for strengthening Jewish commitment and identity for those who are insecure about their Jewishness; Orthodox institutions provide me with necessary social and religious interaction that satisfy my needs and make secular Jewish programming secondary to them.

Though this viewpoint may not speak for all Orthodox Jews, it does reflect the perspectives of the "neo-Orthodox," the modernized, highly educated (in secular terms), and highly professional young religious Jew. In terms of education and profession, they have much in common with the other groups.

The assimilated group could be called "non-Jewish Jews." While a minute number may convert to Christianity, most are indifferent to Judaism and to Jewish concerns. Their Jewish identity is low; their Jewish education is miniscule or nonexistent; their involvement in Jewish affairs is nil. Yet the Jewish community is very concerned about them. These are the "self-hating radicals" and the "self-destructive hippies" that one reads about--or used to. These are the young Jews who are such an "embarrassment" to the Jewish community, the artists and intellectuals who concern themselves with all but Jewish issues. The interesting thing is that the Jewish community probably spends more time worrying about this group than it does about the quasi-committed group, a large group much more amenable to the enticements of Judaism. In any case, Jews are fascinated by this group, first, because it is a possible source of danger to Israel and to the American Jewish community, and, second, because in some cases Jews who return "to the fold" from this group have often been in the vanguard of Jewish creativity. (One of the best examples in history is Theodor Herzl, the highly assimilated founder of political Zionism.)

A 29-year-old Boston feminist, living with a non-Jew, and quite removed from any Jewish concerns, has a few provocative things to say:

How do I view the singles scene?....with contempt! It's just another way of defining yourself by your relationships to other people and devaluating your own worth. It's an extension of certain high school and college attitudes in which your status is determined by whom you date and how often. I don't especially think of my friends in either married or single roles--this might have to do with knowing a hell of a lot of couples who have very good relationships but didn't necessarily legalize them immediately or may never do so. I don't feel that marriage is such a great goal in and of itself, but this seems to be an important, if not frantic, part of the single's philosophy. I honestly believe that the divorce rate would drop drastically if more couples lived together for a year or more before getting into all the legal hassles of marriage....

But the singles scene? That's another story. Singles are supposed to be free in terms of economics, yet they are really an artificially created class whose major function seems to be being exploited by the Playboy-Cosmopolitan thing. Women are expected to invest a good chunk of money in clothes, cosmetics, and other superficial crap, and the men have to foot most of the food, drink and entertainment bills. More singles--both male and female--ought to try to raise their consciousness about sex roles. They might not be so eager to inflict their insecurities and hang-ups on somebody else....

To me, the whole singles trip is a type of psychological oppression that society dumps on vulnerable people who are afraid to be themselves--maybe because they don't know their own identity in the first place.

The overwhelming emphasis on marriage in the Jewish community leads to prejudice against the single adult. Though marriage as an institution is far from "dead," still, its form, especially with respect to traditional sex roles, has been modified; new alternatives to the nuclear family have emerged. But marriage is still a very important goal for the vast majority of Jewish young adults. For most Jews, the single state is only temporary. Though American Jews between the ages of twenty and thirty four have one of the lowest marriage rates of any ethnic group, by the time they reach the ages of thirty five to forty nine, they have one of the **highest**. Furthermore, despite the high divorce rate and the heavy criticism of marriage as an institution, 60 percent of all those divorced will re-marry within five years.

Of the two middle groups, the secularly committed and the quasi-committed, the secularly committed form the central strength of the Jewish community. They have strong Jewish commitments and a strong sense of Jewish identity. They may be weak in Jewish education and often attempt to extend that education later in life. They may have some traditional feelings toward Judaism, but generally their involvement with Judaism is on a secular, political, cultural, and organiza-tional level.

A typical example of this kind of Jew is Esther, a 25-year-old social worker, recently married. She had been active in campus Hillel programs and single-handedly ran a special program dealing with Israel at her college. Her father is an executive in a large Jewish organization in New York. She had this to say about the single life:

> Theoretically, there should be less of a drive to get married today, but personally and psychologically, there's a great need for companionship. Though there is less peer group pressure to marry, there's still a lot of parental pressure. As for Boston as a "singles haven," I have found the town an easy place to meet people. Compared to Pittsburgh, where I went to school, Boston affords a wide variety of activities and religious services. Some of my friends, who are around 24 or so, are getting a little "desperate" and come to me asking where they can find eligible men. I tell them to go to Sunday graduate student brunches at Harvard Hillel or Boston University, or to **onegrei shabbat** around town, or to take a course at the Cambridge Institute for Adult Studies or at Hebrew College. There's any number of places around here to meet men.

This Jewishly committed young woman had no diffi-culty finding suitable social activities both inside the Jewish community and outside. But what about the person in the quasi-committed group? This person has little Jewish background and only minor involvement in Jewish affairs, but maintains a strong "gut" feeling about his or her Jewish identity, even though it will rarely be exhibited in traditional and organizational Jewish life.

Marc, a 24-year-old graduate student in education from New York who starts teaching next year, is a good example of this group. His mother is Jewish, his father was an Italian Catholic. Marc, in a sense, "returned" to Judaism recently and now dates only Jewish women; he has begun to study with a local rabbi for a belated bar-mitzvah. His goal is to marry a Jewish woman and raise children in the Jewish tradition, even though his own home lacked a Jewish atmosphere.

He had this to say:

Frankly, the Jewish community does not do a lot for its singles. Most young singles, however, will not go near a synagogue for, let's say, Friday night services. Young singles have so many more important things on their mind--jobs, marriage, school--than these synagogues or even the Hillel programs provide....and even the Hillels fail because they emphasize the religious rather than the social. There is nothing wrong with having a sense of Jewishness, but too much emphasis on simply religion turns people away....They got too much at Hebrew School, Sunday School, or from their homes--they had it up to their ears with Judaism--so they get turned off by the time they get to college. By then, they want to explore other aspects of life.

One could ask whether Marc's lack of Jewish upbringing was a "plus" factor in this case, since it did not turn him off completely. What he might be saying is that the "lox and bagels" kind of Judaism that most young Jews acquired simply could not withstand the rigors of the more enticing "fleshpots," both intellectual and physical, of the secular non-Jewish world. This could lead to the awful conclusion that programming for young adults may be too late! It questions the very nature of Jewish education--and it should.

-176-

The real question is--how can the community approach such young people?

Where do the young adults live? What do they do? Where do they socialize? What organizations outside the Jewish community cater to their needs--singles clubs, sports clubs, ski clubs, political clubs, etc.? What existing Jewish organizations cater to them-Hillel Foundations, Jewish Community Center groups, temple singles clubs, etc.? What are their activities? Whom do they reach? And most important, what impressions do young Jews have of those Jewish groups that cater to them--positive, negative, apathetic?

We need a composite picture of the "average" Jewish young adult. We will not reach the totally alienated on the one hand, nor the religiously Orthodox on the other, so we need to know what the "average" Jew does Jewishly--his or her attitudes toward Jewish ritual, Israel, intermarriage, the synagogue. This Jew knows he or she is Jewish and will not deny it, but just how will he or she reveal that identity?

Who are his or her friends? Whom does he or she date? Whom does he or she want to date? What are his or her relationships with married friends? With his or her parents? With local rabbis?

Where does this Jew see him or herself five, ten, fifteen years from now? What are his or her dreams? aspirations? professional goals? family goals? Jewish goals? How does he or she see him or herself raising children? What in Judaism does he or she want to inculcate in his or her children? Will he or she join a synagogue? A B'nai B'rith Lodge? The local federation? Will he or she visit Israel? Contribute to Israel's needs?

In short, unless we have some information on these basic questions, even superficial information, programs, and policy approaches will be ineffectual at best and harmful at worst. This very sensitive age is not amenable to the usual organizational approach. This group can only be reached in informal ways by people who know the "scene" well. What is needed is fresh ideas, fresh blood, creative personnel, and complete independence and trust. In short, find the best people to organize such programs, give them sufficient funds, and leave them alone! Program evaluations should take place every few months and changes incorporated as needed. But the main thing is creative independence. The old approaches simply will not work for this highly educated, highly mobile, and highly alienated segment of the community.[1]

After the initial survey of Jewish single adults has been taken, a small number of informal meetings should take place with Jewish (and even non-Jewish) community workers who will deal with this group. Included in these meetings should be local Hillel directors, synagogue personnel who have single adult programs, rabbis (especially those who know and understand the single scene), several representative single adults (including not just the committed Jew, but some on the periphery: the single parent, the divorced, and the elderly single--each of these will have specific problems and needs and will have to be reached in different ways), plus some "expert witnesses" such as local talk-show moderators and journalists, ministers and priests (both to discuss their programs and the issue of intermarriage), singles bar and restaurant owners, and directors of adult education programs.

Out of these meetings a series of issues will emerge: first, the diversity of the population will be shown, and individual programs will be developed to cater to these different groups. Second, an open approach at these meetings will air some of the grievances that singles have toward the general community at large and toward the Jewish community in particular. Constructive criticism is essential. Third, programs that have worked successfully in the past could be described and analyzed and applied to future programs. Fourth, and most important, people will begin relating to each other on a human and not an organizational level.

Many of these activities will have to take place outside the synagogue or Jewish community center because many single adults simply will not go near a Jewish institution. First, because it smacks of old fashioned matchmaking and is seen as attracting only the less attractive elements in the community; second, because it is associated with a married couple approach to socializing; third, because it brings to mind unresolved conflicts relating to a misguided family life and a painful religious experience; and fourth, because of elementary logistics--the synagogue or JCC is often too far away. Most singles live within the urban centers, not in the suburbs.

Furthermore, Jewish social and community workers and rabbis will have to stop thinking in terms of numbers or future temple members. The pitch for either money or membership alienates most of the singles. Another complaint that singles express is that many events are simply huge social dances which are very impersonal, making it difficult to find and talk with someone Jewish. Furthermore, they attract many younger high school and non-Jewish singles; these drawbacks detract from the effectiveness of the event both as a social function and as a religious one (religious in a secular sense--that is, a place to meet a Jewish partner).

Many singles like to attend large dances but also to have them interspersed with "wine and cheese" parties, guest speakers on <u>Jewish</u> as well as general topics, and special events. Probably, the best and least painful way to meet people is at work or at cultural and political places (museums, the Civil Liberties Union, film societies), or within religious fellowships.

A few examples: the Hillel foundation of Boston University has a very successful "graduate student society" which caters more to post-college age adults than it does to graduate students. It is run by working young adults who are unpaid and it meets in a very accessible place: the campus of Boston University in a large rented room or at the spacious Hillel Foundation. It has complete autonomy and is financially self-sufficient. And it works! Last year alone its programs attracted over 2,000 Jewish young adults.

A much different group, more intense and politically involved, is the "Fabrengen" (Hasidic term for "joyous gathering") in Washington, D.C. This fellowship consists of young professionals, lawyers, teachers, social workers, and other post-college adults who engage in a wide range of political and cultural activity. The "Am Chai Community" in Chicago is a similar group.[2]

Havurot, either intensive communal houses or less intensive fellowships, are an alternative for some. The first and most widely-known, the Havurat Shalom of Boston, and the New York Havurah, are essentially for single people. Other fellowships have involved married couples with children. Some are connected with an established synagogue; some have taken the place of the synagogue; others are isolated and independent groups. Havurot and other intentional communities have sprung up spontaneously in order to fill the needs of young Jews, needs that the established Jewish institutions have not met. Though not for everyone, these fellow-ships provide a lifestyle and a sense of community that so many singles seek but never find.[3]

Finally, a third possibility, which is rarely attempted, could be to organize around work places. This has been tried in a few areas. Individuals would bring together several friends and colleagues who in turn would invite members of the opposite sex, and a small informal social group would form and have lunch together regularly. Special topics could be discussed every week: the Jewish position on abortion, the political situation in Israel, or the question of inter-marriage. Each week a different person would be responsible for leading the discussion. The group could expand its activities with evening meetings and Friday night services and study sessions and it could be the basis for political and cultural activities out-side the world of work. The satisfactions would be enormous: it would reduce the alienation and drudgery of the work situation; it would open up areas of sociability in places where such intimacy is shunned and censured; it could lead to further involvement in established Jewish institutions--or it could be an end in itself.

One should look upon this entire phenomenon as an experiment, because it is--one can succeed; one can fail; and one can try again. Each synagogue, each community, and each individual will ultimately decide which of these "experiments" is most suitable for his or her situation. The crucial task now, however, is to make people aware of the plight of the single adult, to dispense with the old stereotypes and false images, and to create meaningful and effective alternatives for them or to help young adults create such alternatives for themselves.

Notes

1. Peter Dreier, in one of the few good articles on the subject, emphasizes the point that we know very little about Jewish singles. He notes that before a Jewish community can embark on such programs, it must first find out more about them. Most important, he advises community leaders and social workers to "ask the young singles themselves what they need." (From his "Young Jews in Limbo," Congress-Bi-Weekly, October 26, 1973.)

2. I want to stress that I mention these communal groups simply as excellent alternatives to the usually superficial "singles scene." Farbrengen and the Am Chai Community did not arise in order to "cater to singles." In fact, they are comprised of married couples, gay people, and others not at all interested in the "singles life." Their purpose is political, not social. In fact, they have a rather low regard for groups such as "swinging singles" or "dating clubs."

3. The Havurot also arose out of political and cultural tensions and not to specifically cater to single people. They too are comprised of married couples as well as single people. But their development was in response to the growing sense of alienation that many young adults feel in both the Jewish and general culture. They too offer a more human alternative to the young Jew interested in meeting like-minded Jews in the same or similar age-cohort. They also have disgust for the shallow "singles scene" and see themselves as a healthier and more natural alternative.

References

A.   I owe a great debt to Morey Schapira, one of the founders of Boston University's Hillel Graduate Student Society and a leading expert in the area of Jewish single life, for his kind advice and for his permission to use previously unpublished material. This paper owes as much to him as anyone. Secondly, I wish to thank Lesley Rovner and Rabbi Richard Israel for their comments.

B.   For a group as important as this one, there is really very little written on Jewish single life or for that matter on American single life, that is useful. Aside from popular journals, there are scattered sources, of course, on marriage, divorce, women, pre-marital sex, and a variety of similar topics, but a major book on the single life has yet to be written. On the other hand, there are several avenues to approach this topic.

        a. Popular and sometimes misleading journalistic accounts of single life can be found in major magazines from Playboy to Cosmopolitan. Beware of cheap distortions such as Alice Wayne and John Harper, Games Singles Play, (New York: Popular Library, 1974.) However, such journals as Society, Social Policy and Daedalus all contain occasional articles on the subject. See for example, Joyce R. Starr and Donald E. Carns, "Singles in the City," reprinted from Society magazine in Helen Icken Safa and Gloria Levitas (eds.), Social Problems in Corporate America, (New York: Harper and Row, 1975.)

        b. Articles on Jewish single life are few in number: Peter Dreier, "Young Jews in Limbo", Congress Bi-Weekly, October 26, 1973, is the only one I could find. Some sources on Jewish women are Response magazine, special issue, "The Jewish Woman--An Anthology," No. 18, Winter 1972-1973. For a quick overview of the Jewish family plus an excellent bibliography, see Benjamin Schlesinger, (ed.), The Jewish Family, (Toronto: University of Toronto

Press, 1971.) For compilations of articles
and statements dealing with Jewish youth
and the Jewish counterculture, see James
Sleeper and Alan Mintz, The New Jews, (New
York: Random House, 1971); Jack Nusan
Porter and Peter Dreier, Jewish Radicalism,
(New York; Grove Press, 1973); and Jacob
Neusner, Contemporary Judaic Fellowship in
Theory and Practice, (New York: KTAV,
1972.)

c. Popular paperback works on sex roles,
marriage, divorce, and other related topics
include: Alvin Toffler Future Shock;
Ingrid Bengis Combat in the Erogenous Zone;
Vance Packard The Sexual Wilderness; Nena
and George O'Neill Open Marriage; Erich
Fromm The Art of Loving; William H. Masters
and Virginia E. Johnson The Pleasure Bond;
and Morton Hunt The World of the Formerly
Married.

d. Sociology textbooks that are highly read-
able and recommended: Lawrence H. Fuchs
Family Matters; Lucile Duberman Marriage
and Its Alternatives; Henry Bowman Marriage
for Moderns; Robert F. Winch The Modern
Family; Janet Saltzman Chafetz Masculine/
Feminine or Human?; Herbert Otto (ed.) The
Family in Search of a Future; and Arlene
and Jerome Skolnick The Family in Transi
tion.

e. Several books that describe the weakened
state of the Western male: Karl Bednarik
The Male Crisis; Myron Benton The American
Male; Charles W. Fergusan The Male Atti
tude; and George F. Gilder, Naked Nomads.

f. Some of the other books mentioned in this
article include: Erik Erikson, Childhood
and Society, rev. ed., (New York: W. W.
Norton, 1964); Robert Jay Lifton, "Protean
Man" in his History Human Survival, (New
York: Random House-Vintage Books, 1971),
pp. 311-331; and Edgar Z. Friedenberg,
Coming of Age in America, (New York: Random
House, 1965.) I would like to add the
classic account of childhood and family
life, Philippe Aries, Centuries of Child

hood, (New York: Random House-Vintage Books, 1962.)

g. A new monthly newsletter for Jewish single adults has just been published. It provides information on social activities, educational programs, and opportunities for volunteer work in the Jewish community. Some of the information is also useful for married couples. The newsletter is published by the Commission on Synagogue Relations of the Federation of Jewish Philanthropies. The Commission has created two task forces to deal with the problems of Jewish single adults. The first task force is for adults between 20 and 40 years of age and the second one will concentrate on those in their 40s and 50s. In order to receive the newsletter, send $3.00 to the editors: Jeff Oboler and Barbara Trainin, Commission on Synagogue Relations, 130 East 59th Street, New York, New York 10022. The subscription is for one year.

Chapter 10

The Jewish Upper Class

This essay was written in response to two phenomena. First, it came out of my teaching experience at a private women's college in Boston that I call "Parkhust College."[1] There, while an instructor in sociology, I first came across not only segments of the upper class but also became intimately aware of the special tensions that Jews felt in this milieu. As usual, they were still marginal despite their wealth. The same tension occurred for black, Japanese, and Hispanic students. Anti-Semitism at the school was never institutionalized on an official level, but it manifested itself at subtle, sometimes petty interpersonal levels ....and it was still painful. The administration was rarely even aware of it. The second impetus to study the upper class and their Jewish component was due to its novelty. The upper class is very interesting, and few scholars tackle the subject. With the case of the Jews, there is almost nothing in the literature on the contemporary interaction between Jewish and non-Jewish upper class members. Like the Jewish poor, the Jewish upper class was practically a taboo subject until a few non-Jewish writers (Stephen Birmingham, E. Digby Baltzell) opened up the Pandora's box. It is ironic that both Baltzell and Birmingham are themselves members of the upper class and have written without the self-censorship that may have inhibited Jewish writers. A second point to emphasize is that one must gain entry in some way. The upper class is not especially pleased to be closely examined and analyzed. I would venture to say that they are as difficult to study as, for example, deviant subcultures such as drug users or skid-row bums. There is much more work to be done in this area.

* * * * *

I.

Until the late sociologist C. Wright Mills opened the Pandora's box in his book The Power Elite, the presence of an American upper class was one of the best kept secrets of its time. Later, other writers such as G. William Domhoff, Ferdinand Lundberg, and E. Digby Baltzell, plus a host of Marxist analysts, went far beyond Mills in not only describing this upper class, but in proving that it was also a ruling class. In short, wealth and power went hand-in-hand. This is not exactly a novel nor radical thesis, but Americans have always been squeamish about discussing class differences, and the upper class has always been tight-lipped about exposing itself. It was only after the publication of the Mills' book and Vance Packard's The Status Seekers in the later 1950s that people began to see that the upper class did not simply consist of "flashy jet-setters" or "eccentric millionaires" but was a very serious and powerful force in national and international affairs.

The reason for this blind spot to class has been the United States' traditional insistence that it is an open society where rags to riches stories are common. A myth developed that with enough energy and hard work plus a little luck one could make it to the top. The myth still persists despite its being a false hope for many people in this society. Discussions of class structure also became intertwined with the name of Karl Marx and Communism and this led to further denial of the subject. Yet, we know that an upper class does in fact exist, and that there is a Jewish component to it. What are the criteria for membership in such a class? G. William Domhoff, a sociologist at the University of California, in Who Rules America?, lists seven criteria for membership:

1) Being listed in the social register.

2) Attending any one of the following preparatory schools listed by him (i.e., St. Mark's, St. Paul's, St. George's, Groton, and Middlesex for men and Foxcroft, St. Timothy's, Westover, Miss Porter's, Emma Willard, and the Ethel Walker School for women).

3) Membership in any of the very exclusive "gentlemen's" clubs; for example, Somerset,

-186-

Piedmont Driving, Pickwick, Knickerbocker, Harmonie, Pacific Union, Idlewild, and Chagrin Valley Hunt.

4) One's father having been a millionaire entrepreneur or $100,000-a-year corporate executive or lawyer.

5) Marrying someone that is defined as a member of the upper class by any of the above criteria.

6) Having a member of one's family fit any of the criteria listed above; and

7) Being a member of a family listed in either Who Killed Society? or The Proper Bostonians, both written by Cleveland Amory.

Here, for example, is how a student of mine, a young 19-year-old woman from Dallas, places herself and her family into these criteria:

Perhaps it is the omnipotent will of Americans to play themselves down that influences me, but until I read Domhoff's book, I would have considered myself to be an exception to those criteria--now it becomes apparent that, according to Domhoff, I am not an exception!

My father, Philip Ross Gagnon, went to St. Mark's School (criteria #2) and then on to Yale. In World War II, he was ranked as a captain in the Cavalry (the last regiment to exist) and from there went to work in Cleveland, Ohio for the Cleveland Trust (a bank). Five years later, he moved back to Dallas (his home town) where he began work with Gagnon & Company, an investment banking firm founded by his father (criteria #4). Gagnon & Company later merged with another firm to become Woodside, Gagnon & Company, of which my father is now president. He did not inherit this position but worked his way up. He is also a member of the Eagle Lake Club (criteria #3); this membership is passed down through the family. I have no idea of his annual income and I do not care to know--that is his business. Now, by Domhoff's analysis, my father and I would be considered upper class.

Had Domhoff been thorough enough to make mention of women of the upper class in his book, he undoubtedly would have listed my mother, using the same criteria. (Domhoff does not list women or women's schools in this book, though he corrects the error in his companion volume The Higher Circles--JNP).

My mother went to Westover School (criteria #2) and continued on to Sarah Lawrence College. Her father was president of Montcalm Mining Company, one of the largest corporate complexes in the country. She is a member of the Garden Club and for some time was president of Planned Parenthood of Dallas.

As far as my own background is concerned, I am the offspring of these two people (criteria #6). I went to Ethel Walker School in Simsbury, Connecticut (criteria #2) and am presently enrolled in Parkhurst College. I would love to go and become president of a huge corporation, but that remains to be seen! In all honesty, although I fit Domhoff's criteria, it is hard for me to consider myself upper class. Perhaps, it is due to the stereotype of the flashy jet-setter, which I am not; perhaps, because I seem to dress and look like most other girls my age; perhaps, because my parents told me to treat all people with respect and to go beyond material things; or perhaps, because my family is going through some real financial difficulties. All this does not seem to correlate with the supposed equation of money-upper class that most people feel is true.

Or perhaps, it is an unconscious dread of being in a minority, of being a member of that "power elite" that everyone seems to be putting down all the time. Whatever it is, Domhoff is responsible for making me realize that there actually is a governing class and in most cases, this is the upper class.

This very honest appraisal by a young student tells us several things: first, the nature of class is hidden from even members of the upper class themselves;

-188-

second, women are still treated as second-class citizens in the power structure of the upper class and, therefore, often ignored even by reputable social scientists; and third, even the upper class have their problems, as we shall see.

II.

F. Scott Fitzgerald allegedly said to Ernest Hemingway that rich people were different from others, and Hemingway retorted: "Yes, they have more money." Actually, both were correct. Members of the upper class do lead different lives; they have different lifestyles, interests, and places to frolic. Yet, they share a common humanity. They may have the same goals as the middle class--to work hard, to save, invest, succeed, and protect one's family, but the difference is that they are more likely to do all of these things more rapidly and in greater amounts than the rest of us. Yet, their problems are only too real. A recent book, The Children of the Rich (Wixon, 1973) poignantly lays bare the social and psychological problems of the wealthy--the money without limits, the absent father intent on success, the absent mother intent on social prestige, the dependence on nannies, maids, and tutors can all lead to a lost sense of self. It can, in fact, lay the grounds for the development of a Patricia Hearst, a "poor little rich girl" who becomes involved in violent anti-social behavior even against her will. In short, money does not buy happiness. I can attest to this from my capacity as teacher and counselor. In fact, the rich may not even receive adequate psychological and family counseling either because counselors are intimidated by their power or fame or feel that money should be able to resolve their ills or because of an inability of the counselor to comprehend the very distinct lifestyle of the rich. In many ways, the poor and the wealthy, at both ends of the class scale, have interesting similarities in how they are perceived by the middle class. For example: There is social disorganization among the upper class: alcoholism, drugs, infidelity, divorce, and mental illness. Private boarding schools ("prep" schools) often replace family life; fathers and mothers are too busy, the one with making money and building a powerful career; the other with often superficial concern for selfhood--dress, interior design, jewelry, and lifestyle. Plus, there are special problems that the very rich have: fear of kidnapping, extortion, and/or blackmail. In one of my classes at Parkhurst College, one of my students, a Jewish women with a well-known and wealthy background (and one with major contributions to Jewish and Israeli institutions, I might add) had to drop out of my classes. Why? Her brother had been kidnapped for ransom. The upper class can afford the most expensive and private homes, apartments, camps, and schools to insure their anonymity and safety. Most often, however, is the problem of boredom and lack of purpose, dilemmas of growth, that plague the third and later generations of the super-rich. The grandfather founded the business; the father and brothers developed it; but what are the children supposed to do?

There is a price that one pays for being wealthy. But the super-rich are so complex that it would be an injustice to only emphasize their problems. I have done just that because, except for a few well publicized scandals, the super-rich do a good job of covering up these problems. Still, one should mention the great contributions to education, science, music, architecture, and design that the upper class makes, and not just as philanthropists but as human beings.

The present Lord Rothschild of England, a warm friend of Israel, is not only a very wealthy patron but a reknowned scientist in the field of artificial insemination and a Fellow of the Academy of Science in London. There are numerous examples of wealth, education, and opportunity linked together to pursue goals with no fear of losing support or of "making a living." There is also a great need to succeed outside the world of finance. Not only do the rich make contributions to culture themselves, they, of course, have long supported others. Long before there were Endowment for the Humanities or Guggenheim awards, there were the wealthy patrons of a Mozart or Michaelangelo. Furthermore, the super-rich sometimes "co-opt" the talented and successful through marriage, social invitations, support, or simply flattery. There has long been a symbiotic relationship between the artist/writer and the wealthy person.

III.

The upper class moves in different spheres. They do different things; they go to exotic places; they even speak a different language.[2] For example:

Where one lives:

Beacon Hill (Boston); Dover (near Boston); Winnetka, Lake Forest, River Forest (near Chicago); Manhasset, Rye, Harrison (near New York City); Grosse Pointe (near Detroit); Fox Point, Mequon, River Hills (near Milwaukee); La Jolla, Hillsborough, Cheviot Hills (all in California).

Where one vacations:

In winter, at ski resorts at Sun Valley or Switzerland, or to Hobe Sound, the Florida Keys, Palm Beach, Palm Springs, or the Caribbean; tennis indoors and out at the Country Club. In summer, at the Cape (Cape Cod), Martha's Vineyard, or Nantucket. Or the cool summer cottage in Vermont or Maine. And, of course, at exclusive yacht clubs.

Where one shops:

Brooks Brothers, L.L. Bean, Shreve, Crump, and Low, Saks Fifth Avenue, Tiffany's, Bonwit's, Bloomingdales, Bergdorf Goodman (never Sears, Zayre's, or Filene's).

What one reads:

Wall Street Journal, Forbes, Barron's, Woman's Wear Daily, Vogue, The New Yorker, Town and Country, and the New York Times.

What one buys:

Crystal by Waterford and Baccarat; Designs by Courreges, Valentino, Diane Von Furstenberg, Halston, Cardin, plus antiques, art, horses, silver, china, diamonds.

What one volunteers for:

Garden Clubs, the Symphony Orchestra, the Museum of Fine Arts, the General Hospital, the Junior League.

The little things:

Coffee in demitasse cups; never ginger ale with whiskey; casualness in paying bills, for instance, to the butcher.

Language:

The affected language of the Kennedys is one
example; a British accent is fine; curtains are
never called drapes; a sofa is not a davenport; a
dinner jacket is not a tuxedo; a person is not
wealthy, but rich; you have a job, not a position;
you go to work, not to business.

What one is called (women only):

Like poor blacks, the rich have distinctive names.
I know why poor people have them; to give them
some distinction in a world that is bleak; but why
the rich have them, I do not know. It usually
starts in prep school or perhaps earlier. I've
seen and known young women with names like Eaddo,
Sioux, Trina, Crispin, Muzzy, Lyssa, Hester,
Lavinia ("Binky"), Terrin ("Misty"), Byrd, Teal,
Valeda, Caro, and Francelia. They often have cute
nicknames like Kip, Bootsie, Winnie, Betts (for
Elizabeth), Bucky, Sunny, Sass, Sam (for Sarah),
Janie (for Eugenie), Popsy (for Priscilla), and
Phyzzie (for Phyllis). And you know with names
like that you naturally are out yachting, sailing,
poloing, and hunting.

Where one "Preps":

Philips Exeter, Philips Andover, St. Mark's,
Groton, Woodbury Forest, Miss Porter's, Miss
Hall's, Emma Willard, Simon's Rock, Concord
Academy, Kingswood.

Schools one goes to:

For men, the Ivy League (Harvard, Yale, Princeton,
Columbia, Pennsylvania) and Amherst, Williams, and
Tufts; for women, the "Seven Sisters" (Radcliffe,
Sarah Lawrence, Smith, Mt. Holyoke, Bennington,
Barnard, Bryn Mawr) plus Simmons, Swarthmore,
Sweetbriar, Skidmore, Hollins, Pitzer, Sophie
Newcombe, and Pine Manor.

Thus, the very rich meet and interact with their
"own kind," from day schools to colleges, from summer
resorts to country clubs, from "coming out" parties
(which are going out of style with the rich) to tennis
tournaments.   They find each other and they marry.
Controlling whom one sees and whom one marries is an

important factor in keeping within one's class, and parents try to guide (some might call it "push") their children into making the correct choices.

The upper class is as complex as any other class, its members as varied as the poor and the middle class. There are not one but many upper classes. At the top are the Protestant "blue bloods," then the Irish Catholic "aristocracy," the Jewish upper class, and finally a black bourgeoise. There are regional enclaves--Southern upper class, New England-Northeastern "Yankees," and Texas-Florida-California "Cowboys." There are also relationships with international sets of the upper class. Thus, it is at times difficult to generalize about "one" upper class. A distinction, however, has to be made between inherited wealth ("old money") and earned wealth ("new money"), and "inter-marriages" between the two is common for all segments of the upper class, including the Jews.

The tradition of the "idle rich" does not exist in America. It had no place in the Protestant work ethic. Upper class members work hard, and they feel that they have earned everything they have. An idle life is frowned upon; in a religious framework, idleness leads to decadence and immorality. Certainly there exists decadence among the wealthy. Yet they subscribe to the ethic that one should work no matter how much money one has; that one should be a productive member of society, not a "parasite" living off mother and father.

For women, the same rules apply. More and more younger women are going into professional and even corporate careers and also finding time for the traditional service to the community in the form of Junior League clubs, philanthropies, and other socio-charity organizations.

IV.

As fate and history would have it, Jews are both part of, and apart from, the upper class. Only after years of assimilation and intermarriage (the Roths-childs' are one example) do they become almost indistinguishable from the Christian upper class. The extent of anti-Semitism in the upper class has been amply documented in the works of Stephen Birmingham (Our Crowd, The Grandees), E. Digby Baltzell (The Protestant Establishment), Vance Packard (The Status

Seekers), and in reports by the American Jewish
Committee and the Anti-Defamation League. Like other
minorities, Jews had to establish their own institutions (hospitals, country clubs, private clubs,
resorts) because of upper class prejudice. Thus, even
the upper class Jew is marginal to the established
upper class, a position reflected by an anecdote from
Europe told me by my father. A wealthy Jewish family
converted to Christianity and became quite devout.
Since they had donated a large sum of money to the
church, they were given front row pews. Yet, some
people in the back would murmur: "You see those Jews:
they're always trying to be so pushy. They even get
special consideration here in church!"

The elevation of Jews into the upper strata of
society came as the result of many years of struggle in
America. The following section from the book by Milton
Goldin, Why They Give: American Jews and Their Philanthropies, strikingly underscores this fact. Goldin
relates the story of the Yahudim, German-Jewish
families, who were quite successful in their adopted
country. They were not only an American success story,
but an important part of the philanthropic and social
life of American Jewish life despite their assimilation
and, in some cases, "disappearance" from the organized
Jewish community:

How could immigrants who spoke no English and
lacked skills find work? For tens of thousands, the solution was peddling. A five-
dollar investment bought a newcomer straw
hats, shawls, leather goods, thimbles, pocket
knives, playing cards, and silk ribbons. He
then started walking towards the frontier,
seeking customers for his wares.

As railroads pushed west to the Pacific,
peddlers established trading posts throughout
the Rockies and the Southwest. Some became
nattily-dressed traveling salesmen represent-
ing wholesalers; other became merchants and
opened general stores in towns and cities. A
typical sequence in the peddler rags-to-
riches story was to walk door-to-door, then
to acquire a horse and buggy, and finally to
open a general store where goods were sold to
other peddlers and to settlers. As propri-
etor, the former peddler served as his own
clerk, looked to a small margin and a rapid

-194-

turnover for profits, and was careful to give his customers value. An astounded Dr. Lilienthal wrote home to Germany that New York had Jewish retail merchants whose businesses amounted to $100,000 or $200,000. "And these people, upon their arrival six years ago, had not a penny in their pockets."

There was Adam Gimbel, who arrived in New Orleans in 1835 and opened a store in Vincennes, Indiana, where he sold a variety of goods and refunded the purchase price of any item with which a customer was dissatisfied. His seven sons were trained to carry on the business. In 1887, they extended it to Milwaukee; in 1894, to Philadelphia, and in 1919, to New York.

Joseph Seligman quit Bavaria for Pennsylvania in 1837. He then sent for his seven brothers, for whom he had an almost paternal devotion. The brothers pooled their money and began peddling in the South, where Joseph opened a small dry-goods store. In 1857, the brothers were reunited in a New York clothing and importing firm, and in 1862, they branched out into banking. During the Civil War, the Seligmans supplied uniforms to Union armies and sold $200,000,000 in Union bonds on the Frankfurt exchange.

Abraham Kuhn began as a peddler, became a storekeeper, and then opened a factory making men's and boys' pants in Cincinnati. He hired Solomon Loeb, a highly emotional immigrant from Worms to help at the factory and to open a New York outlet. After several years commuting between the two cities, Loeb married Kuhn's sister. An accommodating sort, Kuhn married Loeb's sister, the firm was renamed Kuhn, Loeb & Co., and both men and their families moved to New York where they opened banking offices.

An immigrant prospector named Levi Strauss went to California with a roll of tent canvas from his brother's New York store. "Pants don't hold up worth a hoot in the diggings," complained a disconsolate forty-niner. Strauss began manufacturing canvas pants, the pockets of which were reinforced with copper rivets. Under the trademark "Levi's," they became a staple of Western clothing.

And then there were the Guggenheims, Swiss Jews who left Europe in 1848. Simon peddled on city streets while Meyer, his dark-haired, good-looking son, peddled in the anthracite regions of Pennsylvania. On Sundays, the two men separated for the week's work; on Friday evenings, they met for the Sabbath meal. Within four years after his arrival in the United States, Meyer Guggenheim was well established in business. Before he died eight Guggenheims--Meyer and his seven ambitious sons--would comprise the richest Jewish family in the United States, spending Friday nights listening to Meyers's thoughts on business strategy rather than on religion.

The success of the Gimbels, the Seligmans, the Guggenheims, Strauss, and Kuhn and Loeb testifies not only to the rewards of hard work, clean living, perseverance, and inner fortitude, but to the unquestioned adherence of Yahudim to American mores. Tight-lipped and thrifty, Yahudim were staunch believers in free enterprise and Jewish dispersal throughout the nation. Some 3000 Jewish solders served in the Confederate Army, 7000 served in the Union Army, seven won Medals of Honor, and one became the Confederate secretary of state.

An enterprising group destined for great things, Yahudim felt a lack in the ancient laws, commentaries, rituals, traditions, and beliefs that make up Orthodox Judaism. In a burst of energy beginning in the 1840s, they came forth with an American version of Reform Judaism, a religion that would dominate American Jewry until the turn of the century, a religion filled with the optimism of the open frontier and liberal social and political ideas.

(pp. 28-29)

Yet if we sketch a rough typology of the Jewish class structure in America, the Yahudim would not be at the topmost rung. This place is reserved for the

Sephardim, the Spanish-Portugese-descended Jews. Such
a class structure might look like this:

First, the Sephardic families--the first Jews in
America, arriving in 1654. Always small in number and
today dwindling in size because of low birth rates and
little in-migration, they are, nevertheless, the "old-
old" money. Often, their more "raucous" brethren, the
Russian-Polish Jews, overshadow them, both in sheer
numbers and in personality. They are low-keyed,
reserved, and dignified. They also have a high intermarriage rate with Gentiles and are quite assimilated
into American life. They stand higher in status than
German Jews by both Jewish and Christian upper class
standards. There has been an influx of interest recently in Sephardic Jews, but most of it derives from
Jews coming from Egypt, Syria, and the Baltic states.
They are also Sephardic Jews but usually middle class.
The old Sephardic families (Levy, Sassoon, de Sola
Pool, Seixas, etc.), centered in New York and Philadelphia, are a small proportion of a small minority
within a minority called Jews.

Second, the German Jews of Birmingham's "our crowd"
--the Guggenheims, Levis, Loebs, Kuhns, and Strauss's.
They constitute the most visible upper class among the
Jews, played a noblesse-oblige role to their poorer
Ost-Juden immigrant brothers and sisters. Still
eminent, they too have had to intermarry with "lower-
class Jews, that is, the Russian-Polish. The old story
of new money wedded to established pedigree is salient
here. It might come as a surprise to know that the
renowned General David Sarnoff of RCA was considered
"low class" to the German-Jewish aristocracy into which
he married.

This second tier of Yahudim had, after World War II
and the establishment of Israel, intermarried a great
deal, and their descendants had a minimal interest in
Jewish affairs. These defections were soon to be made
up by an infusion of blood by wealthy descendants of
what Milton Goldin has called the Yidn, the Jews of
Russia and Poland (Why They Give, p. 213). While the
Yahudim were conservative and restrained, the Yidn were
adventurous and forthright in their demands for Jewry
and for Israel. They included such luminaries as Max
Fisher, a Republican industrialist from Detroit with
close ties to the White House; Sam Rothberg of Peoria,
Illinois, a liquor distiller and "super-salesman" for
Israel Bonds; the late Samuel Bronfman and his sons, of

Montreal and New York, founders of Seagram's Distilleries; Meshulim Riklis, a creative corporate-conglomerate wheeler-dealer; Lawrence Tisch, the head of the $500 million Loew Corporation; Samuel Hausman, a New York textile executive; the Feurstein family of Boston, also in textiles; the Ratner family of Cleveland; Bram Goldsmith of Los Angeles; Martin Peretz of Boston and Washington, DC; and a host of other "supershtadlanim" who influence both Washington and Jerusalem, while representing Jewish interests in America.

Third, the lowest rung of the upper class, but one that will eventually dominate it in sheer numbers if nothing else, is the Russian-Polish Jews. They have begun to dominate the German Jews in almost every city except New York. They are, of course, the sons and daughters of the offspring of the Ost-Juden who seventy five years ago were looked down upon by the German and Sephardic Jews. There is already a great deal of "intermarriage" among these Jews.

Fourth, the overwhelming majority of middle- to upper-middle class Jews, mostly Eastern European, but including a minority of Sephardic Jews.

Fifth, working-class Jews. A small but dwindling number remain, mostly on the Eastern Seaboard.

And, Sixth, poor Jews, mostly the elderly, the disabled, and those on fixed incomes. They constitute the "lower class" but such Jews are really former working-class Jews, now grown older and more isolated.

From my own observations, the Jewish upper class shares similar problems with all Jews. Most important, no matter how elevated they become, they are still perceived as Jews first. Anti-Semitism unites all Jews, a fact which manifests itself in concern for Jewish welfare by all Jews both here and in Israel. Prominent and wealthy Jewish families devote much time in behalf of Jewish life and culture: e.g., the Littauer family, the Raab family, the Bronfmans, the Regenstein family, and many others. In all cities both in the United States and Europe, it is this Jewish upper class that is the dominating force within Jewish philanthropies.

I do not have definite figures, but I would surmise that intermarriage rates are not significantly different for the Russian-Polish upper class Jew than for the Russian-Polish middle class Jew. Sephardic and German

upper class Jews have much higher intermarriage rates.
I have observed that most upper class Jewish men and
women are proud of their identity and their heritage;
they are concerned and involved with Israel; and they
tend to marry a Jew. But all these propositions should
be checked and researched since there is a paucity of
reliable literature on the Jewish upper class.

An interview with one young Jewish woman whose
parents, using Domhoff's criteria, are members of the
Jewish upper class articulated some of these concerns
regarding marriage.

> My father is president of a large department
> store in New York and he belongs to the right
> "clubs." They want me to find the "right"
> person, preferably someone who "owns a piece
> of the rock" (a phrase that means a student
> whose family has a building named after them
> at Harvard--JNP)--like a Loeb or a Littauer.
> But any Harvard guy is fine, as long as he's
> nice, and hopefully Jewish as well.

Sometime later, I learned that she had, in fact,
become engaged to a young Jewish Harvard student in
business administration. (The Harvard Business School
tops the list of eligible places for both Jewish and
non-Jewish "catches"; next might come the Harvard Law
School, Medical School, Dental School, and then the
other graduate schools.) Here was a case of parental
influence over-riding personal choice. What was important was his Harvard pedigree; other traits could be
overlooked.

V.

The younger generation of rich is not entirely free
from prejudice. Anti-Semitism of a most vulgar form
existed in the small exclusive school in which I
taught. Although I see prejudice and discrimination
slowly being forced out in corporations and banks, I
feel that "social anti-Semitism" will continue to
exist, though lessened and modified when compared to
earlier generations. Thus, the upper class Jew will
continue to be seen as an "outsider." Discrimination
against Jews, no matter their class backgrounds, does
exist and will continue to exist, albeit in small
pockets of society. I mentioned earlier that prejudice
even exists among Jews. There exists separate country

clubs in New York, for example, for Sephardic-German and for Russian-Polish Jews and the differences are reinforced. My hope rests on younger Jews who will do away with this internal form of prejudice. We have enough troubles neutralizing the external type.

Anti-Semitism continues to exist in the upper class. There is still discrimination against Jews in private country clubs, city clubs, yachting groups, and some high class residential areas. However, as Dan Rottenberg (1979) points out in his humorous but straight-shooting article "How to Succeed in Business without Being Gentile:" executive suite discrimination is not a life and death matter for Jews. They have done well enough in companies of their own or in the professions so that their median incomes are roughly on a par with Episcopalians and Presbyterians, the two denominations that control most major American corporations. He quotes Morris Abram, a former president of Brandeis and a ranking lawyer: "It's not a bread-and-butter issue. It's a matter of first class citizenship." Rottenberg notes that Abram himself chose law as a career, because his first choice, banking, seemed to offer no chance for advancement to Jews at the time.

American Jewish Committee and Anti-Defamation League reports over the past decade and a half show that discrimination in the upper realms of corporate life is still a problem at a time when anti-Semitism in other areas of life is at a low ebb. Recent research by Professor Stephen L. Slavin, an economist at Brooklyn College, and Mary Pradt, a research librarian at Time, Inc. (1978:28-33) shows that Jews are virtually excluded from the executive suites of most large corporations in America, especially those in banking, insurance, automobiles, oil, and utilities:

Banks:

> Of the fifteen largest commercial banks in the United States of America (eight of which are in New York City), there are no Jewish senior executives. In New York City, of 1,100 banking executives, only ten are Jews, less than one percent. In Philadelphia, again one percent or less of such executives are Jewish.

Insurance:

In New York City, less than 6 percent of the insurance executives are Jewish. While 10 percent of the sales executives are Jewish, only 4 percent of the home office executives are Jewish. Outside New York City, less than 4 percent of home office executives are Jewish, but two-thirds of them are not in management positions, but skilled "technicians"-- actuaries, accountants, or physicians. (In fact, when corporations try to apologize by saying they do have Jews in executive positions, most often they are in research, engineering, or accounting (being treasurer).

Automobiles:

The auto business has long been rife with anti-Semitism. Henry Ford, Sr. was a major distributor of The Protocols of the Elders of Zion in the 1920s. (To his credit, he repudiated this trash before he died, but the legacy of few Jews in the auto business remains.) Of 128 top officers of General Motors, Ford, and Chrysler, none were Jews in the 1960s. In 1963, of 51,000 white collar workers, professionals, and executives in the "Big Three," only 327 (less than one percent) were Jewish, and there are very few Jews in sales, finance, and even advertising.

Oil Companies:

Of the ten leading industrial corporations listed by Fortune magazine, five are oil companies and three others are GM, Ford, and Chrysler. Even before the pressure of Arab oil, discrimination was high in oil companies. It is hard to find Jewish executives; about 1-4 percent are Jews according to an American Jewish Committee study (quoted in Slavin and Pradt, p. 32). Arab oil connections may increase this discrimination.

Utilities:

> In electric, water, gas, and nuclear
> utilities, less than one percent of the
> executives (and these are <u>public</u> utili-
> ties) are Jewish. These figures included
> A.T.&T., Western Union, and Con Edison.
> In 1963, of 755 officers, only eight were
> Jews. In 1971, of 942 officers, only
> seventeen were Jews. It was not much of
> a change.

And similar problems exist in the railroad, grain,
paper/lumber, and agribusiness: few, sometimes no,
Jews! Where are Jews strong? The garment business,
merchandising, food selling and distributing, diamonds
and jewelry, hotels, entertainment, real estate,
computers, and electronics.

VI.

What are the factors that cause such anti-Semitism?
Some are hoary chestnuts that will not surprise readers, but a few are new. First, business is business,
and in those areas that are energy-related (oil, gas,
tires, autos, etc.), a Jewish executive might alienate
Arab or even communist counterparts. Therefore, anti-
Zionism can be shown to directly increase anti-Jewish
discrimination.

Secondly, Jews traditionally were "allowed" into
high risk, venture capital areas, and when non-Jews saw
profit there Jews were pushed aside. This was true of
banking in its early history, even oil drilling, and
other fields where few Jews are found. Even today,
Jews are often entrepreneurs in high risk gambles.

Third, there are the misconceptions about Jews so
beautifully described in Vance Packard's classic <u>The
Status-Seekers</u>. (Though published over twenty years
ago, the book is still relevant.) Jews are seen as
"too pushy, too aggressive." They "don't fit in,"
meaning into the social life of the city, country, or
yachting club. Packard quoted corporate executives who
maintained that "Jews don't like corporations; they
like to be their own bosses;" "Jews aren't good team
players;" "Jews are too smart; they don't like to take
orders." Even corporate wives "don't like them."
Often, these canards were said with envy and as compli-

ments, but the end result is the same: few Jewish executives hired.

Finally, there is a new wrinkle to this pattern. Professor Slavin has discovered that a root cause is in the recruitment of Jews. A vicious circle develops: Jews are seen as "poor" corporate material; anti-Semitic myths continue; thus, few Jews are interviewed; few Jews are hired; and few Jews are found in the executive suite. Slavin has shown that in schools with a Jewish population of 30-39 percent, there were 5.2 visits by banks to the campus; but this went down to 3.5 visits in those colleges with over 40 percent Jews. Compare this to 9.3 visits for schools that are 20-29 percent Jewish.

This explains why a City College, Brooklyn College, or a Queens College have only one-third as many visits to recruit as, for example, a Harvard, Tufts, or Berkeley. The tipping point, according to Slavin, was a school that was 30 percent Jewish; there was a sharp drop at that level. Thus, it is ironic that in New York City, with its large Jewish student population, there are few visits and few Jews hired for New York City banks, insurance companies, and utilities! The solution, obviously, is to pressure these corporations to increase their visits to heavily Jewish schools. While some improvements have been made through the efforts of the major Jewish defense agencies, there is much more to be done to fight this gentlemanly form of anti-Semitism. If corporations show, and some are beginning to, that they welcome Jews and other minorities, they will be surprised at the number of Jews interested in those areas long closed to them. This is especially true today when fields that traditionally drew many Jewish students (law, teaching, social work) are cutting back in the wake of the economic recession.

VII.

Returning to my pseudonymous Parkhurst College, I must say that even there, despite the veneer of acceptance and camaraderie, subtle forms of anti-Semitism existed. But a new generation of rich is developing. They have been educated to the evils of prejudice; to the perils of genocide; to the quest for justice; one hopes they will begin to make the necessary changes for complete citizenship for all minorities. The young women themselves may not be in powerful corporate positions (and that too is changing), but they may influence their upper class husbands and fathers. These young women at Parkhust have met other Jews in their classes; they have been taught by Jews; they may even marry a Jew. It would be difficult to see them as outright anti-Semites after their college experience. Still, an upper class Jew often feels that he or she must not appear "too" Jewish. Assimilation and money often go hand-in-hand.

One final footnote: after two years of teaching at this interesting college for the rich, I was not re-hired (an oblique way of saying "fired"). There were other reasons, but one teacher (a quietly Jewish one, I might add) told me several years later: "Jack, you were just too Jewish for the place." I think she was right.

Notes

1. This essay is based upon informal interviews with young upper class women. All names have been changed.

2. Most of my examples are drawn from the Boston-New England area, an area crucial to the understanding of the upper class. See also Alison Arnold, "Symbols of Status," Boston Globe, April 17, 1977, pp. 1-10.

References

"Affirmative Action by Provident Mutual Deemed a Success," The National Underwriter, vol. 81, no. 51, Dec. 17, 1977, p. 7.

Arnold, Alison, "Symbols of Status," Boston Globe, April 17, 1977, pp. 1-10.

Amory, Cleveland, The Proper Bostonians, (New York: E.P. Dutton, 1947.)

_____, Who Killed Society? (New York: Pocket Books, 1960.)

Baltzell, E. Digby, Philadelphia Gentlemen: The Making of a Free Press, (Glencoe, Illinois: The Free Press, 1958.)

Beyette, Beverly, "Is L. A. Swallowing Up Its Jewish Community?" Los Angeles Times, Part IV, View Section, Friday, Nov. 2, 1979.

Birmingham, Stephen, Our Crowd: The Great Jewish Families of New York, (New York: Harper and Row, 1967.)

_____, The Right People: A Portrait of the American Social Establishment, (Boston: Little, Brown, 1968.)

_____, The Grandees: America's Sephardic Elite, (New York: Harper and Row, 1971.)

Bloom, Mel, et al, "The Future of Jewish Fund Raising," (A Panel Discussion), Moment, vol. 4, no. 10, November, 1979, pp. 29-37.

Burke, Jack, "The Big Flap Over Club Memberships," Banking, vol. 68, July, 1976, pp. 38ff.

Cuber, John F. and Harroff, Peggy B., Sex and the Significant Americans: A Study of Sexual Behavior Among the Affluent, (Baltimore: Penguin Books, 1972.) (Hardcover: Appleton-Century, 1966).

Domhoff, G. William, Who Rules America?, (Englewood Cliffs, New Jersey: Prentice-Hall, 1967.)

_____, The Higher Circles, (New York: Random House, 1970.)

_____, Fat Cats and Democrats, (Englewood Cliffs, New Jersey: Prentice-Hall, 1972.)

_____, The Bohemian Grove and Other Retreats, (New York: Harper and Row, 1974.)

Gal, Allon, Socialist-Zionism: Theory and Issues in Contemporary Jewish Nationalism, (Cambridge, Massachusetts: Schenkman Publ. Co., 1973.)

Ginzberg, Eli, "Jews in the American Economy," Our Stake in the Urban Condition series, (New York: Domestic Affairs Dept., American Jewish Committee, April, 1979.)

Goldin, Milton, Why They Give: American Jews and Their Philanthropies, (New York: MacMillan, 1976.)

Hamilton, William, Anti-Social Register, (New York: Penguin Books, 1977.)

Howe, Irving, World of Our Fathers, (New York: Simon and Shuster, 1976.)

Isaacs, Stephen D., Jews and American Politics, (New York: Doubleday, 1974.)

Katz, Irving, August Belmont: A Political Biography, (New York: Columbia University Press, 1968.)

Kavaler, Lucy, The Private World of High Society, (New York: David Mckay, 1960.)

Liebman, Arthur, Jews and the Left, (New York: John Wiley and Sons, 1979.)

Lundberg, Ferdinand, The Rich and the Super-Rich, (New York: Lyle Stuart, 1968.)

Manners, Ande, Poor Cousins, (New York: Fawcett Crest Books, 1972.)

Mills, C. Wright, The Power Elite, (New York: Oxford University Press, 1956.)

Newman, Peter C., King of the Castle: The Making of a Dynasty: Seagrams and the Bronfman Family, (New York: Atheneum, 1980.)

Packard, Vance, The Status-Seekers, (New York: David McKay, 1959.)

Rottenberg, Dan, "Supergelt", Jewish Living, September-October, 1979, pp. 41-47.

_____, "How to Succeed in Business Without Being Gentile", Jewish Living, December, 1979, pp. 39-72.

Slavin, Stephen L. and Pradt, Mary A., "Corporate Anti-Semitism," Jewish Currents, vol. 32:2 February, 1978, pp. 29-32.

Weed, Steven, My Search for Patty Hearst, (New York: Warner Books, 1976.)

Wixon, Burton, The Children of the Rich, (New York: Crown, 1973.)

Zweigenhaft, Richard L., "The Jews of Greensboro: In or Out of the Upper Class?," Contemporary Jewry, vol. 4, no. 2, Spring/Summer, 1978, pp. 60-76.

Epilogue:

Insiders and Outsiders:

The Creative Paranoia of the Jewish People

This essay deals with paranoia, a malady that afflicts most oppressed minorities. It touches on the various themes that have surfaced throughout this book: marginality, creative tension, ambivalence, the tightrope between universalism and particularism, and the fact that the more things change, the more they seem to stay the same. The essay also raises one final issue: the role of the minority group itself. An impression may have arisen that minorities always act in response to outside pressure, and that this pressure is always the key variable. By and large this is true, but despite outside pressure, the minority group still makes choices. Sometimes, such choices lead to in-group solidarity and cooperation, and sometimes such choices mean just the opposite--dissension and conflict from within. There is a Talmudic saying that the Jewish Temple in Jerusalem was destroyed, not because of the evil of the outside world, but by <u>sinat chinom</u> (Hebrew for "baseless hatred"). The Talmud was referring not to anti-Semitism but to hatred and mistrust <u>among Jews</u>. Orthodox rabbis say the same thing could happen again-- that because of the "baseless hatred" of one Jew for another, God could bring his wrath down upon the Jewish community in America and by extension upon the state of Israel itself. It is a thought worth remembering by all minority groups. This essay first appeared in a student magazine supported by the UCLA Hillel Foundation, called <u>Davka</u> (Yiddish for "and so"), under the title "Paranoia and Politics," (vol. 4, no. 2, Winter 1974, pp. 25-28) and is reprinted by permission.

* * * * *

<u>Plus ca change, plus que ca reste la meme chose</u>.
The more things change, the more they stay the same.

-211-

So too it seems with the Jewish people in their odyssey since leaving the ghettos of Europe. We Jews keep returning to the same dilemmas, the same contradictions. The Jewish quandary remains: how to maintain a rich and ancient faith in the face of modernism. The old questions keep cropping up again and again, but in different forms with varying intensities: the tension between the universalistic concerns of the host society and the particularistic concerns of one's religion; within Judaism there is a constant struggle between a secular, more radical, more "messianic" expression and a more sacred, more traditional, more conservative, more "rabbinic" one.

Years of anti-Semitism has bred a deep distrust of society. Jews try to keep a low profile. They desire to win and receive guarantees of good faith. They strive to remain within the good graces of the government even if this means at times to defend a status quo even more strenuously than the "normal" patriotic citizen. Jews are seen as a single "race," each Jew is seen as accountable to another, to the entire Jewish community, and to the society at large. There are Jews who do not feel part of their people, who do not wish to be confined and burdened by such commitments, and who wish to strike out in the secular non-Jewish world in any way they choose. If society limits that choice, they are ready to fight to break down inequality and oppression. Their actions, if opposed by state powers, are often seen by other Jews as a threat to the entire Jewish community and to their comfortable status, a status that was reached with great difficulty and drive. The radical, the rebel, the religious heretic, all are seen as a threat. From Jesus to Jerry Rubin, this has been the case.

This has bred a complex form of paranoia among Jews: fear of what the goyim (non-Jews) will do; fear of what the goyim think of the Jewish rebels and heretics in their midst; fear of expulsion, pogroms, and concentration camps. The history of the Jews is a history of persecution. This history of persecution is a history of paranoia as well as a history of internal clashes between Jews.

Examples are not difficult. Jesus was crucified by order of the procurator Pontius Pilate at the instigation of Jewish circles who feared the Romans' reaction to messianic agitation. The Pharisees often clashed with Jesus, resenting the authority which he claimed, the liberties which he took regarding the Law, and his messianic mission and destiny.

During the conquests of Alexander the Great (363323 B.C.E.), Palestine came under Greek rule and Judea was surrounded by an increasing number of Hellenized gentile cities, and in the countries of the Diaspora such as Egypt, Syria, and Asia Minor, Hellenization made rapid progress. Outside Palestine, Greek became the language of the Jews, and in the Third Century B.C.E. the Jews of Egypt were already using a Greek translation of the Bible, the Septuagint. The radical tendencies of such Hellenizing groups as the Tobiads, who were supported by the Seleucid rulers, finally led to the anti-Hellenistic uprising of the Maccabees. Again, Jews clashed with Jews.

After the Maccabean victory, Palestinian Jewry was strong enough to absorb Greek influences without danger of being engulfed by Hellenism. Toward the end of the Second Temple and in the Mishnaic Period, material life was predominantly Hellenistic (synagogue architecture and decoration, tomb inscriptions, art, even certain designations for Jewish institutions and liturgies, for example, the Sanhedrin). The Jewish upper classes moreover adopted a thoroughgoing Hellenistic style of life, which often bordered on assimilation. For this reason, the rabbis opposed too close an acquaintance with, and study of, Greek culture.

This period in history has powerful parallels with American society and is a paradigmatic instance of the capacity of Judaism to enrich itself and its host country without losing itself by contact with a "universal" civilization.

As we continue to jump through history, we can find more examples of this particular kind of paranoia that forces certain segments of Jews to support the established powers, other Jews to oppose these powers, thereby resulting in bitter and demoralizing clashes within the Jewish community.

The movement connected with Shabbetai Tzvi (1626-1676)--the last major messianic outbreak in Jewish history--left a long and tragic aftermath of confusion, kabbalistic heresy, heresy-hunting, and clandestine Sabbatian groups, which divided Jews and led to a reaction against Kabbalah and active messianism. Later Sabbatian leaders such as Jonathan Eibeschutz and Jacob

Frank were hounded by both the rabbis and the bishops of the state.

A contemporary of Shabbetai Tzvi was the Dutch philosopher Baruch Spinoza (1632-1677). Spinoza had a traditional Jewish education, but his own philosophical development, greatly influenced by Descartes, led away from traditional Orthodoxy. His profound and rigorously elaborated pantheistic metaphysics, his radical demand for unfettered freedom of inquiry, and his moral stature have made him one of the great figures in modern European philosophy. Yet his unorthodox views, which came close to "atheism" as understood by the Calvinist authorities in Amsterdam, led to his excommunication by the Sephardic community in 1656.

Over a hundred years later, we will find opponents of the Hasidic movement, the Mitnaggedim, informing on their co-religionists to the Czarist government. Three hundred years later, we will find Jews supporting the early Fascist movement in Italy (see the movie The Garden of the Finzi-Contini), and in Germany, we will find early support of Hitler among Jews. Even during the midst of the Holocaust, we will see groups of Jews, the Judenrate, attempting in vain to deal with a right-wing fascistic government in order to win tranquility for the Jewish community.

In summary then, we have seen that disputes over religious issues have often masked deep political fears, as in the case of Jesus and the Pharisees, the Tobiads and the Maccabees, the Sabbatians and their rabbinic opponents, Spinoza and the Orthodox community, and the Mitnaggedim and the Hasidim. I don't wish to minimize the religious aspects of these clashes, but what I do want to emphasize is the development of a peculiar paranoia, a tradition of paranoia, which pitted Jew against Jew, a form of paranoia in which conservative Jewish elements threatened by Jewish "rebels" or by the general society itself, would attempt to identify with the powers of the state, even if these powers were often oppressive to all Jews. This would accomplish two goals: first, these Jews would (hopefully) win the allegiance and support of the government, and, secondly, they would disavow the "rebels" or "heretics" and isolate them from the general society and from other Jews. Doing this would enable the government to punish the dissidents without endangering the rest of the Jewish community.

Jews brought this "tradition" of paranoia with them to America after it had "matured" in Eastern and Western Europe. What has made Jewish paranoia in America so problematic and complex is the fact that America too has a paranoid style running through its history. Some historians and social scientists have called it the "conspiracy theory of politics"--that is, paranoia on a grand national scale.

Seymour Martin Lipset and Earl Raab in a recent Commentary article, quote a prominent 18th century Bostonian, Jedediah Morse, who declared that America had internal "enemies whose professed design is to subvert and overturn our holy religion and our free and excellent government...."[2]

American history is rich in examples of movements fostering complex conspiracy theory explanations for the subversion of American morals and institutions. These include the Anti-Illuminati agitation of the 1790s, the anti-Masonic Party of the Jacksonian era, assorted anti-Catholic movements such as the Know-Nothing Party of the pre-Civil War Period, and the American Protective Association of the 1890s.[3]

In the 1920s there were even better examples of conspiracy theories which help to explain how discontent among the masses could be effectively channeled onto a scapegoat. This decade, which in many ways paralleled the 1960s, was a period characterized by what Lipset and Raab call "modernism," that is, the breakdown of sexual mores, the waning of church influence, the spread of pornography in Hollywood, corruption in baseball, the deafening cacophony of jazz, and the breakdown of parental controls against smoking, drinking, and petting.[4] A backlash to this "immorality" was imminent.

Henry Ford's anti-Semitic newspaper, the Dearborn Independent, was one voice among many to join in the condemnation of these "decadent" lifestyles. In addition to Ford, there arose a substantial backlash organization, the second Ku Klux Klan. Like its older namesake of post-Civil-War Reconstruction days, this new KKK was not only racist, but encouraged hatred for Jews, Bolsheviks, "foreigners," Jesuits (Catholics), and all participants in the "hip" "groovy" style of the '20s.

Restrictive and racist immigration laws soon followed. A General Intelligence Division was set up

in the Attorney General's office to investigate domestic radical activities and eventually indexed the histories of over 200,000 people. There were widespread
private vigilante groups, lynchings, tar and feather-
ings, and other examples of extremism.

Eventually the Depression and World War II inter-
rupted these trends, but anti-Semitic groups, such as
Father Coughlin's Christian Crusade and the German
Bund, continue to spread their poison.

After the war, there was an economic boom and a
desperate desire for normalcy, but "normalcy" included
a widespread Red scare, the Joseph McCarthy hearings,
and the blacklisting of the Hollywood Ten and culminated in the trial and electrocution of alleged "atomic
spies"--the Rosenbergs.

How did the Jewish community respond? Here at this
crucial junction of American and Jewish paranoia, we
discover a centuries old pattern returning--with a
vengeance: to come to the aid of outcasts is to threat-
en the fragile security of American Jews. At a time
when old anti-Semitic barriers were falling in the
United States, Jews were in no hurry to erect new ones.
They wanted to protect their newly-acquired status.
Thus the "Jews-Commie" stain had to be avoided at all
costs, Jewish leaders felt, and the Rosenbergs were an
embarrassment, a barrier to quiet assimilation. They
were "excommunicated" from the Jewish community in a
sense. They were pariahs. Jesus, Spinoza, and
Shabbetai Tzvi would have understood the plight of the
Rosenbergs very well.

Paralleling the history of paranoia in America has
been a history of "conspiracy trials" starting with
Sacco and Venzetti in the 1920s, moving through the
Rosenbergs' trial of the 1950s, and then into the
1960s--with so many trials--of Black Muslims, Black
Panthers, marijuana-smoking hippies, students, SDSers,
anti-war activists such as Dr. Benjamin Spock, and
culminating in the "Conspiracy 8" trial in Chicago of
1969-1970. As usual, Jews were involved and they were
a painful embarrassment to the Jewish establishment.
Jerry Rubin, Abbie Hoffman, and Lee Weiner were defen-
dants; Leonard Weinglass and William Kunstler were the
defense attorneys; and even the judge was a Jew, as was
also true in the Rosenberg case. Jews prosecuting Jews
defending Jews, all of it was very painful for many
Jews.

In the 1920s, the scapegoats were "international bankers" and "foreigners;" in the 1950s it was "pinkos" and "commie fellow travelers;" in the 1960s it was "radicals" and "hippies." Often, these were also code words for Jews. The paranoia continues--even amidst Jewish affluence and influence.

Today, Jews once again find themselves in the thick of things. As one astute journalist remarked: "The problem for American Jewry is to keep from becoming a problem."

Jews are worried that they will be blamed for a cold and uncomfortable winter as Arab states cut back on oil to the West. They worry that they will be blamed for any difficulties that the issue of Russian Jewry will put in the way of the Soviet-American detente. Jewish leaders may even "sell out" to American and Soviet demands with regard to these Russian Jews. Furthermore, they worry that Israel's intransigence will endanger world Jewry as well as offend others (that is, blacks, left-liberals, the Third World).

What should be the Jewish response? First, let us examine that word 'paranoia', and, then, probe the possible responses to it.

Paranoia is the condition of feeling persecuted when other people tell you that you really aren't. The reverse, not feeling persecuted when other people say that you are, also exists within and among Jews. Sociologists might call the latter "assimilation" and loss of identity. With loss of identity comes insensitivity to the plight of one's group, subsequently, to a soft-pedaling of discrimination and, ultimately, to cultural amnesia.

Paranoia, like body tension, is necessary for homostasis. A little bit of paranoia is crucial for Jewish survival. It is like the needle on a seismograph, a thermometer, a flashing red light. Too little paranoia is unhealthy for the Jews as a collective entity; too much is unhealthy for the individual. Do Jews cry "wolf" too often? Perhaps they do, but history has taught them that the whisper of anti-Semitism has often led to the howling mob. Better too much than too little. But when is too much? Or too little?

It seems the fate of Jewry to be paranoid and thus in conflict between liberal and Jewish interests, between particular Jewish interests and the interests of other groups, between particular Jewish interests and particular national interests, and between universal concerns for, let us say, social justice and the particular concerns of the Jewish people.

Even the existence of the state of Israel has not entirely eliminated this paranoia. In fact it may have increased it. Today, the Jewish-national interests of Israel have come into conflict with world-national interests of America, the Soviet Union, and the Arab states. The issues have been oil and political hegemony, leaving the Israelis in a kind of "Diaspora-paranoia" and world Jewry worried about not only its fate but that of Israel.

Thus one must recognize the inevitability of the Jews' contradictory status--it is the sine-qua-non of Jewish existence. Jews and Judaism have had to live with such contradictions. Each problem must be confronted squarely and defined precisely. Not every issue is either "good for the Jews" or "bad for the Jews." Not every issue must be seen with this kind of "back-against-the-wall" mentality. Because sometimes it is and sometimes it isn't. And, furthermore, which Jews is one talking about? The rich? The poor? The Orthodox? The secular? And when? And where? Without hysteria and with a minimum of paranoia, the Jew must learn to confront the world.

Notes

1. The information on Hellenism was taken from The Encyclopedia of the Jewish Religion, edited by R.J. Zwi Werblowsky and Geoffrey Wigoder, (New York: Holt, Rinehart, and Winston, 1965), p. 181.

2. S.M. Lipset and Earl Raab, "An Appointment with Watergate," Commentary 56 no. 3, September, 1973, p. 35.

3. Ibid., p. 36. See also Richard Hofstadter's The Paranoid Style in American Politics, (New York: Random House, 1965.)

4. Lipset and Raab, p. 36 cf.

5. See Leonard J. Fein, "Liberalism and American Jews," Midstream 19, no. 8, October, 1973, pp. 3-18 for a fine analysis of this conflict. In the end, Fein has no "answers" or political guidelines. Who does?

About the Author

JACK NUSAN PORTER is a sociologist concerned with minority relations, political movements, Nazism, the Holocaust, Israel, and contemporary Jewish issues. He has published extensively in both popular and scholarly journals. His works include <u>Student Protest and the Technocratic Society</u> (1973); <u>Jewish Radicalism: A Selected Anthology</u> (with Peter Dreier, 1973); <u>The Study of Society</u> (editorial board, 1974); <u>The Sociology of American Jews</u> (2nd rev. ed., 1980); <u>Kids in Cults</u> (with Irvin Doress, 1978); and <u>Jewish Partisans</u> (1981, forthcoming). He is the founder and and publisher of the <u>Journal of the History of Sociology</u> and was visiting lecturer at the University of Lowell, Boston College, Hebrew College, and Emerson College. He is listed in <u>Who's Who in America</u>, <u>Who's Who in Israel</u>, and <u>Contemporary Authors</u>. At present, he is studying business management at Harvard University and lives in Boston with his wife, Miriam, and their son, Gabriel.

About The Author

Jack Nusan Porter is considered one of the pioneers in the field of modern genocide studies and the sociology of the Holocaust. He taught the first course in the sociology of genocide (comparative genocide) at the University of Massachusetts at Lowell in 1977; edited in 1982 the first anthology on comparative genocide, Genocide and Human Rights: A Global Anthology (Lanham, MD: University Press of America/Rowman and Littlefield, reprinted in 2002); published the first curriculum on the Holocaust and comparative genocide in 1992, The Sociology of Genocide/The Holocaust: A Curriculum Guide (Washington, DC : American Sociological Association, 1999); and pioneered research into Jewish resistance and the persecution of homosexuals and lesbians during the Holocaust. He was elected Vice-President of the International Association of Genocide Scholars in 1997.

He is the author or editor of 30 books and 600 articles and reviews including: Kids in Cults, Confronting History and Holocaust, Sexual Politics in the Third Reich, Jewish Partisans of the Soviet Union, Conflict and Conflict Resolution, and The Study of Society.

A widely-acclaimed author, editor, and teacher, Dr. Porter is also considered a pioneer in the modern sociology of Jewry, being a founding member of the Association for the Social Scientific Study of Jewry, and author or editor of such classic works as The Sociology of American Jews, The Jew as Outsider, and Jewish Radicalism.

He was founder and publisher of the Journal of the History of Sociology and a contributor to the Encyclopedia Judaica, Encyclopedia of Genocide (1999) the Encyclopedia of Sociology, and The Italian-American Experience: An Encyclopedia.

A former Research Associate at Harvard University at their Ukrainian Research Institute (1982-1984), he has taught for over 30 years either sociology, history, or Jewish studies at such universities as Northwestern, Boston College, Boston University, and is at present an adjunct lecturer in sociology at the University of Massachusetts at Lowell.

Born in Rovno,Ukraine in December 1944, Porter, age 57 (in 2002), came to America in 1946 after a year in a DP Camp in Linz, Austria, (Bindermichel). His parents, Faygeh and Srulik Puchtik (Porter), were partisan leaders in the Kruk-Maks Group in Western Ukraine During World War II. He grew up in the Midwest in Milwaukee, Wisconsin.

He received his BA in sociology with a minor in Hebrew Studies from the University of Wisconsin at Milwaukee and his Ph.D. in sociology at age 26 in 1971 from Northwestern University He had lived on Kibbutz Gesher Haziv near Nahariya in Israel (1962-63) and he studied in Jerusalem (1962-63) and in New York at the Academy of Jewish Religion. He was ordained a rabbi in July 2000.

Today, Dr. Porter is an independent scholar, teacher and a film producer and screenwriter. His latest projects are "Key West Rabbi: A Comedy" and "Partisans". He lives in West Newton, MA where his two children, Gabe and Danielle, also reside.

He can be reached at (617) 965-8388 and at jacknusan@earthlink.net. Look up his complete name <Jack Nusan Porter> on Google and see 217 links to his name.